POOLHALL JAIL LIBRARY

By Loxton Berg

Poolhall—Jail—Library
Loxton Berg

ISBN: 978-0-6484674-9-6 Paperback

Copyright © Loxton Berg

First published 2019

All rights reserved. Without limiting the rights under copyright reserved above, no part of this publication may be reproduced, stored in or introduced into a database and retrieval system or transmitted in any form or any means (electronic, mechanical, photocopying, recording or otherwise) without the prior written permission of the owner of copyright.

This story is true. Most names have been altered.

Published with the assistance of angelkey.com.au

"In the west he (Dean Moriarty) had spent a third of his time in the poolhall, a third in jail, and a third in the public library" – Jack Kerouac, *On The Road*, 1957.

Dedicated to Karen, Ted and Mary, who passed during the completion of this book.

Sincerest thanks to my wife, siblings, friends, mentors and teammates for encouraging me through to completion. A book that is 15 years in the making has relied on your support in so many varied ways.

PREFACE

SHIMMYING through the backstreets of a Brazilian coastal town to the sounds of pagode; the tambourine, the tan-tan and the surdo all being beaten within an inch of their lives.

This is not where my life was headed just a few short years ago.

I look across at the gorgeous woman beside me, twirling along with the parade, smiling back at me as we simultaneously negotiate the cobbles of Rua Francisco Antonio.

Moments earlier she'd taught me to order a caipifruta in Portuguese from a lady in the square.

The vendor, with a smile of a Cheshire cat and ringlets like Shirley Temple, gave me the last drink of the night for free because she decided she liked my face.

I'm a world away from the confused, angry young man who sat for hours at his desk, researching the correct dosage of toxins to slide into his veins, inviting death to come as rapidly and painlessly as possible.

Travelling the world – visiting 52 countries along the way – in the space of a few years has lent everything perspective.

I'm still a ratty-looking kid from the Housing Commission block, child of a deluded dreamer, step-child of a drunk, a bigot, a bully.

Yet there are far worse circumstances in life.

And there's always a path forward.

BRISBANE, 2005
As told by Loxton

"YOU may as well keep this. I won't be needing it."
Eddie looks back at me, concerned. "Are you sure buddy?"
It's nothing more than customary politeness. I know he can use it. He knows I'm happy for him to have it. Besides, it's useless to me now.
I push a pile of Aussie dollars across the table and gaze out of the gigantic glass wall.
"Yeah, buy yourself a beer or something," I suggest.
Eddie grins. You can't deny the little terrier a shiny coin – or an alcoholic beverage for that matter.
He's hardly had enough time to return from the bar and lick the froth before they call my number.
Flight SQ263 to Singapore.
I pat my backpack once more, check the luggage keys are safely stowed and broaden my shoulders.
Eddie shakes my hand, wishes me the best. I thank him for the lift and tell him I'll be home before he knows it.
This is years in the making and the only thing unsettling me is a distinct lack of nerves.
Admittedly, there's a skipped heartbeat passing through security. You always pray they'll chemical test your belongings after you've had a chance to put your wallet back in your pocket.
I'm eventually seated on the plane next to two older men from Redcliffe. They say they are travelling to the Philippines for a business trip. On first impression, I can't resist thinking they're really talent scouts for the local biscuit factory.
There's a running joke in our friendship circle that all the hottest Filipino women in Brisbane have been hired to work on the biscuit company assembly line – and that's exactly why Eddie sought employment there.

Poolhall—Jail—Library

He's landed himself a job amid the digestives and ginger nuts with the primary motive of ensnaring an Asian beauty on home soil. It matters little if they are already romantically attached or otherwise.

I chuckle, shaking my head ever so slightly. Eddie's a wretched bloke, but he's also a great one.

At the very least, booking ahead has allowed to reserve a window seat. I need not contemplate the ethics of Eddie's endeavours or force myself to nod believingly as the men talk of their 'business interests' in the Philippines. Instead, I savour the ascent through the clouds, the hypnotising thrust and turn above Moreton Bay, the disappearing landscape of suburbia.

You'd think after 27 years of living in one country, a six-hour flight above it would be enough to induce sleep. Hardly. The geography geek in me revels in the adventure. I've never seen the outback; the mysteriousness of Mount Isa, Arnhem Land and Katherine touching the horizon.

Somewhere over the Arafura Sea I lose the sun. I am now on foreign territory.

By the time I witness my first international city from the air, Kupang, Indonesia, all I can make out are dotted lights and a few streams gushing from nearby mountains.

Still, sleep does not come. Neither does the sense of trepidation I was expecting.

As told by Karen

ONE-hundred-and-fourteen. That's how many people have died in aeroplane accidents in the last month. Loxton told me I'm "silly and depressing", but I can't help it. He said: "Mum, I would never have bought you a computer if I knew you were going to look up stupid shit like that." Of course, I'm going to use it to find out what I can. How could I just let him fly off without worrying at least a little?

So that's where we are at. My boy's leaving and, you could say, not on the best of terms. According to him we're already distant and it doesn't matter where he's heading.

I keep thinking back to when we first departed England for Australia. Mum, Dad and us six kids. What's it all about? It's like a big international game of pass the parcel.

I guess, when you think about it, there's some symmetry. We would never have left if Dad wasn't so jaded by his past and distant from his own parents. That and being subsidised by the government in a post-war scheme to repopulate the southern jewel in the British Empire.

But Loxton's not being sponsored by anyone. Why's he doing this? How can he expect me not to feel like a failure in some way? Would he rather go broke, leave his friends and live in another country?

He'll find out once he lands. Friends don't just appear.

I was at least lucky to have my younger brothers Howard and Craig when we arrived in Brisbane. The others would go out all day, looking for work, while I'd stay home and take care of the boys. I was all of about 10, but that's how it had to be.

Poolhall—Jail—Library

It was hard back then. They told Dad he'd be certain of a well-paying job. He spent almost six months walking Gympie Road pleading for employment. There was no option but for Mum to join him. As the money dried up, the three older kids had to leave school and try and find work of their own.

I imagine it must have been even more terrible than I thought at the time. There was a period when the only income into the house was through my eldest brother Ronald. He was working as a window dresser for a clothing store, feeding us all by outfitting mannequins in the latest trends, while still too afraid to broach the topic of his 'alternative lifestyle' with my parents.

Mum and Dad eventually found employment at the old Amoco oil refinery, near the mouth of the Brisbane River, where they mopped floors and emptied bins. They worked to buy a car, essentially so they could travel to work on time. Back in England, Dad had been at management level. He cursed his naivety at leaving such security behind, but not as much as my mother cursed him.

On arrival we lived in a house on Suez Street, next to Kedron Brook. It was part of the government sponsorship package.

The floorboards were spaced apart and, at night, you could lay there counting the gigantic cockroaches as they crawled up. One time the brook flooded and I remember our neighbour standing on his back porch, shooting snakes as they swam close to our homes. The neighbour ended up lending us a few spare mattresses too, with ours completely saturated by the floods. They were lumpy as heck and we slept three to a bed. It was not the vision of Australia we had been sold.

Needless to say we couldn't wait to get out of Suez Street. After we eventually vacated, the house was condemned to demolition. From then on Howard, Craig and I always referred to it as 'Sewers Street'.

CHANGI // ZURICH

THIS stopover is killing me. I've heard Changi is supposed to be the best airport in the world; so comfortable you should sleep there instead of paying for a hotel room.

Right now, all it's doing is halting the momentum. We've just flown above Borneo and crossed the equator. I feel like the friggin' wild man, a goddamn explorer. I want to press on.

What makes matters worse is that all along I'd planned to use the gym between flights. Yet I haven't brought any spare clothes in the daypack at all. I could sweat it up in what I'm wearing, but that could make for a slightly malodorous second journey.

So much for my meticulous planning.

I retreat to my journal instead, pressed up on a seat in a corridor full of fast-walking executives.

'Tell me, when do the nerves hit? Aside from a shot of black hair and a tanned bosom a few rows away, all palpitations appear to be present and accounted for. It pains to be so contrived when your aim is to be anything but.'

An old lady eyes the seat next to me. She doesn't seem to notice or care that I'm valuing this time alone. After eight hours trapped on a plane, I contemplate stretching my legs out and taking up the whole bench. The temptation subsides.

"Oi, so that's where you've got to." A gruff Englishman steps his way through the crowd. "What the bloody hell do you think you're doing?"

Now seated, the old lady is ignoring him.

"I said quarter to eleven. We've missed boarding now, thank you very much."

The lady slowly bats her eyes, stares up and purses her lips. The sagging skin around her neck starts to gather, cloaking tensed veins and ligaments.

I feel sorry for her. The husband is not backing down.

"Come on then. I told you..."

Poolhall—Jail—Library

The lady reaches tipping point. She lets fly.

"If you'd blinkin' well bothered to check it, no we don't have to board now. The screen says quarter past. Can I get five minutes of peace from you Gordon? I've bloody had it. Just bugger off for God's sake will you."

I take the opportunity to move to another lounge, further up towards my gate. People continue to zoom by on travelators, even at almost midnight. It could be that they use the travelators simply to avoid the horrible, garish carpet. Indeed, who knows what horrors lay camouflaged on its surface.

As I continue to bide time until my flight, a young mother and infant son stop at the garden bed across from me. She plays hide and seek with him behind her hands.

The child giggles at first and then, as if unable to withhold it, hugs his Mum tightly and bops up and down singing "You are my life, you are my life" over and over.

I can't help but smile and, at the same time, contrast this with the older couple from earlier. It's funny how age and familiarity alter perception, not always for the better.

Without a word of a lie, I turn to the book I am using as my travel companion – Jung's *Memories, Dreams, Reflections* – and begin where I have left off.

The next passage reads: "Time exerts a mighty suction which greedily draws everything living into itself. We can only escape from it by pressing forward."

And onwards I go. Thirteen hours to Zurich.

We're still chasing in darkness. The air above the Bay of Bengal is excited and playful. I find it impossible to sleep until we're somewhere over the west of India. Even then I only manage a mere two hours rest and curse myself for missing the starlit scenery.

The Arabian Gulf sees us pass by Oman and then skirt along Kuwait. I'm on the wrong side of the plane to witness the oil fires, but there's the odd shining city peering out from beneath a sandy blanket.

The lady next to me kicks her shoes off somewhere near Lebanon; the pungent odour almost distracting me from first glimpses of the Mediterranean and the lights of Tripoli. The Lebanese coastline surprises more than anything. It looks stunning under moonlight, although I am sure to live there would bring its own particular challenges.

As if making amends for her wafting feet, my co-passenger offers me her bridnight meal. I'm not sure that's what you call it. I've never eaten a set meal between the hours of midnight and 6am before. So bridnight is what I'll name it.

I begin tucking into the dehydrated portions as we make a pass of Istanbul. The city spreads far and wide, little tentacles of illuminated roads hugging the coast and then venturing inland. I try to imagine if there is any commotion at ground level this late at night. I'm sure there would be. We aren't even flying directly over Istanbul, but it excites me more than anywhere else so far. I picture grittiness, shadiness, decadence all at once.

Too soon it is all behind me. I add it to my list of places to one day visit.

The in-flight display is charting the flight path and counting down the minutes to touchdown, but it drags out far too slowly. I want to see Budapest and Transylvania, Vienna and Salzburg. These places only appear briefly on the edges of the monitor though, teasing out the final moments of the journey.

Arrival in Zurich comes with more than a touch of exhilaration. At first sunlight the city is shrouded in dense fog. The plane leers left and right, adjusting itself in the colossal pillow. When we touch down, a loud collective gasp emits from the on-board passengers, some anticipating there were still several hundred feet left to descend to an obscured runway. Even in his address, the captain admits he did not sight the tarmac until a few hundred metres away.

As cleaning staff and customs officers board the plane, I take the chance to stretch. We have 30 minutes to refuel before taking off again. The delay is made all the better by the cute girl double-checking my passport. She could be a model, but she's in complete business mode.

ASKED to describe my upbringing, I'd contend it was one of many responsibilities and few novelties. It was partly out of necessity and partly due to Mum's experiences during the war. She could be hard and cold – and thrifty in the extreme.

When I finally stopped looking after my younger brothers and attended school regularly, it wasn't for long. I'd like to think I was more than a little smart...I had grand designs on attending art college or studying archaeology. But Mum certainly didn't see it that way.

"Waste of time sending a girl to college. You're better off leaving school and getting a job now."

It still pains me, especially now Mum has provided for one of her male grandkids to follow the exact art college dream I once chased.

I left school before the end of Grade Nine. I was only 14 and my first work was in childcare. Mum started a creche with Mrs Jacobs down the road and it was easy enough to fall into. I'd get some time alone with Mum minus my siblings, which made for a nice escape.

About a year into it Mum began trusting me with home jobs. Most of the work was still at the centre, but occasionally you'd get a baby-sitting task at a client's house. That was how I met Lenny.

Lenny and Cheryl's daughter was only two, and both of the adults worked. They paid extra so I would come to their place. Often Lenny finished a bit earlier, but he'd pay me to stay until Cheryl arrived home as well. That way if he wanted to watch television, shower or rest, I'd still be around.

We would talk. I'd confide how much I hated not seeing my own Dad when he was on nightshift, or how I felt the boys always got more attention at home. I told him about my career and how I was one day going to travel and paint the Seven Wonders of the World. I even made up an imaginary boyfriend to seem more interesting. I'm pretty sure Lenny guessed who it was loosely based on.

Poolhall—Jail—Library

It was during one of our chats that I sat on the bench in his kitchen, something I wouldn't dare do at home. Lenny had been drinking milk straight from the carton and made me promise I wouldn't tell Cheryl. He was so funny, a big boy trying to be a man, but with a nice house and family. I'd imagined many times that I was Cheryl. He'd come home to me and I'd never have to leave.

For some reason that day I felt the urge to grab his hair as he bent down to put the milk in the fridge. At first, I just ruffled it at the back, his blond, straggly locks puffing out. But then I kept my hand there, combing softly through the strands as he turned to face me.

His cheeks reddened and he smiled awkwardly. Standing up, he brought his face close to mine. I could make out where he'd shaved and became fascinated by how alluring his skin seemed. I began rubbing my hand across his stubble, giggling nervously as he leaned in to kiss me.

Hooking me up in his arms, Lenny carried me up the stairs and straight through to the main bedroom.

It seemed like we made love for hours.

This became our ritual at least once a week. Our little secret. For once I felt like I had become good at something.

Although I liked Lenny, I never dreamed he would leave Cheryl for me. In fact, I liked Cheryl – probably felt a little sorry for her more than anything. She was pleasant enough and very pretty, but had lost the joy of life.

Inevitably, after six months or so, guilt became a factor. Lenny and I both agreed to end it, not that it was necessarily as straightforward as that.

Looking back, it might be easy for others to think I was taken advantage of. But I hold no regrets. I loved every minute of it.

To me it was not just a physical awakening. It was my first hint that things could be better in the world.

MANCHESTER

FROM Zurich, Manchester is a hop, skip and a jump. Compared to the rest of the journey from Australia it is anyway. Thick clouds continue over the north of Europe, so much so that all I can see are sections of the Alps and a little of eastern France. At least it will remain a secret for when I tour the Continent in December.

My first impression of Manchester from the air is that it is made of tiny, brown Lego blocks, perhaps a Fabuland kit. It's a weird, fulfilling experience to be landing in your motherland. All the old television shows, the stories from your grandparents; they start to make sense in a way they didn't before.

This is a reality, something that has always existed and been experienced by others. Yet at the same time I feel like I alone have discovered this parallel universe.

The whole experience strikes me as a kind of rebirth; having to relearn all of society's constructs and guidelines. I feel incapable of the simplest things and find myself asking for directions at the train station, despite having a map and timetable at my disposal. Even crossing the road or finding the right platform seems like a major accomplishment. Thank God they speak the same language here.

Coordinating my body and brain is a major issue. For the past day all I've been is a consciousness. When you're sitting on a plane, experiencing life without physical involvement, you wonder if it's all perhaps a cinematic façade. My body has now grown distant. Moving and touching just doesn't seem right.

There's little time to give extended thought to the issue as the express train to the city pulls away. An overwhelming sense of fascination prevails, even just looking at the shape and colour of the seats, what people are wearing, what's on the front of the newspaper. On one hand I feel as though I have truly accomplished something, like I could just turn around now, go back home and say "Hey everyone, *I've* been overseas".

But there's so much more to this. I have to prove myself. The inspector asks for my fare and all I can offer is a blank expression, despite holding the receipt safe in my front pocket. There is a lingering suspicion that I've somehow been caught out and that everyone knows I don't belong here. But I hand him my ticket, he gives it a cursory glance, and he hands it back with a disappointing lack of fanfare.

Manchester's main rail hub is Piccadilly Station, not to be confused with Piccadilly Circus from Monopoly, which is actually in London. When we arrive, I load up my 90kg frame with my main backpack and daypack. Together they weigh about 35kg, clinging to me like two obstinate koalas. They dig in at the shoulders and strain the lower back.

The late autumn air strangles the breath from within me and I focus solely on getting to my hostel without having to stop.

Down the ramp to the city centre, a group of boys in tracksuit pants and baseball caps approach me. Carrying all my luggage, I feel like a roving target for street youth.

"Ay fella. Got any Rizzler? Know wot I mean?"

How deliciously, delightfully English. I wish my mates were here for this moment. I most certainly know what he is alluding to.

"Sorry mate, I don't smoke," I reply, smiling and keeping my stride.

It takes a while to locate my hostel, The Hatters, but the walk is thoroughly enjoyable. I still feel like an astronaut taking their first steps on the moon.

Jetlag is definitely taking its toll. It's 9am and I've been awake for roughly 34 of the last 36 hours. The receptionist at The Hatters takes my money, but tells me I can't check in for another six hours while guests leave and the beds are remade. Thankfully she at least allows me to store my heaviest backpack.

I wander off through the adjoining streets, past the trams on Market Street, the Arndale shopping complex, the Urbis arts precinct and St Ann's Square. I contemplate forking out £3 for a black pudding, just to say I've eaten the real thing off the streets of Manchester. My budget is extremely slim. I've estimated I can only afford to spend £30 per day. That has to cover meals, accommodation, transport, everything. It's a measure of my desperation that I've allowed such slender margin for error.

Deciding against the black pudding, I walk on. There's a giant Ferris wheel near the Arndale and some alluring tucked-away pubs close to the Printworks Centre. One has a long garden bed of flowering chrysanthemums out front. Another has a thatched roof and a striking black-and-white Tudor exterior.

Further along, at the extremity of Deansgate, I stumble upon the Boddington's brewery. Instantaneous thoughts arise of the time my mate Jabba and I sat drinking the famous drop on The Strand in Townsville, overlooking Magnetic Island. I take out my camera and add it to a growing image library.

For the next few days it seems all I do is sleep, take photos and load up on 99p pasta from Tesco's.

I'm consistently waking at 3.30am, a combined legacy of jetlag and the amount of noise my Polish roommates make when returning from nights out drinking. Several days in a row I meet the same people for a bridnight meal in the kitchen.

There are brief expeditions around town, most notably to the consuming hovel that is Affleck's Palace – a four-story maze of thrift shops. I buy a couple of rock'n'roll badges for my jacket and a black stretch earring.

Other than that, I do some sit-ups, some push-ups, read and conserve money.

It's all with a purpose. Saturday will be the first major event on my schedule, the Super League grand final. I've planned to have my first beer on foreign soil at Old Trafford, preferably

Poolhall—Jail—Library

while singing something inappropriate and silly. Restricting my activities now will only make that particular occasion more enjoyable.

As it eventuates, I last all the way until midnight Friday without touching alcohol. Even then, the beverage comes free.

Kinato is a six-foot-four African American, dressed in a thick khaki jacket, jeans and trainers. He's watching *The Negotiator* with Samuel L Jackson in the recreation room and drinking Foster's. The standard conversation ensues about how nobody in Australia actually touches Foster's.

"It's cat's piss mate," I eloquently inform him.

Kinato has a stash of Carling in the fridge. He grabs one out and offers it to me instead.

"Perhaps this is more to your liking?"

By the time the movie finishes, there's roughly 10 other guests in the room, either joining us on the couches or using the pool table. One of the Polish guys brutishly rips out the coin slot so he can play for free.

A few beers in, I get to talking with Kinato. He seems like a cool dude; very well-spoken and worldly. Kinato's been living at The Hatters for over a month, so he's seen a lot of my type come and go. His aim is to get together enough money to study music or sound production, then maybe even try his hand at playing football.

It's inescapable. Dressed in that military coat and talking about his dreams, he reminds me of Uncle Howard.

A girl from Virginia hears us discussing music and slides down the couch.

"Hey did you guys know that Badly Drawn Boy once did a recording in this building?" She lights up in a look of total amazement. I'm impressed, but obviously not as much as her.

Kinato seizes on her over-animated expressions and sits upright. They start talking about all things American and after a few minutes, I realise I'm superfluous to their needs.

Scanning around the room, there's a pretty girl with flame-red hair and round glasses, sitting cross-legged on a beanbag. She looks deep in thought, one hand clutching an apple and the other a novel.

Her eyes flicker up and she catches me staring. Feigning interest in the hijinks at the pool table, I look away. It's only momentary however, and soon my eyes return. She really is quite beautiful. Her face is remarkably attractive, a porcelain complexion and a dainty little chin. She doesn't look like one for sports, but her figure is slim and petite like a ballerina.

Now reading her book, the girl twists her head to bite from the apple and catches me out once more. I'm more than a little embarrassed, but again and again my eyes keep returning.

Eventually it reaches a point where she puts down her book and stares straight back. It's not an angry stare. In fact, I'm not quite sure what emotion it conveys at all.

If anyone were to look at us right now, they'd clearly see what is going on. But nobody cares. They're all too engrossed in their own conversations.

Maintaining the gaze, my lungs swell until they're uncomfortable. I'm self-conscious in every way. I'm incapable of this. I look away, bid Kinato goodnight and get up and leave.

IT WASN'T exactly smouldering glances across aisles of ox tongue and offal, but it's true I fell for Marty Nichols in the meat section of Woolworths. Having resigned from the Mills and Boon world of baby-sitting, it was now the supermarket life for me. Marty and I worked side-by-side as apprentice butchers and one day he asked if I'd like to go for a drive to the Sunshine Coast on the weekend...not that either of us had a license back then.

What started as a deli dalliance escalated rapidly. We soon lived in each other's pockets and I revelled in the wondrous attention that accompanied my first romantic relationship with someone of my own age.

Poolhall—Jail—Library

Neither of us was close to our parents and there were countless nights spent escaping to Paddington skate bowl and poolhalls of Brisbane's inner western suburbs. Marty had the fashionable haircut of 1975 – unbrushed shoulder length brown hair, thick and fluffy. His family lived just down the street from Enoggera Army Barracks and when he wasn't cutting meat at Woolworths, he sold porno magazines to soldiers for extra money. I didn't agree with everything he did, but Marty had me hooked.

He was a natural artist at everything he turned his hand to and we would lay together, talking about plans to design jewellery, illustrate children's books and sell our paintings.

I was probably the only person who saw beyond the accomplished exterior back then. I'll never forget the first time I went to dinner to meet Marty's parents.

Marty was one of seven kids. The middle one in fact. Although his older siblings had left home, it was still a tight fit when everyone packed into the Nichols' tiny kitchen. You'd have only the slightest gap between the bench and table to squeeze your chair and quite often you'd end up on the very corner.

Mrs Nichols, Peggy, was a lovely lady and that was evident the first time I visited. She'd been a nurse at rural Esk Hospital and was of a most genial nature. It was while at Esk that she met John, Marty's father. He'd only just returned from war duty and had been riding around Lake Somerset when he came off his motorbike. His left leg had to be amputated.

To say John was a study in contrast to Peggy would be an understatement. Whether it came from his accident or his youth, he possessed the most infernal bitterness. Not surprisingly he became a local school headmaster.

That first night at the dinner table, the kids all went quiet when John walked through the door. Peggy was still scurrying around, cooking the last of the dinner and tidying here and there. She was very eager to make a good impression, yet I suspected she'd tried to do the same thing each night for John.

In the presence of her husband, Peggy and her shadow were hard to differentiate.

Although she was loath to discuss it, Peggy descended from people of colour somewhere in her bloodline. There was talk her paternal family had Spanish traces, and a more uncomfortable suggestion that perhaps the Aboriginal workers employed on her grandparents' property had something to do with her darkened skin. However, this was in the days when to raise such issues was sacrilege. She didn't wish to identify as being anything other than Australian.

When we came to be seated for dinner, John was at the head of table, where he could still see the television in the loungeroom. Heads were bowed and voices lowered for grace. They stayed much the same throughout dinner.

"So, Dog, is this your girlfriend then?"

That's when I heard it – 'Dog'.

Marty winced and there was a sideward glance between us, his being of embarrassment and mine of shock. His father was not calling him Dog affectionately. It was derisory, dripping with contempt.

Later that night when Marty walked me to the bus shelter, I asked him about the name. It had remained ignored since it left John's mouth. Marty was reluctant, but he revealed he had worn the name for as long as he could remember. For some reason, he believed his father straight out hated him. Not that I think John particularly liked anyone.

One of Marty's earliest memories of being called Dog was when he had to sit in the 'kennel'. The 'kennel' was a deep cupboard with a large void where the glass doors had been removed from the crockery section. If Marty did anything wrong, John would make him sit in the 'kennel' on a thin perch. If he moved or fell off balance, Marty would get the strap.

I was horrified. The first bus came and went and neither of us hopped on. I remained in the shelter cradling Marty's head in my lap. He had completely broken down, sobbing *uncontrollably as he curled up, anguished and tormented beyond belief. I heard it all that night – how his Dad hit his Mum, even to the extremity of using his prosthetic leg to beat her. I heard how John had touched Marty when he was younger. Another bus went by as the realisation came to me that my own problems at home could not even compare to this.*

Marty was either going to go crazy or kill his father.

That night at the bus stop we decided we would move out together.

OLD TRAFFORD

ON days like today, the sun, the atmosphere, the alcohol; you don't drink them up, they drink you. The Old Wellington Inn is one of the most famous pubs in Manchester. It's the black-and-white Tudor building from my earlier reconnaissance and has stuck in my memory firmly enough to warrant a beer there.

The city populous has responded accordingly to the unusual warmth and brightness for Manchester in October. Saturday shoppers, mingling teens and a steady influx of rugby league fans are streaming through the Millennium Quarter. I plan to consume just enough pints to make for a pleasant walk to Old Trafford, but not hurt the hip pocket.

I may be headed to the 'Theatre of Dreams', yet The Old Wellington is an item of fascination on its own. Connected to the similarly antiquated Sinclair's Oyster Bar, it dates back to the 16th Century and has lived through the Great Plague and the odd bomb or two. Most recently in 1996, eerily enough on a busy Saturday morning, it was close to the centre of an IRA attack. It has since been dismantled, moved and reassembled a short distance away, part of a regeneration project for the area.

Half-timbered on the exterior, inside the Old Wellington is a rabbit warren of musky rooms in which you can pull up a pew and take any number of vantage points over the square below. But today is too nice to waste sitting under a roof. To keep with the Super League grand final theme, I select a fine and fitting pint of Tetley's and stroll to the far bench in the beer garden.

Seats are at a premium here. There are more young, preened women here than I have seen since leaving Australia, but each arm is attached to an equally well-manicured young man. They're chatting at tables in groups, savouring hot chips from greasy baskets and allowing the sun and the alcohol to consume them too.

Within time a group of middle-aged men wearing Leeds Rhinos jerseys plonk themselves at my table.

Poolhall—Jail—Library

"Mind if we sit here?" the heavily-bearded man enquires.
"Happy to have the company."
The hirsute fellow, I learn, is Fozzy. He works in information technology and has been a mad Rhinos fan since infancy. He also looks a lot like my Dad. Graham is a school teacher. Peter is another IT boffin. Then there's Tony.
"What do you do?" I ask Tony.
Thin and wiry, Tony has a gentle face and a look of respectability. "I'm actually a physio for some of the Rhinos boys," he says covertly. "What do you do then?"
I tell them I'm the media manager for a leading rugby league organisation in Australia.
There's a look around the table. "What bullshit is this young Aussie git, dressed like a hobo, with a name like a fairy, feeding us?" But they continue chatting politely, mindful there are no free seats elsewhere.
Usually I'm overcome with a sensation of boredom and depressing ambivalence in the presence of men this age. Yet they keep me entertained and I wonder why older people don't stimulate me this much normally. Is it my own preconceived prejudices that don't give anyone over 40 a chance?
The Shambles is what the locals call this precinct and I'm well on my way to feeling a little shambolic myself after 3pm. Sensing my slender budget, the lads have taken it upon themselves to introduce me to some previously untried beverages – John Smith's, Young's, Oranjeboom. They repeatedly insist I put my wallet away.
To the backdrop of a dimming sun, an African drum band sets up on the edge of the beer garden. Their deep rhythm suits the mood perfectly. Fine company, fine drink and that surge of adrenalin that comes when alcohol mixes with anxiousness. As if carried by the beat, we arise and begin the long pilgrimage down Deansgate.
Old Trafford is far from what I expected. I had been duped to thinking it was merely a world-famous stadium, an

impressive steel and concrete structure that houses the most renowned football team known to man. It is much more. There are lovingly-painted murals along the entrance, the smell of tomato sauce smothering deep-fried delights and everywhere children tug at the hands of parents to get inside. Groups stop in front of me and stare upwards admiringly, as if cast in the shadow of the Grand Pyramid. Yet at the same time this place has similar charm and character to the local football club where I spent my youth.

I agree to meet my new-found friends after the match and, in the meantime, squeeze through to my allocated row. I have been seated with more Leeds fans. One is dressed as Friar Tuck, the other a giant Pokemon character. Lord knows why. I unwittingly find myself purring along to their passionate chants. "Neck him you tosser" or "You're a right bastard referee". The first 20 minutes of the match is a complete blur. An utterly surreal sensation fills my body and I cannot keep from gazing around in 360 degree turns. Disbelief and weightlessness take over.

"Fuck, I've actually made it here."

Outside of taking amphetamines, I have not felt this rush of exhilaration for years. The ambience and atmosphere are incredible

Themes of destiny swirl through my mind and I look for meaningful signs everywhere. Even as the game wears on and the Rhinos fall behind on the scoreboard, the blissful, childish joy barely dissipates.

Foz and the lads keep their word and, despite their evident disappointment at the loss, we link up afterward at the Pizza Hut across the road. On the long walk back into town, thus follows the after-match strategic dissection, seemingly a uniform ritual no matter what part of the planet you belong to, or what competition you follow.

We reach a trendy little bar called the Atlas Lounge and I sneak away from the group to buy them all a round of drinks.

Poolhall—Jail—Library

I know the others wouldn't stand for it, but I feel I owe them, even it costs me a relative fortune. The beer is starting to go down hard, however the experience is still keeping me entertained.

As the lads head for the train station I give them my sincerest thanks and take their contact details. They've opened my eyes to more than just a new city.

That said, my surrounds continue to intrigue me. Last pit-stop for the night is Corbieres, found down a narrow flight of plastered stairs that descend from ground level on a laneway. I've made a promise from the outset of this trip to look around every corner that grabs my interest. Descending to a breathless, windowless cave I find myself in a room of Generation Ys, sitting back in multi-coloured scarves and listening to Pink Floyd, The Rolling Stones, The Beatles and Queen. That shit just doesn't happen in Brisbane. It's a perfect spot for a nightcap, a pint of Hoegaarden on a rickety stool by the bar, exchanging smiles with anyone that bothers to smile first.

Back at the hostel I am well and truly ready for bed, but I bump into Kinato before I reach my bunk. He's more drunk than I and asks if he can recite some of his poetry to me.

"Yeah why not," I say.

Kinato comes across as a very passionate guy. Deep and thoughtful. He loves his words and I admire that. It's another thing I think is hard to find back home.

But there are some disturbing themes in his prose. I'm no angel, but he pushes the comfort zone. Violent homophobia, heavy drug abuse, intense paranoia. They underline nearly every one of his verses.

I see pain in Kinato's eyes and I want to help him, but I know I will be gone in the morning. It's not just his army jacket that reminds me of Uncle H.

UNCLE Owl, that's what Loxton called Howard when he first learnt to speak. A lot of kids seem to struggle with the pronunciation of H.

My brother and my son have always been undeniably close. No doubt it stems from the time that Marty spent away from home when Loxton was young. It was such a thrill for Marty to be accepted into the artistic community, and have the ability to travel, that he probably missed the best years of his only boy's life.

Howard becoming a surrogate father figure was quite peculiar in itself. He was the most insecure of all us Bergs and he remained utterly convinced that everybody despised him. Then again, maybe that's what drove him to treat Loxton so well.

Whatever people thought of him, Howard's intelligence was beyond question. He could recite geography and history with fascinating colour and precision. At Trivial Pursuit he was virtually unbeatable and, in matters of music and military, he could absolutely bore you to death with detail.

There is no way anybody would guess he had left school at 14 and been fired from every job he ever held.

One moment that sticks firmly in my mind was a day when Howard was visiting and we took the regular trek from our flat to Toombul Shopping Centre. For an infant, Loxton loved walking. Not so much did he love holding hands.

On one particular trip, for some reason Lox took off across Sandgate Road – all four lanes of it! Needless to say, I was in a mad panic. With a postman's van bearing down, Howard scampered over like a Saint Bernard and hoisted Lox out of the way. When my brother returned, he looked more nervous wreck than godly savoir, but he had proved his courage and love.

Although Loxton's vocabulary was rather limited at the time, the way he stuck close to Howard thereafter spoke volumes.

Together they'd spend hours in the back yard, digging holes and throwing macadamia nuts at toy soldiers from opposite sides of 'No Man's Land'. Eventually Howard melted *down a couple of old bullets, made them into metal figurines and painted them for Loxton. They were to be his special set of soldiers, but they still buried them in dirt and threw nuts at them anyway. One ritual I never understood was them drawing pictures for each other. Even though Howard was around our place every second day, he and Loxton would sketch and scribble, then mail off little packages to each other.*

I guess in the long run it suited a purpose because Marty was soon after bequeathed a house and land in Toowoomba when his aunt passed away. It meant the three of us moving two hours west and up the Great Dividing Range.

For both Lox and Howard, their geographical separation was a shock to the system.

They kept in touch by sending each other sketches on a weekly basis and, on the rare occasion they got to catch up, they would sneak away and keep to themselves. Sometimes they would breakdance, other times they'd play with robots and cars. It didn't seem to matter as they were inseparable.

Marty was only fleetingly jealous of the relationship between the pair. My husband's sum contribution to being a dad at that stage was to illegally gift Loxton a frill-necked lizard as a pet and to nickname his son 'Wally' after a monkey on a television commercial.

In many ways Marty had gained his own surrogate father and they too were spending plenty of time together. Andreas was a Greek artist who had become somewhat of a mentor to Marty at that same time. They met at a gallery at Clayfield and within months were touring up and down the east coast of Australia in a vintage orange-and-white striped bus which had been converted into a mobile exhibition room.

I never quite figured out Andreas at all. Thickly bearded, pushing 50 and more than a little overweight, he was married to a beautiful young girl in Tina, almost two decades his junior. Andreas could be either outlandishly generous or incredibly surly. Tina on the other hand was unwaveringly positive, and her fondness for flowers, food and children made her difficult not to feel warmth towards. That they should not have any children of their own seemed a mystery to me. As a couple, Andreas and Tina were altogether puzzling.

Though Andi shared a love of nature with his wife, his artistic predilection was for painting the female form and not always in the most flattering of poses. He was passionate about his work and would cover their house with artwork, often splashing vulgar creations directly onto the timber walls. It was uncomfortable to be around at times.

Thankfully Marty found his specialty in another area. His inspiration harked back to family origins on the Darling Downs, particularly the villages surrounding Toowoomba; the likes of Allora, Clifton, Leyburn, Ravensbourne and Crows Nest. He delighted in capturing gums and billabongs, sunsets, yellowed grass and wooden sheds in his brush strokes.

While Andreas encouraged Marty's work, I also suspected he nurtured other emotions and attitudes. To be controlling, imposing and downright disrespectful was not something I had ever expected to see of my husband.

YORK

HURRAH! Finally, I've snapped out of my jetlag cycle of waking before dawn. I'm thinking the consumption of alcohol on grand final day may have assisted somewhat.

It's 9.30am before my eyes take their first blinks of the day and that means just enough time to hurriedly dress, check out of the hostel and scamper to the train. Goodbye Manchester! You've been a wonderful virgin experience for this traveller.

The journey to York is packed. It's standing room only as Leeds and Bradford fans return along the eastern railway, many the worse for wear. I myself am a touch bleary, but a bottle of water and the continuing fascination with my surrounds keeps me alert.

We pass by Salford and Dewsbury, flitting through tunnels under the Pennines until we start hitting beautiful, tranquil country towns. I'm most impressed with Walsden and Todmorden. They sit cloaked in lush valleys on all sides and evoke a stirring of the subconscious, as if sometime, somewhere I've seen them on a postcard.

By rail, York is perfectly gift-wrapped. You cruise right up to the heart of the town, but the journey gives away none of its secrets. Stepping off onto the platform, you notice the station is a well-preserved, early century design, but not totally unlike any other number of English rail stops. Then you climb the steps, turn and head to the exit, make it past the taxis and buses and...find yourself staring straight at a medieval fortress wall.

My head is permanently creased to one side, scanning the old stones for hints of history as I walk alongside the towering structure and then around to one of the immensely impressive city gates, Micklegate, from which my hostel is only a few doors away.

Never had I imagined being able to sleep 50m inside an ancient rampart and castle wall. I'm conscious of being rudely brief with the receptionist as I make a hurried introduction, quickly stow my gear and return to the street to continue the exploration.

The laneways to the very centre of the city are narrow and cobbled. I call them laneways, even though they seem to be the main route. Pedestrians reign supreme here. People amble comfortably, as if shank's pony is the only form of transportation known.

A bus has the temerity to try and squeeze through on one tight intersection. Taken by complete surprise, an Italian tourist steps out in front as the bus turns sharply behind her. It necessitates me lunging forward, grabbing her by the shoulders and whisking her away inches from an unhappy holiday. We both draw a sharp breath, she thanks me and I continue on my way.

Crossing over the River Ouse, just enough room exists on the sidewalk to pull the camera from my backpack. Leisure boats split scenery which would otherwise belong to a William Turner canvas. On the far side of the bridge, steps lead down to a cobbled dock. Barely a spare inch remains as young lovers eat fish and chips, watch the watercraft and enjoy a beautiful Sunday's weather.

I've been lucky indeed to fall into this city, almost entirely by accident. York was a dot on the map – a stopover – which I knew very little about until this day.

Continuing, I take special notice of the antiquated shops, cluttered together, leaning forwards towards the pavement, as if they are listening to conversations below. Each street has a mind of its own and curls and twists with no intention of meeting another thoroughfare until chance should make them cross.

There comes a point, deep into this area of commerce, that you cannot ignore the massive shadow being cast over you. It belongs to the York Minster, among the largest houses of worship known to man. It's a monolith and would otherwise

Poolhall—Jail—Library

dominate most cities. Yet there is so much to be discovered in York that it bides its time.

Not being one for religious leanings, I opt not to tour inside the Minster and instead walk a circular path that brings me around Monkgate, Bootham Bar, an art gallery and the former kings' manor. Henry VIII stayed here, so did Charles I. Today a shabbily dressed man with a cigarette and a pit bull terrier stands outside; the new royalty as it so happens. With his thick Yorkshire accent, he's hassling a girl who looks to be under some illicit influence and everyone is giving them a wide berth. They stand out like sore thumbs in York, but I can appreciate the yin and yang. It's all blissfully English to me.

Back towards the hostel is a plastered white pub with thatch roofing – The Priory. I order a Black Sheep and watch the barmaid pump it from the tap. It flows like charcoal soap suds, slowly and thickly.

Today I believe just one beer will do me, so I sup in a most genteel manner. Small mouthfuls. Swished from cheek to cheek. Pressed with the tongue back against the esophagus. Savouring the palate. Never have I drunk like this before. It's sad. I'm 27 and for the first time I'm tasting ingredients, appreciating nuances, not guzzling with the sole aim to be legless.

I quite like this new method of drinking. What say I shall have another?

The second Black Sheep comes accompanied by a serve of chicken breast and vegetables. I'm being rather outlandish with my spending now. It's my first meal that's cost more than £3. Not to worry, I should save money in the coming days. It's only the quiet north after all.

There's maybe 20 metres separating The Priory from my bed for the night. If only the next pub down hadn't put out a sign advertising the soccer. Manchester City versus Newcastle.

Montey's is not exactly your average sports bar. There's Bowie, Hendrix, Presley peering down from the walls, leering over platinum records and hand-me-down guitars. Three boys with dyed black hair sit on the next table from me. They have multiple piercings, tattoos and a protective shield of hairspray. Beside them is a family with two kids, running from inside to the beer garden and back to the table again.

Together with the barman, everyone is watching the big screen intently, praying one of these hapless teams can produce something special. The vibe to the place is incredible and the Bombardier, I decide, has a much fruitier, zestier tang than the Black Sheep.

Still, I think I may need another to be sure.

Further samples confirm my suspicions, corroborated later at The Windmill, which coincidentally shows another game straight after that at Montey's.

"I really like this place. So historic, friendly, comfortable in every way," I think. I'm climbing the strata of alcoholic euphoria, unfazed by the chilling wind as I walk my way up the street. "I have to figure out a way to live here one day. Maybe play rugby league here for a year. Study could be on option. I bet I'd find the perfect girl. Pure soul, perfect complexion."

The doorman at The Parish only gives me a slight glance as I pass by. Clearly, I'm not as intoxicated as I feel.

Large Viking horns, draped in blue and red ribbons stream down from the ceiling, and woolen baubles hang to the bar below. The York natives rejoice in their Scandinavian links, even though as one patron puts it: "It's hard to understand. We got our arses kicked by them".

Next to the horns, the beer lines run, wrapping their way in spirals and delivering the amber fluid impressively, as if straight from the Nordic gods. The Parish is an old, dark grey-stoned church and has been restored carefully with utmost stylistic consideration. All the wording is in a powerful, thick silver design, with furnishings and window frames gleaming the same colour. The chairs are high and well-padded, gathered around thick mahogany tables and occupied by the best dressed in

Poolhall—Jail—Library

town. There's a pack of English roses laying down roots around a settee on ground level, giggling and growing progressively louder. By now I am in contemplative mode and I watch them only in glances between deep personal philosophical debate.

The bouncer is eyeing me like I am some oddball, as if it's heresy to be anything other than mind-numbingly chatty and boastful when tipsy. But I ignore his attempts to impose on my thoughts and recline peacefully into the chair. I want to stay here forever. I've felt an instant bond with a physical location for the first time since I was a teenager.

THERE was a certain darkness to Lox, I suspect even before things turned bad for his father and me. His run towards the traffic on Sandgate Road was like a foreboding of things to come.

When Kim was born a few months into our time in Toowoomba, Lox was absolutely terrible to his younger sister. Once, he pushed her pram as fast as he could downhill towards an embankment. Luckily the pram spun around rather than tipping over. Another time he covered her in thick red clay from head to toe and just stood there laughing as she cried and gasped for breath. On several occasions he found Kim's baby bath and used it as a toilet.

While Marty was down south selling his paintings, Loxton grew out of control. He would constantly run away from me and yell "You can't catch me, I'm the Gingernut Kid". I wonder how amusing he would have found it if I had actually been able to keep up with him. More worryingly, he would do things to purposely scare me – like hiding when we were out shopping. There was a particular day at Myers department store in Toowoomba that I can reference. Lox had secreted himself behind a rack of clothes, pressing up against a window. When I found him, he was staring at a long crack through the thick pane, eerily transfixed. Before I could grab Lox, he ran his palm over the length of the crack, slicing deeply along his hand. He barely whimpered, instead concentrating intently on the thick redness gushing all over the glass and his shirt. The more passers-by that stopped to watch, the more he was amused.

Loxton really did some strange things for a kid. He'd stand out the front of the house and throw big rocks in the air as an apparent display of strength to others in the neighbourhood. That lasted until the day he cracked himself heavily on the forehead and received a pronounced scar. When my youngest brother Craig visited, Loxton would constantly test his patience, goad him and then roll on the floor and giggle uncontrollably when Craig lashed him with the cord of the kettle.

Poolhall—Jail—Library

Extremely idiosyncratic would be one way of describing my boy. Unsettling would be another. I don't think I even knew what autism was back then, but these days I certainly question if he was on the outer fringes of the spectrum.

Whether it be capital cities or flags or insects, machines or even languages, Loxton would intensely focus on a topic and hunt up every piece of information he could find. It was a source of pride for me to educate my son and, before the time most kids were in kindergarten, he could already count to 20 in four different dialects. We taught him to complete jigsaw puzzles back-to-front, so that he could not 'cheat' by being guided by the picture on the front. His advancement in that respect, I took as a blessing.

Yet, at the same time he also pursued activities that had absolutely nothing to do with me or his father. I was never one for sports, but Lox would take his plastic tricycle down to the dilapidated velodrome, which sat in the middle of the parkland between our house and the sawmill. He rode monotonously around for hours until completely breathless. After months and months of this, eventually he split apart the frame on his trike. Other times he would run for as far as he was allowed. It was a good idea to let him keep going, because any unspent energy would inevitably come back to haunt me in the form of temper tantrums.

Our long walks into town for shopping expeditions and visits to the public aviary were frequently interrupted by Loxton's haphazard wanderings. Passing Downlands College one afternoon, he caught sight of a rugby match and stood still, hypnotised. It took all my strength and persuasion to rip him away so we could continue. Soon after he was given a hard plastic moneybox in the shape of a rugby ball. He never placed any coins inside. Instead he would play imaginary games in solitary, diving to the dirt and squeezing the air from within himself, booting the solid polymer ball until the top of his foot was raw.

Not that I could have ever known, but that one game at Downlands probably saved Loxton's life in the long run.

Another factor from this time that would leave an indelible mark on the future was the continuing relationship between Lox and his uncle. Despite the tyranny of distance, they still kept in close touch. Without fail each week they would swap drawings. Loxton's usually consisted of a few words he'd learnt and whatever else he could manage to scribble at that age. Once more proving his misdirected talent, Howard would respond with artistic works of precision, flair and imagination. Receiving his work became the highlight of my week, not just Loxton's. First it was pictures of fire trucks, buses and steamrollers, then of relatives in funny situations and as it progressed, ongoing gags with regular characters. Howard was fascinated with insects, most of whom he called 'Eric' for no decipherable reason. Aside from the effort and regularity of his work, the passion in the subject matter was clear. No matter how difficult it was to capture one of Loxton's interests, he would attempt and somehow succeed.

Among the most memorable sketches was a mock drawing of a photo which had appeared in the local paper, The Toowoomba Chronicle. It featured a young Loxton at the Carnival of Flowers, inspecting one of the many parade floats as they prepared in Queens' Park. The newspaper photographer had snapped at the very moment Lox looked underneath to the wheels, bending and baring his bottom to the entire crowd. It became a running joke among the family and, over time, Howard managed to harvest a tendency in Loxton to show his affections through light-hearted mockery.

It was fortunate that Howard's attention often diverted mine. My relationship with my own parents was becoming more distant and Marty was scarcely around the house, even when he returned from travelling. His painting work had dried up significantly and, ever the dreamer, he toyed with bohemian ideas like making pottery and living a subsistence lifestyle, using the vegetable patch in our back yard.

To that point I thought he was simply idealistic – finding his way in the world.

That was until the day he phoned me, from somewhere else in Toowoomba, and said he wanted to invite two of his friends to come and live with us. They were both women.

"Don't you think it's possible to love more than one person...really when you think about it?"

NORTH YORKSHIRE MOORS

THERE doesn't seem to be a point defending the fact I am a tight-arse.

I've worked out that on my budget, if I subject myself to three meals of pre-packaged pasta, I will have about £5-10 to play with a day after accommodation and travel are subtracted.

In this instance I've tried to squeeze about four days' worth of activities into one, just so I can see everything, but only pay for one night at the hostel.

The lady at the information booth doesn't seem to understand this equation as she surveys my itinerary.

"Well for starters, at this time of year the bus doesn't go anywhere near Castle Howard," she frowns.

My heart sinks. Out of all the places I will see in the next three months, Castle Howard is definitely top 10 material.

"Where's the nearest it stops then?"

A look of incredulity sweeps her face. She's already told you once buddy. Not possible. Now scram.

Instead I board the bus for Malton and ask the driver. He's much more affable, but still scoops his neck out the window to survey the overcast sky.

"You sure pal? It's a good four mile from the stop on the highway. And that's over the countryside."

I can't begin to explain to him what the trip means to me. My uncle – my best friend and surrogate father – owes his name to the landmark. I've dreamt of this pilgrimage for years.

"And don't forget you'll be carrying that," the driver adds, pointing to the bulging backpack which resembles a particularly chubby adolescent.

I give a nod of consignment, not mentioning the additional bag in my hands, and offer a hearty thanks for his help. We take off. After a meandering journey through a dozen sleepy villages, the Coastliner doors open and I'm pointed in the approximate direction. I cannot even see the castle on the horizon.

At about half-a-mile the larger backpack starts pinching awkwardly at my shoulder blade. A mile or so later and the knees and ankles are complaining in unison. The heavens begin to spit with rain.

It was close to freezing in York when I left, but now I am steaming up like a glasshouse. Two jumpers, a t-shirt and a singlet make sure none of the sweat or heat escapes. Stopping to remove layers is the last thing I want to do and, as I push on like a repugnant engine, I'm sodden both on the outside and the inside.

My mindset is soothed as I pass through a speck on the map called Welburn. It shares the same name as my old woodwork teacher, but is infinitely more interesting. Humble cottages snuggling together, neighbours chatting over fences between proud and pristine gardens, not a scrap of litter or a speeding vehicle in sight. It's exactly the type of place I want to elope to when I retire.

Past the last house on the street, there is a slapdash sign, a broken crate with the words 'Castle Howard' and an arrow pointing down a muddy trail. It looks far from the beaten path. That said, I have no real idea where I am going anyway.

By the appearance of the trail, the only people to come this way previously did so in tractors. And they appear to have had a rough time of it too. The boggy thoroughfare leads past an old turnip mill that looks untouched since the 19th century, a graveyard of disused machinery, and then ends abruptly in an out-of-season crop field. Inexplicably, there are dead rabbits strewn across the paddock.

I pick my footing carefully until I can see where the path resumes at the opposite fence. It twists sharply downwards and to the right, through a grove and over a small creek. The trail becomes less and less distinguishable until I am forced to vault a gate that has rusted onto its latch. I am wandering aimlessly when I cross the path of a shepherd, walking with his wife and dog in tow.

They quiz me about where I am headed and nod and say 'aye' in that typical Yorkshire way that gives nothing away. Eventually I decipher they are happy to show me the way to Castle Howard. Indeed, they become chattier with every step, leading me through a sequence of gates which would have been otherwise unnegotiable.

We exit a field full of draught horses, goats and sheep, stopping at the base of a stony ridge that is unfenced.

"Well I guess you'll be in a hurry then," the shepherd says, creating an opening for me to walk ahead and scale the hillside alone. From where I stand, I can see the crumbling ruins of an old erection and assume I've made it onto the castle grounds. But as I stride further through the long grass, heaving my luggage with me, it becomes clear I have a way to go yet. The ridge unfolds and I meet winding bitumen which I pursue in pure hope. Mercifully it connects to a main road, passes through a rather impressive archway and, after another half-mile, finally delivers me along a row of fir trees to the entrance. The castle itself has been cloaked by cunning gardeners, so that only slender glimpses are possible through the wall of bushes at the entry point.

"You look like you've come a distance," chuckles the lady at the turnstile.

"Only from Australia." She accepts my dry humour warmly.

"I tell you what," she says as I strip off two layers of soaked clothing and gleefully stow my backpacks, "I'll let you in for kids' price."

It's a neat gesture, as fitting as it is charitable. Because since I was a little tacker, this place has been part of family folklore.

I purposely do my best to initially ignore the castle as I first inspect the grounds. There is a large and well-tended rose garden, over 2000 blossoms hidden between walls of hornbeam hedges. Its expanse and intricacy are suggestive of an Elizabethan maze or a stage for Lewis Carroll's Queen of Hearts. Passing through concentric archways, you reach

Poolhall—Jail—Library

a round fountain, an island amidst creamy blooms. Though each plant is manicured and perfectly sculpted, nature cannot be denied and, in the stems closest to the water, a clutch of spiders weave their own artistry.

After pausing briefly on an ornate bench, I exit the garden, wait for a miniature train to pass and walk downhill into a lush valley of greenery. Trees give way to acres and acres of playful grassy hillsides, lollygagging about until descending into a gluttonous lake, spilled wide at their feet and fed by fresh rain. Indeed, precipitation begins to drop on my shoulders with increasing regularity as I move to the woods at the rear of the castle.

A criss-cross of paths leads you in multiple directions through the dense and cool forest, where it is necessary to once more assume a jacket and hood. They lead to ornamental statues dubbed 'follies', amusements to the wealthy line of occupants, many of who were avid connoisseurs of foreign craftsmanship. Not content with a palace the size of several football fields, the Howard Family dotted these works in the corners of their estate to entertain guests and further demonstrate affluence. I am walking specifically to see the Temple of the Winds, an Italian-inspired construction which has caught my eye in a guidebook.

There is no disappointment when the woods finally open to a strange, lowering sunlight. The imminent thunderstorm has created a yellow hue, which sneaks through and bathes the temple before my eyes. It is a breathtaking work of art, touched on this particular day by a divinity of the skies. Towering female carvings on the edge of the temple ponder over the dales below like massive sentinels. As I round the structure, a lone escaped sheep is also quizzically tilting its head at the sublime masonry. It is a beautiful snapshot, one that should be ideally shared in company.

But for now, a balance must be struck between appreciation and available time, so I head back to the castle along an alternate pebbled route, passing by an elaborate pond and into a barricade of gushing fountains.

Finally, I am before it. This is not so much a castle as a sprawling manor of opulence. I open my eyes fully and accept the complete significance of being here. My diaphragm inflects and exerts with the extremities of pride and heartbreak, pure happiness and extreme sadness. Bending down to rub the ground, I comb the grass and push into the dirt with my fingertips.

In the corner, where the paving and long fountain ponds meet in skyward outbursts, there is a statue of a calming, all-knowing man cradling a new-born baby. He seems familiar.

With little time to waste, I line up for the guided tour. The attendants inside talk through their noses in haughty tones and offer instructions not to photograph any of the rooms. You get that sickening feeling of class privilege surrounding you. It is admittedly disconcerting to my socialist tendencies, and I know my uncle would share the same thoughts. But this is definitely one of those times when the old cliché rings true. The journey has been my reward, not so much the destination.

The guide informs us the Howard lineage traces back to Lord William Howard, the youngest son of the Duke of Norfolk, beheaded in 1572 and known commonly as 'Belted Will'. Other entertaining facets of the tour include tales of the inferno that once gutted the castle – leaving scorch marks on the high domed ceilings – and a spartan lunch involving some particularly arid scones.

Little time remains for me to scurry back overland to the bus stop and complete the rest of my day's tasks. I summon the cheek to jog portions, propelled by a new familiarity with the landscape and a searing adrenalin rush of destiny fulfilled. I have just crossed off one of the major items on my 'Do Before You Die' list.

Still panting when I board the bus, I begin a trek further out towards the North Sea. The North Yorkshire Moors are a national park of scenic wonder, predominantly in a pleasant way, rather than a breath-taking one. Whatever isn't green is covered in dense heather, lending a scarlet flavour to the countryside. Occasionally gushing streams will converge to plunge into dramatic crater-like valleys, but for the most part it is undulating hills, rollicking winds and villages of quintessential Englishness.

I have intentionally pursued this British essence, formed through years of being parked on my grandparents' musty brown sofa. As if clutching a Union Jack to their chests, they would religiously tune into shows like *Coronation Street, Eastenders, The Bill* and *To The Manor Born*. In thick Yorkshire accents I'd be told stories of what it was like to live in Britain – some of them repeated many a time – and always England was made to seem so much more sophisticated and fantastical than Australia.

Truth be known, I was a diehard *Thomas the Tank Engine* fan when I was a kid. Had all the books, all the trains. I also had a soft spot for *Heartbeat,* mostly for the constable's unwaveringly sweet wife. Both of these dramas, from opposite ends of the spectrum, were set in a tiny little dot on the map called Goathland. It is my next destination, one of the UK's most isolated towns, dropped smack bang in the middle of the Moors.

Perfectly on cue, a steam train passes under an impossibly steep and narrow bridge, just as the ageing bus crosses overhead and pulls into the stop. You can see automatically why Reverend Awdry picked this place and why PC Rowan didn't mind being stationed in these criminal backblocks. It is as though the whole place has been preserved perfectly from the 1940s. The train station boasts on a sign that it has 'stood still for 100 years', a claim supported by old grey milk canisters, leadlight street lamps and retro carriages shunted down quiet sidings.

Opposite, up a small ascent, is the Goathland Hotel – more commonly known as the Aidensfield Arms in *Heartbeat*. One must hunch to fit under the low ceilings, the walls are covered in memorabilia, and the tables and stools look to have taken care of arranging themselves in a cosy manner between the fireplace and bar. Enough time exists for just one beer and a stroll down the main street, where shops sell preserves, candy and lacework and where the garage has an old metal Shell pump with a Pegasus insignia. Out the front of the general store is a stunningly restored early-century police squaddie, a baby blue and off-white vehicle that seems prehistoric by today's technological standards. There is an endearing craftsmanship, innocence and splendour.

Before long I must leave, or else be left behind in this hypnotising time warp. I catch the last bus to Whitby, another isolated spot in the atlas. All I know is that in Whitby I can catch the morning train to Middlesborough and then to Edinburgh. Grandad has also told me it is one of the best places on Earth for seafood. When I arrive it is dark. I have a bed booked at the YMCA for the night, but possess neither a map nor the faintest clue which street to take. In a small place like this, how hard could it be to find?

Bemused passers-by initially give short shrift to pleas for directions, as I begin a flustered and fatigued stroll into the unknown. Eventually, after crossing a split bridge and evading a chorus of feeding seagulls, I encounter a couple who can at least give vague assistance. I follow a narrow laneway seaward, passing several lively hotels, before being met with a cascade of stairs and a YMCA signpost. The magnitude of the climb is not immediately apparent, but my legs are already sapped of energy and it only takes a few dozen stairs before pain commences. These steps keep going and going...and going. It is one final test of mental desire for the day.

At the summit there is a hippy dwelling, a shed-like hostel, a cemetery to one side and a truly startling set of ruins for what looks like an old cathedral. It's all intriguing, but my priority is checking in, dumping my bags and getting some food in my stomach. After unloading, I make sure to grab a guide pamphlet on the way out to dinner.

Among the harbour-side amusement fairs is a rough-and-ready locals' bar called The Jolly Sailor. Following my grandfather's advice, I order the cheapest portion of fish and chips, along with a side of mushy peas. Everyone inside is drinking Old Brewery Bitter on tap and talking about trawling and jigging (which I discover has nothing to do with dancing). The overtly gay barman sticks out like a zebra among a pride of lions.

While I wait for dinner I read from the pamphlet. One-hundred-and-ninety-nine steps, the literature informs me, is how many I scaled with my bag. It rings a bell and, reading on, I realise that Whitby was the inspiration for Bram Stoker's English scenes in *Dracula*. The cemetery at the top is St Mary's, a pivotal location to the iconic dark tale. Listing eerily above the cityscape, the ruined facade at the very top is Whitby Abbey.

I feel both energised and naïve to stumble upon these facts. Any proper traveller would have researched well in advance. More red-faced, I learn Whitby is also the former haunt of Captain James Cook, the South Pacific's eminent explorer and a staple of my childhood education. His statue stands out near the crashing waterfront and Endeavour Harbour is to my back.

True to advice, the dinner is delicious. My drooping eyes and contented belly give me just enough energy to cross back over the harbour and rescale the 199 steps, each one counted this time. As a last exploration before bed, I open the creaking gate to the graveyard and circle the grounds. Now I can see that on the far side is a cliff face, a sheer drop to the icy North Sea, the same body of water my maternal grandfather patrolled in the Second World War. Soft foundations encourage the headstones to rest at obscure angles and the unrelenting salty air has eaten through them in the most grotesque ways.

Tired pupils begin forming elaborate figures from the eroded stone and at once I am starkly aware of being alone in pitch blackness. At night, there is an eeriness and presence here that introduces men to a fear they don't admit to knowing.

Poolhall—Jail—Library

WE started running from Marty at regular intervals.

The kids would just get settled and we'd be up and on the move again. Without fail, he'd track us down, get friends to double-cross me and inevitably leave some sort of haunting calling card. I lost count of the number of times the police were involved.

From the day my father covertly drove us back down the Toowoomba Range to Brisbane is his old Ford XT Falcon, we were effectively fugitives, crimeless but hiding from a man I no longer knew.

The first place Marty traced us to was Albion, hiding out in a little dogbox of a flat that fronted the main road. It was downstairs, starved of natural sunlight, but flooded by the noise of banking traffic. The plasterboard walls only went within six inches of the roof, allowing gusts of wind to rudely intrude, along with the sound of endless daytime TV from neighbouring apartments. Indeed, Loxton used to whistle along each and every time the kids next door watched 'Skippy'. Outside, the communal laundry was a dilapidated row of chipped and dirty concrete tubs which stunk to high heaven. It was an absolute hovel; dark, noisy and cold.

My parents and siblings dubbed our flat 'The Black Hole'. It was a time when I really could have used some emotional and financial support, but instead I was left feeling incredibly humiliated and isolated. Kim had already celebrated her second birthday by now and I was still to lose the extra weight I'd gained during pregnancy. I was 24, divorced, fat, broke, unqualified and completely useless.

Reflecting, there were some pretty clear reasons why I yielded the first time Marty came crawling back. Despite everything he'd done, he showed up on the doorstep with presents for us all, flowers and offering to help out with the bills. Sometimes there is no pride in doing what you need to do to get by. The rosiness lasted about a fortnight before I was reminded what I had hoped to escape. Marty would lay in bed all day with the door closed and the blinds drawn. When he'd finally emerge, he'd yell at the children loud enough to let the whole block know. Our violent rows would echo in ferocity and he'd denigrate me with a perverse pleasure. It got so out of control, he smashed out sections of the plasterboard, just so he could walk easily between rooms and keep an eye on us all.

There was no money to pay for repairs, or in fact any money to keep up the lease. While Marty was on a mystery outing, I gathered our meagre belongings, called my father, and took off again. As embarrassing as it was, I was forced to borrow money from my youngest brother, Craig, who at 19 was already out-earning us all via his electronics business.

With what I could muster, I took on a piddly little flat on the Redcliffe Peninsula, at the time the furthest extremity of Brisbane City. It was still a little 'Wild West' in those parts and under-developed. Not only was our laundry communal, our bathrooms and toilets were too. Dad let me put the rental agreement under his name so the tenancy authority didn't have a record of our details, and we purposely omitted our number from the phone directory.

Most imminent in my mind was Loxton starting primary school. Government payments barely allowed me to cover his stationery and uniform costs. My son and I were also at loggerheads non-stop. When we'd left Albion, he'd tucked one of Marty's paintings under his arms. I took it more to heart than I should have, and made several comments to Loxton about either letting go of his father or choosing between the two of us. Lox couldn't comprehend what was happening. It resulted in him being even more withdrawn and odd.

Walking along the waterfront at Margate one day, he jumped headfirst down the gnarled bitumen stairs for no apparent reason. He didn't put his hands out to break his fall or anything. It still makes me cringe to think about it now. He was left with the most hideous scab, stretching the width of his forehead and all the way down both cheeks. Truthfully *it was like a dog had mauled him. There was pain and there were tears, but Lox also had a totally disconnected stare which bothered me.*

Not long afterwards, he disappeared down the rocky escarpment across the road from our flat, an almost vertical drop to Sutton's Beach which could have killed him. Marble-sized chunks of flesh were missing from his legs when he limped back and one flap of skin on his knee covered a deep cut almost to the bone. It was incredibly sickening and no surprise the scars have stayed with him into adulthood.

Were the incidents just coincidental; par for the course for a growing boy?

Of all the times in my life, those first few weeks on the peninsula were as great a challenge as any. Aside from the money, the kids and Marty, I was always looking over my shoulder at the obnoxious family which lived next door to us. They'd steal our toiletries and clothes from the shared amenities, they took off with Loxton's prized Batman cape and they made me feel incredibly intimidated, if only with their mere presence. Several times I caught their kids defecating in the backyard, more than once forcing me to clean it from my feet.

Regrettably, Howard had also gone back into hospital at this point in time. He'd starved himself stick-thin and been trying to hide it under heavy jackets. But his face had become so gaunt and, when spotted in a t-shirt, he looked strikingly akin to an emaciated prisoner of war. I'd chosen not to tell Loxton about the first time his uncle had been sent away, and on this latest occasion, I only said that he was 'sick'. Figuring Lox was old enough to at least handle that, we would catch the bus to visit Howard regularly and both the boys seemed to benefit from the interaction.

The drama and pressure were building and building. Quite honestly a few times I felt like I needed to see a psychologist myself.

An overwhelming sense of pride and relief came when Loxton was finally due to start school. Plenty of obstacles had been laid in our path, but we made it there. Giving both of the kids a strong education was at the top of my priority list. And he looked so damned cute in his little uniform too. Not that he could bear to hear me say that now.

Rising early in anticipation, we took almost a whole roll of photos once he was dressed and rearing to go. Some on the stairs, some near the banana trees out the back, a few posing with Kim, and then a couple at the cliff face overlooking Moreton Bay. Loxton was one of the few kids I knew that genuinely looked forward to going to school. He had an insatiable thirst for knowledge. It couldn't hurt for him to mingle with some boys his own age either.

With not long until assembly, I took the kids back to the flat. In total, we had only been taking photos at the cliff for 10 minutes, roughly 60 metres away on the gently curving esplanade. You could still see the front door from where we had been standing. I did not, however, see the wire mesh cage on the front lawn until we had just about stumbled on it. It had not been there when we'd left. On top there was a note.

Without looking at the hand writing I knew who had left it. It had all the hallmarks of his mind games. My eyes flicked up and down the street, my neck swivelling to see where he was hiding. To my knowledge he didn't even have a vehicle. How could he have made it this far so early in the morning? More importantly, how did he know where we were? I continued to scan suspiciously. Men walking into the store down the road, glimpses of people passing in cars, others strolling into the distance.

Before I had the chance, Loxton ran to the cage and grabbed the note.

"Dear Wally," Lox read in an excited panic, "A present for your first day of school. I hope he can become your friend. Love from Dad."

Poolhall—Jail—Library

Crouching, all three of us inspected the contents of the cage, long grass poking through the bottom. To me it seemed completely empty. I exchanged confused looks with the kids. What was this all about then?

"Oh cool!" Loxton yelled all of a sudden. "A turtle!"

When I finally dragged my son away from his new pet his entire mood had changed. He was flustered and fidgety, no longer thinking about class. Loxton didn't understand why I was upset and didn't comprehend why his father hadn't stuck around.

Unbelievably, on my return to collect him from school, Lox was being disciplined by his teacher for fighting on his first day. He lasted three weeks maximum at Humpybong Primary before we were gone again.

EDINBURGH

ESPIONAGE. That's the name of this game.

Less cryptically, I have found myself at a bar in the Scottish capital, just off the popular Grassmarket area and up a slight rise. It is called Espionage and proudly advertises £1.50 drinks all night on a Tuesday. Cartoon monkeys crawl across the windows. All up it looks like a winner.

Truthfully, the inside décor is not nearly as tacky as one would expect. It is modern and clean and cascades over three levels, the lowest of which is just 20 paces from my hostel entrance. For now, though I am on the second level chatting with a kindly barkeep named Amy.

Unmistakably English, she's in Edinburgh studying art, history and languages at the university. Her enunciation is near-perfect, almost of the plum-in-the-mouth variety. She asks how I'm finding her new home and I confess I've just practically arrived. There was only one train that allowed me to get from Whitby to Edinburgh in a day and it meant waking with the sparrows. Not until mid-afternoon did I reach my destination, a journey which started at a quaint rural station and ended in a heaving metropolis.

From Whitby to change-over in Middlesborough, the thin, humble track weaved slowly through its surrounds, offering shy salutations to babbling brooks and lavish emerald hills. In contrast, the second leg was on a plushly outfitted train, powering overland like a jet fighter but still taking in a sweeping scenic montage.

As I speak of the waterfalls, grazing sheep and horses on the approach to Edinburgh, Amy turns her lip down and emits an exaggerated sigh.

"You're making me miss home now. At my parents' place in Hertfordshire, I used to ride horses every day. We had dozens of animals. I want to go back and see my horses...make sure they're being looked after."

I tell her I've always been a city-slicker, lots of times didn't even have a garden. Once, when I was six, I tried riding a horse at my cousin's property at Samford and I'm sure I fell off then.

"Ha! Oh my gosh! No, I bet you'd love riding. You can't be a proper gypsy unless you can handle horseback. It's one of the most wonderful things in the world. You should learn scaredy-cat."

Amy tilts her head downwards as she polishes a tulip-shaped Duvel glass. At this early stage of the evening we are the only people on this level and I wonder if I should give her space. Nobody likes the guy who harasses the barmaid.

But then I catch her glancing sideward through her fringe, making sure I haven't taken offence to her light-hearted taunts. I decide to stay for another.

Amy pipes up. "Anyway, go on...what else do you make of Edinburgh?"

The immediate thing that struck me when we pulled into Waverley was the overpowering moodiness of the city. History and culture ooze through the grey stonework, peering down on the intrepid newcomer. Waverley station sits amid a chasm, and buildings all around rise sharply into the sky. This is a city of accomplishment and – until you can contribute to the grandeur that already exists – the visitor is interned to a nagging feeling of insignificance. Carried from the central brewery and trapped underneath low clouds, a thick, hoppy aroma fills the air. It attacks your olfactory senses in a distinctive and emotive manner. Combined with the dim winter sky, hilly terrain and gothic architecture, physically Edinburgh is confronting, at least initially.

That is not to say I find the inhabitants unfriendly. There is a learned, vibrant style to the people and they mill about unhindered by the sterilised design and ordinance of many modern hubs. These people walk cobbled streets that follow few architectural laws, crossing over archaic bridges that take them past buskers, comics and the towering monument to Sir

Walter Scott. All of this is done under the shadow of Edinburgh Castle, perched with dignity upon a rocky outcrop at one of the highest points in town.

Perhaps the greatest compliment that can be paid to any city is when you struggle to spy anyone wearing a uniform. It is a pleasant and liberating aesthetic.

And obviously Edinburgh has its various tattoos, festivals and sporting attractions on which to hang its hat. My friends have all raved about the nightlife. Gig posters line the alleyways and sociable types have a wealth of independent, creative stores from which to pick their threads.

I'm hoping to catch some decent live music in the two days I'm here. My drumming has gone downhill in the last year, I tell Amy, on account of work commitments. But I still love getting out to see bands.

"Yeah I sing a little," Amy casually responds when I ask her if she has any musical talent.

"What style? Go on give us a taste then."

For five tantalising seconds the mostly vacant room fills with a crystal-clear operatic voice, sweet and powerful all at once. It reverberates off the polished wooden floors and shelves of glass, finally absorbed into the burgundy couches nestling in the dimly-lit alcove. This girl, all five-foot-four of her hidden behind saucer-like green eyes, is clearly bluffing me.

"You don't just sing 'a little' do you?" I shoot back, eyebrow lifted in disbelief.

"Ah," she blushes, "What did you want me to say? Yeah, I'm a classically-trained musician with a big head? Pfft."

"So, are you in a choir or something? Do you have an evangelical show that tours the country, pocketing donations for your uni fees?"

"Very funny. Actually, I've got a couple of bands on the go and sometimes I do solo work or guest vocals for other groups. Would you believe burlesque and rockabilly?"

Tilting the stool back underneath me, I deliberately accentuate the action of choking on my beer. Amy meanwhile, has her face screwed up in mock shame. Angelic to look at and shy in gesture, she almost makes me feel guilty for forming an attraction. Whenever deep in thought, she innocently tongues at a small gap between her left incisor and front teeth, the only blemish in a sparkling white mouth, on a milky clean face. I can't believe she can deliver that voice, let alone entertain the thought of her in a corset, raunching it up on stage.

"So, let me get this straight. You study art, history and languages, sing in a handful of bands and you work here a couple of nights a week? That's crazy. What do you do in your spare time?"

"I like to paint also," says Amy, oblivious to the intended sarcasm.

Another £1.50 is stacked together and pushed across the bar. "I'm not annoying you if I stick around? I mean if you've got things to do..."

"Truthfully, I've already decided I am quitting this job," Amy says. "I don't feel like doing much work anyway. And shut up, you're good company."

Looking Amy over, I'm guessing 19. A couple of years too young to think any more of that last sentence. But gee it sounded good rolling off her tongue. Just a simple compliment, but overdue from someone like her.

Amy tells me she has just come back from a trip to Croatia with her girlfriends. Amongst other places, she's been to China, to Hong Kong, India, Italy and the Netherlands. The benefits of growing up with well-to-do parents she admits. Ideally, one day she'll get to Russia.

Aside from Jung, the other book I have stowed in my backpack is the autobiomythical tome *'The Shameful Life of Salvador Dali'*. There is so much to simultaneously admire and despise in him. As Amy is a budding artist, I ask for her impressions of the great man.

"Are we talking aesthetically or conceptually? I can't say I've taken too much notice of Dali, because I'm more into the impressionists. No doubt he's an interesting man and had some fabulous ideas, but I'm concerned with how it comes out on the canvas. To me, the real skill is being able to represent something perfectly, beautifully, like it's captured. I love the subtle details and the colours...the emotions. That's what I study for. Sometimes being abstract or surreal seems like an excuse, you know. I'm sorry, does that sound a bit posh of me?"

Far from being affronted, I'm relishing the answer. Dali may be someone who intrigues me greatly, but Amy has just used half-a-dozen terms I've barely ever heard on my third pint. A little over a week ago I was in Byron Bay on a football trip and "She's got cracking tits, but a shithouse personality" was about as close to dissecting aesthetics from concepts as anyone could manage. If I'm to be honest, it's been that way for a long while.

"I think you know what you're talking about more than me," I concede. "Say have you been to Spain at all?"

"Only briefly. I've visited Portugal a few times though. A friend of mine lives there."

"I was just asking because I'm going to Barcelona and wondered how far it was to Figueres. That's where Dali was born. It's a tiny place by the Mediterranean, connected to the rest of civilisation by a solitary road. Once it was predominantly a fishing village, but now I think his gallery is the main attraction in town. I've seen pictures of the building and it's as kooky as you'd expect. But his book paints such a grimly enchanting picture of Figueres in his youth; this dusty, dry isolated, outpost where he developed this sense of disconnection and imagination. I'd like to see both sides – the old and the new."

"Yeah it does sound cool. I've never heard of it before though. I'll tell you what – if you are going to see some art galleries around Europe, make sure you go to Amsterdam. The Van Gogh is my favourite. I could spend days there, just brainstorming and sketching. And you can catch a tram just up the road to the Rembrandthuis and the Rijksmuseum. They're fab too."

Indeed, I will be going to Amsterdam. I have planned my trip to end there on New Year's Eve. Admittedly I am entirely skeptical as to how much artistry I will be appreciating during that period. Pure or impure, I decide Amy doesn't need to know that part.

"I should be able to make it there. And I plan on going to the Louvre when I get to Pa...," I am cut short as two Americans walk down the stairs. Mike and Chris. Software developers from Chicago. Late 30s and in town for just four days.

"So, what's the craic? That's what you say around here isn't it? Two Millers sweetie," Mike asserts, holding up a pair of phalanges as if instructing a child.

"Uh no, that's Ireland, but not to worry," deadpans Amy, snapping the lid off two bottles and turning to roll her eyes in my direction.

Mike spends the best part of the next hour trying to engage Amy. He's clearly had a few drinks already and it becomes uncomfortable for all concerned.

"So, art hey? I'm scouting for a few new pieces for my collection. I'd like to see your work," he salivates from his open-neck shirt, nonchalantly rolling the drink in his hand.

To his credit, Chris is not nearly as loathsome. He can hold a conversation, even if he is a little depressing. At the moment he's worried about his father, who is undergoing cancer treatment. Being away from home means he also misses his children. As Mike alternates between orally assaulting Amy and tapping on his Blackberry in the background, Chris sarcastically notes his work partner is obviously uncomfortable being apart from his kids as well.

Around us, Espionage is starting to fill up. Amy has her work cut out for her, sliding along the bar to field orders until another staff member finally arrives to lend a hand. Aside from

Chris, I am also now chatting to an Irish student, Sean, and he is giving me tips on visiting his home country. Namely, he advises, stay away from Limerick unless I want to be stabbed.

In the moments when the crowd lulls, Amy returns to the section of the bar in front of me and continues conversation while cleaning glasses. We talk intermittently of siblings, of movies, music, career aspirations. It's the type of conversation that makes drinking worthwhile.

Eventually we also discuss Amy's boyfriend. It figures she should have one. She'd be a catch for any guy.

The revelation at least removes that tension from the dialogue and I am glad. I've spent the last few pints looking over at Mike and praying to heavens that I am nothing like him. At my age, I don't want to be a cliché just yet.

I'm merely thankful to know that people like Amy are still out there. Better still, they don't seem to mind people like me. She's invited me to a club called the Opal Lounge tomorrow so she can introduce me to her girlfriends.

"I AM so incredibly sorry Karen," wept Sandy down the phone, the start of a conversation scalded into my memory. "I saw Marty out drinking the other weekend and ended up doing something really, really stupid. I just want to…want to clear the air with you. I don't want to keep secrets from you and I know I don't deserve it, but please can we stay friends? It's terrible and I feel sick to my stomach."

"Hmmm?" That was all I could manage. Absolutely shell-shocked. Sandy had been my best friend for almost 10 years. We had worked together in Woolworths as teenagers and she was now godmother to both Loxton and Kim.

Sandy also knew Marty from our days at Woolies. Apparently, now she knew him now a whole lot better.

"He was at the poolhall with some guys I didn't recognise. Didn't leave me alone, but I didn't want to be rude either. He was pestering me at the end of the night to share a cab. Must have said it 20 times or more. In the end I agreed just to shut him up. He basically invited himself in and fell asleep on the living room floor. Then in the middle of the night I got up to get a drink of water and kind of forgot he was there. You know, Karen, I was a lot more drunk than I realised at the time. I tripped over him and we were sort of laughing about it. Things ah, just kind of happened. I figured you two weren't together anymore and it wouldn't…"

"Stop! I don't want to know. How on Earth could you do this?"

"I know, I know. I'm so so sorry. I was drunk out of my mind. You have to believe me. I would never have even dreamt of doing it. Please forgive me. And I need to tell you something else, because I still want to be your friend. You should know. Please don't be angry."

"What?"

"I told him where you live…"

It all clicked. The note and the cage with the turtle on the landing. Marty had found us through Sandy's big mouth. I slammed down the telephone and ran to the toilet to be ill.

Gradually over time Sandy and I patched things up. She never double-crossed me again and was always there to lend support when needed. Admittedly though, I didn't tell her of my change of address for quite some time when we moved to our next house, a duplex just around the corner from my parents' home in Gordon Park. Nor did I ever tell my children what had happened between their Dad and their godmother.

Thankfully the period immediately following our arrival in Thistle Street was one of the happiest junctures in my life. Marty was completely gone. There was not a single temptation to even speak with him, let alone see him. Loxton enrolled at the same tiny primary school that I attended 20 years earlier, Wooloowin State, while Kim commenced kindergarten.

Quite noticeably Loxton began to settle down. He made friends with two classmates who lived close by, Robert and Juhymn, and he totally applied himself to not only schoolwork, but especially to sports. Even at such a young age, he would beg me to come and watch him race on athletics day, as if it were the most important thing in the world. For the first time Lox reveled in group situations and would delight in setting the tone for fancy dress days, carnivals and anything competitive, from spelling bees to tug-of-war. While it felt as though my life revolved around my son to a degree, I really enjoyed making him costumes, working on projects together and the many afternoons spent at the local park.

Not surprisingly the period of contentedness coincided with a renewed closeness between my parents and I. Being physically close-by meant I could visit them most days and either lend a hand or at least mull over matters with a cup of tea. Howard came out of hospital and seemed much healthier in body and mind. Naturally Loxton spent whatever time he was permitted with his uncle, poring over atlases and encyclopedias or

Poolhall—Jail—Library

pretending to be ninjas and soldiers in the back garden. Their vivid imaginations and eccentricities were perfectly matched.

That Christmas, when Loxton was six, will always be remembered by the entire Berg family as the best yuletide spent together. Every single one of my brothers and sisters, my nephews and nieces made it along. My mother and father put on a massive roast and platter along their back deck, overlooking Kedron Brook and the valley between Lutwyche, The Grange and Enoggera Reservoir. Even with our Yorkshire accents, it was a typical feast of Australiana; the boys all in singlets, the girls in skirts, the macadamia trees nodding in a light breeze and a kookaburra attacking a lizard just above us on the shade cover. My brothers were wearing silly party masks and drinking XXXX, teasing my sister and me as we laid out the table and tried to keep the kids in check.

Loxton, Kim and their cousins were enjoying the attention of their first experience with a video camera, bought by their Uncle Craig. He filmed them having foot races around the clothes line and staging a military battle beside the old tool shed, jumping into a pile of leaves to hide from imaginary helicopters. Kim still had blonde hair back then and an unrelentingly squeaky voice. She looked and sounded like a little doll. Loxton was cute in his own way, but for completely different reasons. He sprinted his matchstick legs out in the running races and gave his younger sister no quarter. At the finishing line he would flex his tiny arms and snarl his face, exposing a gappy smile. In terms of hilarity, it was only rivalled by Lox's later attempts to breakdance on the kitchen linoleum, facing off against a mop-haired puppet controlled by Howard.

Copies of the '84 Christmas video are treated like gold in the family. For it was the last time everyone was able to assemble in the same location, able to put aside their differences.

After our six-month lease on Thistle Street had come to an end, it seemed like a shame to move on when everything was at last running smoothly and stably. We signed on for another three months until the adjoining duplex to us became available. It was a little larger, looked down towards the brook and had large bay windows. So, we got set for the world's shortest house move, 10 metres along the footpath.

But there came a week in January that was like no other. It began with a terrifying electrical storm, described in news reports as the worst in a decade. Rain pelted the exterior of the flat and lightning cracked like a whip as it tried to snatch the timber and tiles. For three days it continued without relent. On the Wednesday a man two blocks away died when powerlines were brought down on the road. So many electrical wires scattered the ground in our neighbourhood that barely a soul dared to venture out. At first the kids were amused and would sit by their windows with the shutters open, watching the lightshow and allowing the teeming rain to graze their faces. But as the weather grew wilder, forcing the roof to leak and threatening to buckle the foundations, more than once we found all of us huddled together under the kitchen table.

Outages of electricity meant whatever food remained in the refrigerator had to be consumed. There were three small crème brûlées that I had bought as a treat, complete in their own self-saucing cup. With caramel seductively drizzling down the sloping dessert, the picture on the package certainly made them appeared delicious. However, when put to the taste buds, it was more like a greasy venom that sharply knotted the stomach. We screwed our faces at each other. There was definitely something not right about the dish.

With the storm unabated outside, Loxton, Kim and I took turns at heaving our insides that night, ill to the core. The food-poisoning not only struck us down with an aching and lethargy, but also delivered the strangest dreams and hallucinations. Gnomes were running rampant in our unit, utilising the darkened, gothic atmosphere to lay in wait for an ambush. They hid under our glassware cabinet, rubbed the legs of the bed like demented Comedia characters and positioned themselves *under my feet in the shower as I stood on the drain. When their chance came, they attacked my legs like cannibalistic swine. They threatened to chew all the way to the bone when, suddenly, armies of black ants sprayed forth from the showerhead like bullets. A draw burst open in the bathroom cabinet and even more ants filed into a latex glove en masse, acting as one. The glove took a cutthroat razor, scurried across the tiles and lopped off the heads of the offending gnomes. Together the millions of insects suffocated and consumed their decapitated foes, celebrating while I sunk into a pool of my own blood.*

This one incongruous dream played constantly in my mind, inescapable while condemned to a hazy coma of sickness.

In combination, the freakish weather and horrid food poisoning meant I could not shift anything next door until the following weekend. An exercise that was supposed to be a piece of cake had been transformed into an ongoing saga.

Clear skies finally arrived and, unexpectedly, my brothers and father strolled down from Aberdeen Terrace to help cart the furniture the small distance. Their assistance and presence were a godsend. For, while we worked, Loxton was playing around on the raised garden near the fence, running and jumping in his typical hyperactive manner.

A white van zoomed down our street – a popular shortcut between shopping precincts – and Loxton stopped dead in his tracks.

"Dad!" Lox screamed out.

It still chills me now to think of it. Serenity shattered.

The entire family glanced up disbelievingly as Marty screeched his rust bucket to a stop. Loxton had blown it all. Initially I suspected my ex-husband had known our whereabouts all along, but reflecting, I have to stomach it simply as one of life's terrible coincidences.

Marty appeared just as stunned as us when he emerged from the van, leaving behind three passengers, a dark-skinned *lady and two little kids. Approaching the fence, he had a smirk like the cat with the proverbial cream.*

"Wally!" he shouted as Lox jumped over to hug him. Kim remained at a distance, glued to the stairs, unsure of the appropriate response.

Marty had some cheek. He tried to buddy up to my brothers and father, at the same that he chastised me for 'taking away his children'. But my four brothers and father crowded around, all well-built men on the upwards side of six feet. They let him know in no uncertain terms which direction he should be headed. Gradually Marty retreated to his van, but he was still grinning that stupid grin. I knew it wouldn't be the last we saw of him.

If that was an unsettling experience, the next chapter was utterly terrifying.

Not more than a fortnight later Marty's vehicle was in our shared driveway. It was full to the brim. He and his new family were moving into our old apartment right next door, treading the same floorboards, sleeping and showering the other side of the wall, aware of our every move.

SCOTTISH HIGHLANDS

I LOOK and feel like crap. As much as I'd like to brag to my mates back home, I'm not going to take up Amy's invitation to the Opal Lounge. I just don't have the confidence for it. My wallet and energy are already depleted enough from last night. What do I have to gain anyway? Say I did meet one of Amy's friends and we got along okay. What then? I doubt anything would happen. In any case, I leave tomorrow and I don't want to give the impression of some international lothario. No, meeting Amy was plenty enough for my stay in Edinburgh. We swapped email addresses when I said goodbye and I'm content to add her to the list of regular travel correspondents. Not every interesting girl has to become a love interest. You sad, desperate, contrived loser.

Whether or not it's the amount of alcohol I consumed at Espionage, the darkness is welling up inside me today. It was a struggle to get out of bed, I did none of my usual exercises this morning and even when I was climbing Arthur's Seat or hiking to Calton Hill I couldn't shake the black dog. The only time at all I felt like I was having fun was when I caught the bus to Portobello Beach and a bunch of strangers invited me to join their five-a-side football game. Again, relying on the acceptance of others to fuel your self-worth. You make me sick in the guts.

No, there'll be no hitting the tiles tonight. I've fallen asleep in the communal room once already this evening, woken by an attendant concerned for my well-being. Cultural immersion for these last few hours has consisted of a Perry Mason re-run, a reality show pitting celebrities as commandoes and a cinematic masterpiece called 'Dumber and Dumberest' – home videos overdubbed in thick Scottish.

I'm presently enraptured by a documentary about the Arctic – narwhals, polar bears, walruses and Inuit. The isolation and disconnection strike a chord. Convincing myself this is much more dignified than being laughed at by a half-dozen rosy-cheeked girls, I drift off again on the couch as the credits roll. This time the attendant wakes me at 2am with a vacuum cleaner, no longer worried about my health. Dreams and consciousness become blurred and at 6am I have somehow managed to find myself on the bottom bunk of a dormitory, suffering an embolism from a Japanese boy's nuclear-powered alarm clock.

My schedule feels like Fartlek training. Constant movement, occasionally slowing, but never coming to a complete stop. Days and activities jerking each other along like discordant railway carriages. The placid waters of the Firth of Forth pass under me as I head north, telling me to wipe the nagging regrets of Edinburgh. Oranges and yellows replace grey, nature's reminder this is one big adventure. Don't let a solitary day of idleness and insecurity weigh you down so soon. Every 24 hours somewhere new becomes the furthest you've ever been from home.

Today I move the marker on the map to Inverness, a trip that squeezes through Inverkeithing, Pitlochry, Kingussie and Perth. The Highland countryside only improves with distance and poses a poignant question. Why is the planet most beautiful when battling against itself? Hard rock denies groundwater a simple course. Instead it drops from craggy edges, plummets to unwelcoming ground, bucks at right angles, swishing in violent slaloms until it finds its level. Stone's price for accosting the icy flow is to be sculpted and worn into arches, channels and otherworldly formations. Combined, the two elements become an ornament to their own unending duel.

Inverness strikes me as more of a large village than a city. Single lane streets charge off over hilly terrain and intersect where they please. Some become paved malls, others skirt non-geometric residential blocks, taking obscure shapes on the steep rise near the castle and the drop-off to the River Ness. Quaint bars at the city heart become a meeting point for a throng of students, tourists and those from surrounding rural districts. Scotland's 'Ned' brigade is well-represented too, underaged smokers and tracksuit wearers insulated from the Scandinavian clime.

I've made it in time for lunch (a pack of digestive biscuits from the pound-saver shop), giving myself enough free hours to catch a Jacobite tour to the Loch. My guide has wrinkled, smudged tattoos down both forearms, markings from his time in the Highland Regiment. He's an entertaining character and it seems a pity the trip to the Loch's shores is much briefer than it looked on the atlas.

This outing is mainly for my youngest sisters, Pip and Alyce. They told me before I left that Ness was the one place they wanted to visit most. Personally, it seems a bit tacky, an attraction for the unimaginative. But as I may only be headed this way once in life, well I should see it with my own eyes.

Thinking of Pip and Alyce, I wonder how much they will change, grow up, by the time I am back? I've missed a lot of their childhood and they probably don't fathom how fond I am of them. Before the boat cruise boards, there is just enough time to snaffle two small, stuffed Nessies from the gift shop and a photo of a curious indigo-coloured plesiosaur, a 15-foot plaster creation.

A powerful wind blasts across the surface of the Loch, coercing troughs and peaks that tickle the underside of our craft. In response the boat lurches and rollicks, flicking a fine spray into the dim afternoon sky. Legends have much to do with the notoriety of Loch Ness, but they fail to convey just how impressive it is as a geographic feature. Deeper than the North Sea. More fresh water than all of England and Wales combined. Nestled on a tectonic fault line that stretches 23 miles in length, but only one mile wide.

Sailing towards Urquhart Castle, the western horizon is constantly consumed by a haunting fog. It is foreboding and mystical. Pure chance and scattered light allow capture of the greatest photo of my lifetime. My role is to simply press a button. The picture crackles black, grey and silver. Only those ripples blessed by shards of illumination from above are detectable on an otherwise ebony slate. Hills frame the distant condensation until it is a pointed representation of deliverance. The photo could be of the dawn of creation or the inevitable apocalypse.

Despite freezing my gluteus off, I'm so very glad I made the journey; monster or no monster.

When back at the hostel, I wrestle temptation to jump straight under the fleecy sheets while dressed in my hooded jacket. I'm still burnt by the hangover from two days previous and the falling temperature does not encourage nighttime liaisons. Yet the fellow on the counter tells of a bar called 'Hootenanny's' and I cannot deny myself a trip there. Hootenanny is at least in the top 20 eminent words in the Anglo Celtic lexicon. And when I force myself to go, I again silently applaud my dedication to adventure. Otherwise I may have never believed of a place with three levels of live music, where you can buy inflatable sheep and handcuffs side-by-side in the toilets, but not condoms.

Dreams follow of deflated livestock in the surrounding hills, left stranded – manacled, immobilised and impregnated by drunken Scotsmen on their way home.

But even before the sun surfaces, I am woken in my shared dorm with the sound of beds creaking, bags unzipping and teeth being vigorously brushed. The Backpacker's Symphony.

***   ***   ***

MENTALLY and physically I am back on track. On track, as it so happens, in the direction of the very tip of Britain at John O'Groats. My intention is to hop off a few stations short at a tiny place called Culrain, which is home to Carbisdale Castle. One of the few castles in Britain where members of the public can rest affordably overnight, it sits on the edge of the stunning Kyle of Sutherland.

I'm disorientated when I alight from the train and begin to follow what looks the longest and most important road. As it winds through tall dark trees, I hear footsteps trailing me, quickening in pace.

"Hey!" a voice calls out and I twist to see a chubby blonde girl, freckly and pale. If not for her accent and Hawthorn Hawks beanie, I'd assume she was a Highlands native. "You were at Inverness last night, weren't you?"

"Oh...ah yeah."

"Yeah I saw you at the hostel. I noticed the little Aussie insignia on your bag and was going to say hi. I'm Nat anyway." She thrusts a mittened hand forward. "Say, I don't suppose you know which way is the castle?"

I try not to be thrown off by her rapid-fire conversation. I wouldn't recognise her from a bar of soap. "Not really. I'm kind of walking from memory – from instructions I read off the website. But I am not sure which way is north."

"Well that makes two of us. Hahaha. Are you sure it's not that road over there? It connects to the main road. Seems to be more houses over there you know? But then again it did say to go past the camping ground. But you know camping grounds are different over here hey? It could look like a field or something. Do you think where those benches are...maybe that's the camping ground? Gosh I hope we don't get lost. It's chilly already and I am starving and it would be..."

I resist the temptation to break stride and interrupt her verbal assault as we pass by a stone cairn with a sign that says 'Castle >'. Instead I subtly point at the marker and raise my eyebrows.

Having lived by the motto 'Everyone has a story to tell' I am all ears to Nat's plight. She is a teacher, 26, from Melbourne. Has been living in London for the past year, but has packed up to do more travelling. She hasn't dated anyone serious for a while. Well, there was kinda this one guy, but you know how traveling is? She's followed the Hawks since Dipper and Dermie and Dunstall delivered them all that silverware in the 80s. Her parents are worried sick about her. This trip was meant to give her direction in life. But money is low and the world seems even bigger now.

"Ah, I'm just going to check in and get a few hours shut-eye. Was a big one for me last night," I lie blatantly as we finally reach the front desk.

Insofar as castles go, Carbisdale appears fairly plain. It doesn't reek of boiling oil, battering rams and archers from the watch-tower. Instead it presents itself as somewhere an aristocratic family might hold a wine and cheese night. Nonetheless I can't say I've ever laid my head to rest in an actual castle before. Plus, the interior contains all the expected trappings. Animal heads mounted and growling from the walls, suits of armour dotted throughout corridors and furniture fit for the nobility. The proprietors have done a grand job of preserving the building and it does not feel at all like a hostel.

When I park my backpack upstairs, I admire a grand view that stretches over what seems a never-ending expanse. It's similar in many ways to the wilderness and lakes around Castle Howard, but it also triggers a searing flashback that's closer to my home in Brisbane.

A long-gone sense of comfort reignites and for more than a minute I am daydreaming of being 20 again, in that abandoned cheese factory on the Downs, laying on the floor of the attic office, spooned behind Jen, peering out over countryside. My wooly brown jumper seems 10 degrees hotter all of a sudden. Time to get a grip, I think, somehow convincing myself yet again that it's the first time I've thought of Jen in ages.

And I make sure I don't think about her again for the rest of the day.

Not when I creep outside my room and clamber throughout the upstairs levels, ignoring the 'Staff Only' signs, walking over raised doorways and snooping my nose around artefacts and detailed masonry. Not when I squelch my way downstairs to the muddy path that takes you through the woods, to a footbridge across the Kyle. Nor when I reach the other side and set forth for a three-hour uphill hike to the falls, even though the salmon have long since finished jumping. I don't think of Jen one bit. Honestly.

This is especially the case when I can no longer pre-occupy myself and wind up at the Invershin Hotel, beer in my hand, gazing out over that same transfixing landscape. Jen who? Doesn't mean a thing to me.

ONCE Marty and his new family had interred themselves in the adjoining flat, the kids witnessed some things I wished they'd never seen. Truth be known, Loxton had been around for it as a baby, but his comprehension was nowhere as sharp as it had become.

My immediate response to the situation was as intelligent as it was edifying. I invited around one of my oldest friends from high school, Julie, who loaded the boot of her beaten-up blue Datsun with a case of Foster's and a bucket of Kentucky Fried Chicken. So long had it been since my last serious drink, from the initial sips I was riding into oblivion. Led Zeppelin went on the stereo first, followed by Black Sabbath, Billy Thorpe, Alice Cooper and Bowie. Loxton and Kim preoccupied themselves watching Ghostbusters on our tiny Solid State television set.

As I lapped from the bowl of self-pity, a sickly odour of beer and greasy poultry swilled around the room. Never before had I drunk in front of my children and not since high school had I smoked. Above the music, Julie and I began to holler insults to our unwelcome neighbours; childish cussing in front of two kids that were behaving far more maturely.

The nonsensical barking heightened the alcoholic euphoria and as the evening wore on, it took a grip on the internal machinations of my stomach. My mind followed, growing irrational and divisive.

Loxton holding my hand as I fell to my knees, sobbing and vomiting across the carpet was a low point which I swore never to recreate. I hugged my boy and told him how deeply I loved him. But the eyes of a six-year-old stared back at me, scared and embarrassed.

A shoddy early-hours attempt to scrape the offending mess from the floor failed to clear the flat of the marauding stench, much the same as we could not rid ourselves of Marty's nagging presence. My ex did not react to our taunts that night, but for weeks after would call past the front door at all hours, checking on our welfare. It was never overtly aggressive, but I recognised it as yet another of his mind games.

Another of his favourite charades was to parade about his newfound love and offspring. Daksha came from Fiji, mother to both Kanishk and Mohini. Her first husband had been a white land-owner, a sadist who kept her locked in a caravan just outside of Suva. Apparently on one of Marty's many art excursions to the Pacific he heard of Daksha's plight and set about rescuing her and the children. At least that's the story we were all told.

I was filled with hatred towards this new woman, but also held a degree of pity and concern. To make things worse, she was incredibly, incredibly umm...nice.

Loxton and Kim enjoyed the company of Kanishk and Mohini as well. There was only three years in age between any of the kids at most, so they would constantly play together outside, even when instructed not to. Quite often I would catch them sampling the Fijian-Indian food, fouling up their hands and accosting my nostrils with disgusting spices and sauces.

I confronted Marty about encouraging the children's disobedience and he laughed in my face. It precipitated a blazing row. Daksha took the children and led them outside to buffer them from the violence in our voices. Behind her, Marty slammed the door and proceeded to unleash a barrage of abuse upon me. Simmering to boiling point, I innocuously threw a plastic plate in his direction, though not directly at him.

"Why the fuck don't you just leave us alone?"

My foolish impulse provided the necessary excuse for retaliation and Marty picked up a thickly-backed hand mirror and aimed it straight at my forehead. As it struck, he lurched across the room, lacing one hand around my neck and the other pulling tightly on my hair. His hands rubbed over my skin, repulsing me to the very core. Struggling, I tried to claw and slap him away. But with every effort he responded by firming his grip or punching back.

I'd hate to imagine the words that came out of my mouth or what the rest of the neighbourhood could hear. Wrestling and grunting, we stumbled into the dresser, my head slamming dangerously close to the corner. Then, out of the corner of my eye, I saw the door now open and a tuft of red hair poking out from behind the upturned coffee table.

Loxton was screaming at us to stop, but was caught between brevity and fear, his cries muffled and seeking protection.

"Don't worry Wally. Your Mum's just being very silly," chuckled Marty, tightening his grip. "Aren't you?" he asked rhetorically, ripping my skull around until our eyes were mere inches apart.

I submitted in hope Loxton would be spared further anguish. As I dropped all my weight towards the floor, my assailant could hold me no more. What a weak excuse for a man.

Marty outstretched his arms as if to welcome Loxton for a hug, but our son refused to come towards either of us. Instead he left the room and dealt us the silent treatment for days to follow. Certainly, a noticeable rift between Lox and myself had opened since his father's reappearance. I admit with a certain shame that I'm not entirely convinced the resentment was solely on my son's behalf either.

Driving a wedge further into that gap, there came an incident on our back stairs, which were elevated some five metres above a pile of disused timber. I suspect the bleached wooden planks in the pile may have come from an old fence, never properly cleared away by our landlord. Nonetheless, I heard Loxton playing in the vicinity and ran to the steps to check on his whereabouts. Had I realised Lox was using the stairs for monkey bars, gripping on to them from beneath and swinging up from one level to the next, I may have avoided treading on his fingers. Startled, he had no option but to plummet straight down. As he hit the heap of wood, his body seized solid and his eyes exploded wide as if opened by electricity. The sense

Poolhall—Jail—Library

of shock was so powerful that it stopped Lox from crying instantaneously.

Glued to the spot, I watched as my son rolled to the side, stood up and tried to drag free of the makeshift ski his foot had become firmly impaled upon. Finally, he yielded to the onset of tears, his vision transfixed downwards and his legs unable to desperately shake away the bloodied plank of wood. It was my duty to then fight the nauseous sensation as I pulled the rusted nails from the sole of his foot with a struggle. How they didn't pierce all the way through I do not know. There was a stand-off as I bandaged Lox's gushing feet and called for a taxi to the doctor's. He needed my help, but would not forgive me for causing such hurt.

That infernal, deep rage of his formative years in Toowoomba was returning. Indeed, had it not been for a number of related happenings, I fear I may have lost Loxton altogether.

As much as I suspect my son hated me at this point in time, he was not a great deal kinder to his Dad. Marty had recently moved his orange-and-white bus – his travelling art gallery – down from the mountains to our adjoined back yards, saying the children could now play in it. He reconfigured the insides so it was more like a mobile home-cum-cubbyhouse and painted 'Gus the Bus' along the front of the roof. It seemed he had given up his nomadic lifestyle and was focused entirely on winning the attentions of his kids back. But true colours, as is said, inevitably shine through.

There was a relatively minor matter of Loxton one day pushing Mohini over in some sort of game, a fairly usual occurrence that arose from his competitiveness. But Marty's reaction was harsher than expected, very protective of his new golden child. The contempt in his voice spat forth like buckshot from his grotty beard. A dressing-down as such had been a long time coming for Loxton, for he had always held the power in the relationship with his father. Attention and affection were normally at the younger's whim and fancy.

Loxton didn't take kindly at all to the sudden turn of the tables and, after the scolding, he disappeared behind the bus. Latching onto the side mirror, he swung violently, warping the metal and ripping several screws out of the corroding shell. The brutality increased until the mirror was at right angles. Puffing and possessed, he picked up a stone and then punched his fist straight into the mirror. Not satisfied, he then added a final touch, dropping his shorts and urinating all over the side of the bus.

Scarce time passed until Marty discovered the rampage. Loxton was dragged downstairs to a concrete slab where his father had set aside an exercise area. I had joked it was the least used portion of cement in the known universe, but in honesty I had packed on more pudding of late myself. Plus, on this particular day there was no room for witticism. Unbeknown to me at the time, Marty had taken out his thick, brown skipping rope - not an object I would wish anyone to be belted with.

"Step up!" he yelled as he swung it against Loxton's behind like a rusty anchor clanging against the bow. Each strike grew in its ferocity and Lox fell to his knees accordingly. There was none of the unnerving comfort or enjoyment my son displayed when experiencing pain in the past. Part of me wanted to shriek as the brushstrokes painted my son black and blue. But then something else took over, a combustion of fear and anger, and I bounded down the stairs faster than I knew how to. I did not so much confront Marty, as tackle him. Using my superior weight, I bustled him backwards into a pebbled retainer wall and freed one arm to slap his face. The temptation to further strike Marty was incredibly strong, but instead I pushed myself free, turned to grab Loxton's hand and walked back up the stairs without another word.

Secretly I had commenced plans to move us north to Banyo, still on the train line, but separated from surrounding suburbs by industrial estates, a large cemetery, wetlands and a sprawling monastery. It was a pocket of isolation still within *the city limits; a place where I knew nobody else and where few people would pass through. This time around I was not telling the kids or any of my friends about my intentions.*

There was the lingering fact that Marty had recently set the wheels in motion for a custody battle. But after his recent explosions, neither Lox nor Kim were overly keen to spend time in his presence.

Together, my father and I planned an ambush to cement the kids' allegiances. Loxton was the key, because, for all the turbulence, he was the more attached and familiar with his Dad. We had to swing his unpredictable decision-making in our favour.

Just a few days before a crucial hearing at the children's court, Loxton arrived home to find his bedroom completely spotless and clean. There, perched on his bed was his Grandad, holding a picture frame with a yellow background. As Lox moved closer, he recognised the familiar sketch of a smiling clown's face. At the bottom of the freshly painted picture, his Uncle Howard's signature dashed from side-to-side. We were pulling at every heart string we could find.

"What are you going to do my boy?" my father asked Loxton softly. A great deal of respect and affection existed between the two.

"I'm not sure. Mum has had her turn with me. It would be unfair not to go with Dad...wouldn't it?"

"Then what? You're a smart kid Loxton. You must have thought about what that will mean. We won't see you."

"But I just make everyone so unhappy here."

"Who? Your mum?" my father said as my ears pricked from the hallway. "Oh, she's unhappy all the time."

I could hear the two trying to muffle their giggling.

"But it will hurt your Nan and I a lot if you choose to go. We want to see you grow up and become something great. Your Mum will help you do that."

"I know," Lox conceded.

"Do you still want to join the Navy like I did? I can show you some of my old war books...with all the ships?"

Dad was playing his cards perfectly. Lox dreamt of nothing more than following in his footsteps, seeing the world and tackling adventure.

So, it was at the eleventh hour we torpedoed any attempt by Marty to steal the children back. At the mediation Loxton consistently gave a tepid response to questions about his father. The court still saw fit to grant Marty access one day per fortnight, but finally our family was secure and legally shielded.

ISLE OF SKYE

I AM perplexed by the concept of the advertised 'Puffin Hydrotherapy Pool'. Is it for puffins? Run by puffins? Or in fact connected to pelagic seabirds in any way, shape or form?

Pondering this Scottish riddle takes up half my time in the lovely little town of Dingwall, initially a mere transitory location on my next leg from Culrain to the mystical Isle of Skye. The sign at the train station tells me Dingwall is also known as Inbhirpheofharain, a Gaelic translation that I wrestle with phonetically. Aside from that little trivia piece, I have nothing else to sustain an hour's layover in this tiny outpost until my connecting train arrives.

Yet in a short stroll I find a town deep in history and heritage and with no shortage of pride. Once a royal burgh, it was a meeting place for Vikings and a community that was touched by conflicts from the dark ages to last century. Tributes to fallen warriors are prominent from the first steps toward the city centre. Less meaningful, yet similarly prominent, are the delicious bakeries and the confusing billboard advertising the puffin pool.

I thank Madame Fortune for tossing me this unexpected gem as I board my next railway chariot to the western isles. Recently a magazine article rated the Great Highland crossing among the top five rail journeys in the world. It is wistfully described as a 'symphony', melding the beauty of lochs, stark mountain ranges, countryside, streams and an abundance of wildlife. The crescendo is reached with a stunning sequence through the towns of Stromferry, Lochcarron and Plockton; miles of white stone cottages on the water's edge, dotted far enough apart for authentic isolation, adorned by row boats resting in the shallows. An artist could barely dream such marvel.

Lochcarron is hosting the Highland Games and I am extremely tempted to stop by for a dose of caber tossing and bagpipe tooting. However, I ride until the end of the line at Kyle of Lochalsh, just in time for the bus to Dornie.

We then snake alongside 'Alsh's frozen beachfront to the destination, a town of 300 or so, home to a solitary shop, a lonesome hotel and a poorly patronised shinty club. But as I disembark in this one-horse town, I smile the breadth of my face. All I have done today is pay the fare for public transport, yet I am whisked up in a searing sense of fulfilment and accomplishment. Strangely, even more exulted than the day of my university graduation.

The reason stands before me, clearly visible and just a short walk from the carpark. I pay the entrance fee and pass through a wrought iron heraldic gate onto a stonework bridge. Crossing the reeded moat, I find it impossible not to outstretch my arms triumphantly and snatch at the crisp blue air. After these many, many years, after so many, many dreams, I am metres from Eilean Donan Castle. To get here from Brisbane has not just been a great distance of planes, trains and buses. It has been against a mentality that has weaved a crooked fissure through my consciousness. Inside, I have never stopped being the kid who grew up in a housing commission block. That ugly, useless child from a family of few aspirations. I have never been deserving of success, neither in my eyes nor others.

I have never once felt worthy...until today.

Bringing myself to this tiny islet at the fork of Loch Duich, Loch Alsh and Loch Long has taken me somewhere money, career and fruitless searches for affection failed to ever reach. The sensation is wonderful. Burden lifted. Blood rushing uncontrollably. Today I am not afraid to say I'm a good person. I've worked hard. I deserve this happiness.

My feet feel as though they are scuttling much too fast to imitate the broody pace of Connor MacLeod when he crossed the same bridge in *Highlander*. This very site is steeped in endless chronicles of feudal raids and regal bloodshed, but my great attraction is because of a 1984 Christopher Lambert film.

Poolhall—Jail—Library

It was the first movie of my childhood to receive a prestigious four-star rating in the trusty notebook where I diligently reviewed every rental cassette played on our second-hand VCR. That was geeky, freckly Berg in his prime.

I must have watched *Highlander* close to 100 times, fantasising of one day leading my clan across a fog-shrouded moat and refining my swordsmanship with Sean Connery on an impossibly inaccessible outcrop several thousand feet above glistening glens. Deep down however, I was convinced for many years that I would never travel anywhere more than one tank of petrol from my home.

In a weird marriage of my adolescent awkwardness and this newfound sense of deliverance, I actually kiss the archway as I walk through. It's by far the oldest thing I've managed to snog.

An hour of exploration later and I meet a super-friendly Israeli couple waiting for the same bus back to Kyle of Lochalsh. Bashful and baby-faced, the young man hesitantly reveals he has just completed national service, "visiting Lebanon in tanks". He and his girlfriend have walked overland from Glasgow to this spot, to clear their minds, experience the countryside and because the castle is featured in a James Bond film. Others have come because it appears in *Monty Python and the Holy Grail* or because it is depicted on the tin of a famous shortbread biscuit. I warm myself with this knowledge, standing among learned trivia buffs and fellow pop culture tragics.

The approachability and demeanour of people in these parts is remarkable. I fail to learn the names of my Jewish friends, but we talk non-stop, swapping tales, maps, timetables and photos until transport finally arrives to deliver us to the Kyle. No sooner do my fleeting associates depart for Inverness on the train, than I meet 'Lucky John'. He stands, feet wide apart and arms crossed at the entrance to the town's sole supermarket, itself positioned on a remarkably steep hill. From a short distance away, I can tell 'Lucky John' has Down syndrome. As customers enter, he points where they should park and presides watchfully over the store entrance – in fact the whole settlement – as if he is the mayor. The townsfolk go along with the act, address him affectionately and show a playful respect that manages to fall well short of patronising. 'Lucky John' stares me down as I enter the store. I smile back, nod my head and his stern façade melts instantaneously.

From the cashier at the supermarket to the next bus driver, everybody wants to stop and chat.

"Ah a good old Kiwi hey?" the man behind the wheel says as I board the next bus for Portree.

"Get out. Not on your life mate. I'm an Aussie," I reply stiffly, screwing my face up and trying to broaden my accent.

"Oh really?" he snickers sarcastically, knowing his playful barb has hit its intended mark. "I would never have guessed that."

What used to be a ferry from Kyle of Lochalsh to the Isle of Skye is now a parabolic bridge that dominates the otherwise pristine natural landscape. The clash of progress and wilderness divides me, for after a day of non-stop travelling I am thankful for the shortest route possible.

While I possessed premeditated, definable reasons for visiting Eilean Donan Castle, I have forever held an inexplicable, inescapable attraction to Skye. I never even realised the two locations were so close until I sat down and mapped the trip. In my head Skye does represent an ideal of purity and peace, but there is also something deeper.

Jung once wrote "people are established inalienably in my memories only if their names were entered in the scrolls of my destiny from the beginning, so that encountering them was at the same time a kind of recollection". The statement perfectly reflects how I consider Skye.

A longer-than-expected road winds past the Red Cuillin mountains, which are formed of gentle granite rises, and then the Black Cuillins, igneous and more jagged in appearance. Tranquillity permeates the air. I have caught the constituents in hibernation and holiday mode, but I suspect the pace of living here rarely accelerates. The distance to the picturesque community of Portree accentuates the sensations of remoteness and discovery.

Portree is considered the 'capital' of Skye, which is somewhat akin to being the tallest student in kindergarten. My reasons for booking accommodation here in preference to somewhere like Kyleakin, Broadford or Uig were not particularly meaningful. Simply, it is more centrally located and has a prettier website. Most striking of all things in Portree are the pastel houses which sit by the harbour – baby blue, daffodil and pink abodes starkly contrasted against rickety brown fishing trawlers.

There is an atmosphere of togetherness in this chilly garrison and the central square is the focus. Banks and bars, estate agents, bakeries, butchers and restaurants circle around, facing inwards on a gathering of souls. At the witching hour I am motivated to leave my dormitory, which smells unmistakeably of rotting seaweed. Drawing men like mice to the pied piper, the sound of cèilidh floats from The Isles Inn directly across the square. Immersed in an acoustic jamboree with an assortment of roustabouts, I swallow my first beer of the night. We rhythmically stamp our feet on the hard floor as a dreadlocked man and a banshee of a lady trade haunting verses back-and-forth in front of the fireplace. For spontaneity and authenticity, there is no beating moments like these.

But soon the band is departing for another village in their vehicles and I am left alone without a party. Several cafes and clubs line the street, but even on a Saturday night, there are few places brimming at this early time. I walk up and down twice, casual so as not to look desperate, before I hear a faint wail from an upstairs window. Climbing the banisters, I am greeted by a modest, varnished room called The Caledonian. Only half-a-dozen or so people are milling around, but the barman has a delightfully creamy Belhaven on tap and that clinches my decision to stay. Self-conscious, I try to hide the fact I am on my lonesome, shielding behind a table near the rear bathroom and occupying myself by studying the clippings on the walls. As I read of nearby mountain hikes and local-DJ-made-big Mylo, I am starting to pick up a few accents as more people filter in. Most are Americans, but there's also another, with a low, mysterious half-Scottish, half-Aussie twang.

Tracing the vocals to near the top of the stair well, I see a broad-shouldered man of the same vintage, standing by a girl that looks remarkably like Sasha. Ouch. Too soon for that not to hurt. What is this – two girlfriends returning to haunt me on successive nights? I'm not entirely sure what I am being punished for. But it's undeniable. The wide blue eyes, short pixie hair, killer smile, well-proportioned in the cleavage region. Maybe this one is a little bit taller.

My inability to look away from the two is painful. Consciously dragging my eyes to the other corner of the room, I can't help but struggle as my vision flits back-and-forth to the subject of my attention. The boy has noticed and caught my eyeline more than once. Eventually, after finishing his second beer, he strolls past, his barrelled chest just missing the point of my shoulder as he heads to the men's room. Upon return, he props just in front of me, thwarting any attempts to feign distraction.

"You right mate?" he blurts loudly. I casually drop my right foot back, firm my grip on the pint glass and watch his collar bone for the slightest movement. What odds everyone in this bar knows him? Even if I can get a punch in before him, is it going to be worth it?

"Ah, I'm okay yeah."

"What you doin' here?" Big pause...... "I mean you be a fair way from home, no?"

"Yeah, Australia? How'd you guess?"

The potential assailant stares me long in the eyes and just manages to crack a smile before raising his right palm to my shoulder, perhaps feeling the tension still nestled under the skin.

"Come join us for a drink." His voice has become less abrasive, yet as I'm introduced to his partner Francine, I'm no less hesitant. There was already a lump in my throat before I stood toe-to-toe with her. Alarm bells tell me the prospects for danger are large when her boyfriend turns to the bar and graciously buys the next round. Francine is pretty, witty and flirty. Conversation flows effortlessly.

"I'm Lachlan by the way," the man pronounces as he slides back in between us and hands over a frothy beverage.

"Haha. Well I'm Loxton," I say and shake his hand.

"So where'bouts in Oz you from? You travelling by yourself?"

"Yep. I'm from Brisbane. Do you know where the Gold Coast is? It's kind of north…"

"Get out! We both know where Brisbane is. We used to live there. Five years ago."

"Unreal. It's lame to say, but it really can be a small world sometimes."

"Yeah we were living in Ashgrove. Nice area. Franny was out there backpacking and I met her while I was working in town."

"I don't suppose you'd know where Nichols Avenue is at Ashgrove then?"

The two of them look haunted and glance sidewards at each other.

"What?" Fran asks sharply

"What a strange thing to say mate. My surname is actually Nichols. Why do you ask? And yeah, Nichols Ave was just a few streets from us," replies Lachlan.

I sink back in my chair, the air taken from my chest. Half of me is on the verge of laughing in disbelief. The other half is totally unnerved and blown away.

"Well…Nichols Avenue is named after my grandfather. He was headmaster at the local school there for 40 years."

"So, your last name is also...?"

"Yep it's Nichols too. Well I use my mother's maiden name now, Berg, but yes technically it's Nichols. Not many people know that."

"So, you don't get along with your Dad then I take it?"

"You could say that. I haven't seen him in yonks."

Lachlan begins to tell a similar story of a fatherless childhood, not that it is a rare coincidence these days. But after everything else that has just transpired, leading to us both being in this bar tonight, it is beginning to feel as though I'm conversing with a mirror.

Both of us grew up playing rugby league. Both of us were mysteriously drawn to Skye. Lachlan says even before he met Francine he had dreamt of the place. Side-by-side we are roughly the same height, the same weight and we have established we are the same age. I marvel how we have never crossed paths previous and how we cannot be related at all.

Something like this was just meant to happen here and it makes me question how much I know about true consciousness. A small part of me is freaked out, imagining I am a pawn in a game. Perhaps I have been lured by some sinister calling to this far-flung extremity for death. Is this night some sort of cryptic epiphany? Has the image of Francine, who reminds me so much of my own devilish ex-girlfriend, been made to represent a siren detouring me to my final place of resting?

I consider that I am quickly approaching my sixth pint and have been known to let my imagination escape throughout the years. Plus, Francine does not come across as a totally evil wench, despite whatever her Sicilian lookalike may have done in the past.

"So, I take it you have come here to see the monument?" Lachlan asks.

"You mean the mountain, Old Man Storr? I saw it in a brochure and thought I might climb it tomorrow."

"No, I mean the MacNeacail Clan monument, Scorrybreac."

"A-what-what?" I joke, merriment prevailing over accuracy of hearing.

"It's called Scorrybreac. You do know this is where all the Nichols and Nicholsons come from? We're all descended from the MacNeacails of Portree."

"You're pulling my leg? I would have had no idea unless you just mentioned it."

"For sure, that's what I thought you were in town for. There's a big cove with a monument just north of here. Maybe 500 metres. It's a dedication to the land they used to hold. You should check it out. It's worth your while."

"This is entirely unbelievable. What a bizarre night."

The more the story progresses, the more I realise my friends will never believe this. For I am struggling with the truth of it myself. I am not afraid to say I detest my Dad, so why would I travel the globe to trace his lineage? The multiple parallels with Lachlan defy logic. What if I'd never come to this town, never walked up those stairs, never eyeballed them across the room? Would I have gone through life not knowing from whence I came?

My two newfound friends invite me back to their farm when closing time falls, but I decline amidst the swirling surrealism and the promise of adventures in the morning.

As I unlock the front door to the hostel, I am met by a half-dozen American girls, sitting around the communal television and watching *Dirty Dancing*. They have stayed in for the night to save money.

"How was your evening?" asks one dressed in pyjamas.

"Umm...was interesting."

AGE seven was when Loxton first displayed a clear willingness to take his own life.

His temperament eroded disturbingly after the custody hearing and his strange mannerisms amplified.

A couple of incidents at school led to him being placed with a counsellor. He had openly begun calling his Grade Two teacher, Mrs Williams, 'Mrs Dumb-Dumb' after she one day made a mathematical mistake on the blackboard. The lady was fragile and Lox seized on this by yelling out her new nickname to earn laughter from classmates.

Around the same time, Lox had told me of being involved in a fight with up to 10 older girls who had been teasing him. "I punched them right in the guts. They were crying," he said. Initially I was unsure if it was a boastful flight of fancy or had actually occurred. Then both Loxton and I were summoned before the principal, Mr Wolff. In a school of less than 100 students, the ripples my son created were not going unnoticed.

"Well Master Nichols, don't you think we've had enough of your bad behaviour?" A balding, but imposing man, Mr Wolff took to stroking his grey fuzzy beard when in a serious mood.

"Yes," Loxton offered meekly.

"This term you have been a constant disruption. I'm always hearing of Mrs Williams having trouble with you. I don't know why this has all come about, but the situation has to change."

The principal's eyes followed across to me, addressing the next question in my direction. "Have things been a bit tough at home?"

"What?" Loxton snapped back in full voice, before I could even reply. He then sat staring into space, tapping the side of his chair rhythmically. I could see his chest rising sharply with rapid breaths and heard an almost demonic hissing noise from his throat.

"Are you okay Loxton?" we both asked in quick succession.

"Hate you...hate you."

"Why? Why are you saying this?" I pleaded, becoming upset myself.

"Nothing. Fuck them. They won't tell you. They won't help." Lox looked ready to combust.

"You're not making a great deal of sense sorry," chimed in Mr Wolff.

"Doesn't matter...doesn't matter. People keep it here. Show no one."

"I think, um, we might get you to the sick bay Loxton," said the principal gently as he stood up and tried to take Lox's hand.

Loudly objecting, my son ripped his arm free and cocked it back as if to throw a punch. But instead of striking out, he skipped backwards, exited the room and disappeared down the steps towards the playground.

"Err Mrs Nichols. I say this with the best of intentions. I think perhaps you should take Loxton home today. And when he is rested and ready to return, I would very much like for him to start seeing Mrs Corgan for some one-on-one remedial work."

Even though inside me I knew this made sense, I couldn't help but sob. Mrs Corgan was a nice woman, a behavioural counsellor, who I had met briefly before and I'm sure she could assist. But at the end of the day, I had failed as a mother. There were a lot of things wrong with our family.

Eventually I tracked down Loxton to an alcove outside a seldom-used fire escape. He was sitting on a bench, underneath the dappled light of a tea tree, eerily quiet and deep in thought. According to the teachers, he regularly disappeared there when troubled. I noticed him becoming generally a lot quieter at this stage and developing several of these 'havens' where he would escape to and sit and ponder. Another was Bradshaw Park near Kedron Brook, where he would often deviate from our walk home and climb the blocked-off back stairs of the scout hall. It bothered me, because it was a known area for drunks, vandals and drug takers, scarred by numerous arson attempts and littered with broken glass.

Thankfully his other place of seclusion became what he dubbed the 'Magical Mustard Kingdom' – Mrs Corgan's brightly painted yellow remedial room. The 'Mustard Kingdom' was an elongated shape, annexed off the main assembly area, where

Loxton would visit at least once a week. He developed such a bond with the counsellor that even when we moved to Banyo, I kept him enrolled at Wooloowin Primary. It necessitated at least two train trips per day and an awful lot of walking. But I saw it as a sacrifice on my behalf to try and right the wrongs I had brought to the children's lives.

Many moons later in his adult years when I mentioned the counselling sessions to Lox, he shocked me with how vividly he could recall them.

"Nearly every time I would be asked to draw a picture of our family doing something. Mostly I would leave Marty out of them. It would be just you, Kim and me. And I'd always make Kim look like a monster. She'd be very ugly and growling or annoying. You'd be happy and look pretty. And then I...lots of times I'd be sitting in a corner or standing apart and I'd be putting a gun to my head or falling on a sharp stick. For some reason, I was fascinated with drowning too. Then of course, when Steve came along..."

It shocked me to think that a kid of seven could have such violence and self-loathing in their thoughts. The extremity of his feelings towards Kim also came as a surprise, until adult Loxton went off on his high horse as per usual.

"In childhood I always thought Kim was selfish. And I grew up always believing the single thing that stops human kind achieving utopia is selfishness." That's Lox, always judging and trying to sound more intelligent than everyone.

As alluded to, next came the period in my life when I met Steve. The kids and I had lived in our new home at Paradise Street, Banyo for a good few months before I began to date again. Steve Reimann was not the first man I was courted by post-divorce, but he was by far the most charming. A work colleague of my sister Jean's, he came from a farming family and worked much of his life in a metal smelting background. He was more man than Marty could ever dream to be.

Poolhall—Jail—Library

Introduced at an informal barbecue one Sunday, we instantaneously hit it off. Steve came home with me that afternoon and by the Wednesday had moved in with us. My philosophy with love is 'When you know, you just know'.

Watching on, my parents didn't hide their disapproval and chose to take an instant dislike to Steve. It didn't help that one of the first occasions he visited them, he wore very short Ruggers without underwear. When invited to sit with my mother and father for a cup of tea in the lounge room, he unthinkingly crossed his legs and accidentally let slip a testicle out the trouser leg. My poor old Mum almost needed the Heimlich after choking on her Scotch Finger biscuit.

Lox and Kim too were initially cautious, protective of the tight trio we had established. However, they soon warmed at the novelty of a new household member. They were undoubtedly thrilled that Steve owned a gold-coloured Ford Fairlady, the first time they had regular access to a family car. It provided day-trips to places like the hills of Dayboro, the fruit market and mangrove flats of Deception Bay and the yachts and fish'n'chips of Wynnum. Because Steve came from a large family like me, his arrival also meant an exponential increase in gifts and hand-me-downs for the kids.

Prior to Steve, we had been living extremely frugally. Money was thinner than at any other time. There were weeks where we lived off Weet-Bix and hot water. Once I even caught the children stealing dried cat food from the neighbours. That said, amid the poverty the kids were possibly at their happiest.

Oddly, there was no real resentment from the children that Steve took the place of their natural father. Kim held little attachment or affection to her Dad, while Lox said he was pleased to see me safe and happy again. After witnessing Marty's physical outbursts at Thistle Street, I sensed that Loxton liked having a male protector in the home.

Not long after I entered the new relationship, Lox also startled us by ending all contact with his Dad, telling Marty to his face that he no longer wanted weekend visits. He said he preferred to "Stay home on Saturdays and watch Transformers and Inspector Gadget". It was Lox at his moody and flippant best, but surprisingly he stuck to his guns and cut Marty out cold. I didn't try to influence the outcome. I thought it important that he should know his Dad while growing up. But even with legal entitlement, Marty gave up battling against his son's icy attitude and, for a while at least, disappeared completely.

Gradually however, it was the same propensity for fantasy and strong-headed impulses which also drove a wedge between Loxton and Steve. They came from completely different moulds. Loxton would be happy playing by himself for hours, hiding down the back of the garden in the banana trees or drawing in a book, imagining himself as a super hero, a robot or a famous sportsman. He also remained very close to his Uncle Howard and the special bond between the two elicited a degree of envy from Steve. More comfortable with a frosty ale and an afternoon of car racing on television, Steve was affronted if the children chose not to join him. Admittedly, his insecurity grew the more he had to drink.

With a weekly pay packet now coming into the home and Lox still requiring behavioural counselling at Wooloowin, we decided after a few months that it was best to move back towards the city. I had shifted home so many times in the previous five years, I'd just about lost count. But the Banyo house was tiny and could hardly fit all four of us now, plus our new dog, Tinker. Instead we found a sprawling high-set white Queenslander at Lutwyche, the nicest place I had rented under my own name.

That's not to say my surname remained the same for too much longer. Eight months after first crossing paths, Steve and I got married. As it was a second wedding for both of us, we steered clear of churches and lavish trappings. Instead we took two of our closest friends with us to the city registry office and confirmed our union quickly. Back at home, our families *assembled and awaited, celebrating long into the night when we returned.*

Our upgrade from fibreglass to a timber home, and from holding hands to wedding bands should have heralded in a bright new beginning for the family. Instead it practically signified the onset of hostilities. Steve no longer hid his resentment for Loxton, who he could not relate to and who served as a constant reminder of my previous marriage. He would bark feverishly loud at the children to 'Shut up!' when they were chattering and playing harmlessly. After being initially hesitant to discipline either Lox or Kim, he turned it into an artform. Belittlement and brute force crept through. It concerned me, for he seemed to take enjoyment from asserting his power, often smiling as he dished out punishment.

Steve's expectations grew by the day. The children had been helping with household chores since they were small, but he decided they were not pulling their weight. One of their new tasks was to clean up after Tinker, a dark kelpie with boundless energy and a remarkable growth rate. Given paper towels to pick up her droppings, the kids were disbelieving. Still only five, Kim most times vomited at the thought and refused to do it. In an attempt to deflect Steve's anger, Loxton took up the slack, but sometimes became nauseas himself from the putrid smell and repulsive texture. The pen we built for Tinker was downstairs in a dark corner and was half-dirt, half-concrete at the base. It trapped the odour and it was nothing for her to leave a half-dozen stinking piles per night. I tried to explain how the undeveloped senses of the children made it a traumatising experience, but Steve laughed me off and said they were too 'soft'. Not surprisingly, Loxton grew to increasingly resent his stepfather.

Another time Loxton was given a fish tank by his cousin Graham, my sister Jean's eldest, which was full of calicos and shubunkins. Soon after, Steve went netting for freshwater crays and catfish in the forested hinterland of Cedar Creek and caught a heap of yabbies in the process. He dumped them in the fish tank, then cackled as they subsequently cut the fins from Loxton's plumed goldfish, either killing them or leaving them to hopelessly flail about, attempting to swim.

Lox was convinced his stepfather was purposely goading him into conflict. I struggled to cast the situation in a better light, particularly after an incident at my son's eighth birthday party. The first real celebration in his honour, it brought a house full of hyperactive schoolfriends, cousins and relatives. One of the biggest presents was a giant Lego castle from Steve's parents. Prior to the day I had already spoken with Loxton about being considerate and paying equal attention to both sides of the family, not only the Bergs. You could say there was a degree of perceived favouritism. In any case, Loxton was blown away by the gift and thanked Steve's parents profusely. However, his stepfather, who had been drinking most of the day, was out of the room. When he returned, he unleashed an abusive tirade at Lox for being ungrateful and punished him by isolating him in the corner of the room. Classmates and relatives chose to start leaving the party early. I suspect Loxton never forgave that unwarranted outburst.

Things were heading in a worrying direction. But after raising the children by myself for so many years, I was convinced they needed a father figure. I didn't want to be alone for that long again. After what had happened with Marty when we broke up, I'd learnt that sometimes it's best to maintain the status quo. I was sure these were only teething problems until everyone became properly familiarised.

Then there came a night when I was watching quiz shows with Steve, while the kids did the washing up. Kim came in and tugged at my skirt, standing there oddly. She whispered under her breath and motioned for me to follow her to the kitchen. Looking across at Steve, he was occupied with a packet of cheese rings and a jug of home brew, so I left him be. The blare of the television was still strong as I walked to the back of the *house, but faint chills of spluttering also caught my ears. Knelt on the linoleum, as if praying, Loxton had a tea towel wrapped tightly around his throat and was pulling on it with all his weight. I shouted at him to stop, but he barely flinched.*

Lox's grip remained taught as he strangled himself. His face white, pink, red, purple, blue, then white again.

OLD MAN OF STORR

IAN is convinced we are on a mystical hobbit journey.
   This is one of those moments when your intuition reaches a murky crossroad. Is he a complete fruitcake, an annoyance on an otherwise marvellous day? Or could this bloke just be the perfect comedic foil to offset a day of adventure and furnish future anecdotes?

"It does feel as though we are approaching Middle Earth though doesn't it?" he prods again, as we trod a scrappily laid bitumen road, pursued by a flock of equally maddening sheep.

"Like I said before man, I haven't watched any of the *Lord of the Rings* movies, so I'm not sure what you're on about," I laugh, shaking my head.

Moments earlier we had stood on the far side of Portree Harbour, looking back from the impressive lands of Scorrybreac to the picture-perfect pastel cottages of Quay Street and the tower upon Sron a'Mhill. A lush peninsula jutting into equally serene waters, Scorrybreac also stares reflectively at Portree's Royal Hotel, the site of the last dalliance between Bonny Prince Charlie and Jacobite heroine Flora McDonald. Legend has it that here McDonald distracted loyalist knights from finding the prince by performing a highland dance.

Thanks to Lachlan's instructions the night before, while on Scorrybreac I successfully located the cairn listing famous descendants of the Clan MacNeacail.

"Ah the virtuous peoples of the Clan MacNeacail. What worthy warriors they be," piped up Ian, his tribute clearly not sounding as schmaltzy in his head as it did out aloud.

Wearing a matching flat cap and vest, round spectacles and fluffy muttonchops, he had encountered me walking the curved road around the harbor, stopping to offer me a biscuit and then asking my plans for the day. Initially I thought him a local, then as the fake accent was dropped, I discovered he was in fact from Vermont, USA, currently a student at the University of Edinburgh, undertaking Gaelic history and literature.

"Oh, I say, do you think I could join you? We might just strike upon some highland coos."

We've got almost three hours of walking ahead of us to Storr, so I decide early that it is best to tolerate the rather amusing loner and enjoy the trek ahead. Our course twists through yellow and brown hillside on a road that barely fits one vehicle at a time. It is more like an elaborate driveway into oblivion. Waterfalls constantly erupt from the areas where soil has eroded from roots of towering trees. Splashing into gullies either side of the thoroughfare, Mother Nature's tears trickle into two massive lochs that stand between us and our destination.

Mercifully, by now Ian has progressed from talking about *Lord of the Rings* to *The Princess Bride*. In terms of theatric quests, I can relate to it more enthusiastically. The horde of sheep that has been following us the last two miles like a pack of loyal canines has now been joined by numerous horned goats. We lead the procession onwards, towards the object of our conquest.

Old Man of Storr rises out of a national park, a thick roundish mountain, whose top is flat towards the southern end, but climbs sharply at the northern tip. Several obelisk-like structures have broken away and stand in solitude at this end, giving the mountain its stunning and ominous appearance. My goal is to make it to the very tip of the north face and bask in a 360-degree panorama of perhaps the most idyllic island on Earth.

We have no maps for the climb, so elect to start the approach from a siding where several well-prepared hikers have assembled. The climbers are elderly and mill about talking too long for our liking, so Ian and I decide to set off alone. A magnificent waterfall, bigger than any previously seen today, greets us in the very first footsteps. After the long trek from

Portree, Ian takes off his shoes, folds his socks and decides to wash his feet in the pure water.

"You'll get blisters now mate," I chuckle to him, wondering how long it has been since his last outdoors exercise.

But the joke quickly turns on me as we scale up to our first plateau and I sink my foot into deceptively marshy terrain, soaking right through to the bone. The water is freezing cold and my socks grow gritty with swamp muck. It should figure that the stunning waterfall below us could not alone come from the thin stream which runs to its head. A huge amount of groundwater surrounds us, squeezing out of the spongy, uneven turf. Soon, we pass a hiker headed back down to the carpark

"Got 'bout 45 minutes 'head ya. 'Ave fun with that grass," the man snickers, eyeing our poorly considered footwear and ensembles.

On face value, I accept 45 minutes to the summit as a blessing, but as the thorny blades below us grow thicker and the terrain becomes more uncertain, I realise the man means 45 minutes merely to our first vertical climb. Eventually we squelch our way to the footings of a steep mountain goat trail. It is already well past lunch and we have only just managed to make it to where I initially thought our ascent would begin.

Conceitedly determined to prove my superior athleticism, I bound upwards from foothold to foothold, not using my hands at all. Ian is taking a much more measured and hesitant attitude, still quoting from books and films as he lags behind, struggling for breath. At least a handful of times I feel my soles slide slightly underneath me, but persevere with the rock wallaby impersonation until the gradient is perpendicular to the sky. I try not to show, but I am feeling the pinch in my lungs myself, a combination of the weather, altitude, exhibitionism and a few too many beers on my travels.

At this point it becomes necessary to scale with my body pressed firmly against the rock. Ropes and harnesses were an afterthought to our adventure and, looking upward, I can see some points where they will be sorely missed. Ian is actually beginning to catch me as I tire noticeably. My eccentric colleague has presumably never played rugby league and does not have the bulky, arthritic shoulders and unforgiving center of gravity that I have been bequeathed. Spider-climbing, needless to say, appears to come far more natural to him and his slender frame. I've never done any sort of rock climbing prior to this, but I consider myself the alpha male here. I opt to keep my fatigue quiet.

At several points we are forced to stop and assess what looks an insurmountable route to the heavens. Yet, after shuffling along the rock face sideways, we always manage to work our way forward. Conquering this intriguing formation has suddenly become something I MUST do on my travels. Failing to reach the peak, I become convinced, would make the whole experience of these next few months incomplete. Safety and common sense increasingly take a back seat.

Upon reaching the top of the southern face, we realise the adjustments in our climb have deviated us even further off track, towards a long ridge which stretches to the west. The other realisation is that the long, sloping plain which separates us from the northern edge is much bigger and steeper than first perceived. From ground level it appeared the length of just a few football pitches. Up here it seems 10 times as long, particularly to our tired and dehydrated senses. Underfoot is not quite as swampy as the first plateau, but it is far more unpredictable and nobbled. Nettles grow rampant, making it a dangerous proposition each time your footing is lost. As Ian stops thrice for photographs whenever I stop for one, our progress verges on glacial.

Concerns and complaints become a moot point though, as the arc of our journey takes us to a point where we can see out over both sides of Storr. Wild rabbits and goats are racing by in the dimming light, allowing our eyes to follow to a spectacular perched lake, cradled by the mountain some 600m above sea level. To the east, the clouds seem to sit below our feet and we can gaze clearly across the Inner and Outer Sound to tiny granite islands and snowcaps on the mainland. Privately I wonder if one of these icy specks on the map is home to Mr Leppard, the most tattooed man in the world. I have heard he lives a life of subsistence in these parts, only occasionally kayaking to the store for emergency provisions.

The mesmerising horizon draws me tantalisingly close to the most unprotected and dangerous edge of Storr's cliffs. For pure brevity alone, I force myself to walk right to the edge and stare down until I feel sick to the stomach. One false move and I will be joined with the mountain for eternity. Splashing against the cliff face and then twisting, tortured in circles, the wind has started to chill Storr noticeably as the sun has dropped.

Early Scottish evenings mean light can fade by 3.30pm, a fact my fluffy-cheeked friend is keen to remind me of.

"Come on, we've seen it from the top. Maybe we should start to head back. It's going to be some time before we get down, and I have hardly any water left."

I am freezing cold, possess only a mouthful of water myself and have been starting to have very minor hallucinations. But I conceal these facts and instead convince Ian to press on, at least for the time being.

"But the whole reason we are here is for the northern face. It's what makes it special. We could climb any old hill if you just wanted a lookout. I bet it's spectacular on the other side."

What is this? Have I developed 'summit fever' on a mountain that is not even one kilometer in altitude? How pathetic. We stumble onward, constantly tripped by the uneven ground, Ian continually looking over his shoulder at the darkening heavens. A weird sensation starts to develop inside me. For the first time I consider I am stuck in a potentially dangerous situation, a million miles from home with a man I do not know. Will he hinder me? Can I trust him if my life is on the line? Strange as it seems, I begin imagining how I would subdue or even kill him if need be. I wish it was unexpected that my imagination would take such obscure tangents.

"Look, I thank you for today, but really I am going to turn around," Ian says after a mere 20 minutes further. "I'd advise you did too my good man."

Sadly, his hobbit adventure has come to an end.

"No worries," I say, calmly walking forward. "Take care." I wait until there is a small ridge obscuring our line of vision, then I break stride from my purposeful, collected stroll to a flat-out, desperate run. If I kept at the snail's pace that Ian had established, it would take close to an hour to reach the peak. It is liberating to sprint free at this height, slicing the wind like an arrowhead.

Though my target now approaches quicker, negating the danger of nightfall is offset by the distinct possibility of snapping my ankles on the godforsaken terrain. My legs are sore all the way from calf to buttock and I know my lungs are not giving me the output I would have expected. An increasingly delirious mind switches back-and-forth between the ecstasy of the enchanting view and the shame I feel at the condition of my body. Partway up the last rise, I am convinced I spy a young lady in a blue jacket to my far left, wearing leopard-print galoshes and flying a kite around a bend. But I pretend to pay her no attention and maintain a forceful uphill jog. When I finally give into temptation and look back, the apparition is gone.

At the finish point of the exhausting quest, I am again reunited with an intense exultation that signifies a goal achieved. This trip has so far given me more feelings of this divine compulsion than the previous five years. There is a near-triangulated point to the mountain where I am closest to the once volcanic formation known as The Old Man, where several wide chasms and crevices abound. Alone, I ponder again that which I considered a day earlier. Have I been brought to Skye all this time to fulfill my destiny? Is this where I pass on; where

I come to rest? Does that take everything full circle and right all the wrongs?

I am staring, glazed in the eyes, rocking in the Hebridean tempest, thinking about attempting to jump one of these chasms. I could die up here, be happy with what I've achieved, escape further inevitable heartbreak.

But I am still as weak as ever. I cannot do it. When I move closer to the edge, my legs lock painfully in fear, like nothing I have experienced except in dreams. What if I plunge to the ground and become a cripple or an amputee? What if I damage my brain, my body, but am kept alive and can no longer do those things that make life bearable?

Suddenly, I am walking down a mountain that has taken all day to climb, the ashy sky magnifying the atmosphere. Descent is far quicker than the ascent, so much so that it is lulling me to a false sense of security as I continue my inner debate.

After a while I reach a point where the ground drops off into sheer darkness, the edge of Earth as it were. I recognise it from when Ian and I pulled ourselves over that first ledge, clearing the vertical climb that had us clinging chest-to-rock. Stupidity alone has stopped me from previously forecasting how to negate this section on the way down. I look to the gentler gradient to the west and decide that path will take far too long.

But as I pan the scenery, my footing comes free and I hurtle earthwards, the embankment disappearing behind me. The romantic ideals of death that I carried just moments ago now seem like a self-fulfilling prophecy. I am clutching at the smallest clods of dirt, holding my breath and pressing my backpack to the rock as I slide, hoping it will slow me somehow. The reality is that my lower back and bottom are being sliced to shreds by the weathered stone, but adrenaline lets me feel none of it. I've courted fatality before, but never has nature brought me this close of its own accord. It is a humbling experience.

A good 50m later, just as I prepare to be spat through the mist onto the unforgiving marsh, I manage to halt momentum by digging a foot into the ground and latching to a ledge with both hands.

As disrupted pebbles continue to roll past me, I cast one softly-spoken word to the cold, desolate air.

"Fuck."

From this juncture, all movements are slow and closely monitored. I have experienced an unsettling, unexpected instinct which I cannot ignore. When I was flying downhill, I wanted to stop. I wanted to stop because I look forward to my coming travels and adventures. The afterlife can take me later, not now. All this time of being an eternal pessimist and considering suicide honourable – 'The One Truth' – and here I am, wanting to remain alive for my future on a very basic level.

Two days on Skye has left me enlightened, exhausted. It also leaves me shoeless. On the very last step of the entire descent, jumping down from the waterfall to the car park where it all started, I land in a bog, ripping my foot free and tearing the stitching to the sole. Wrapping the muddy monstrosities in a plastic bag, I slowly walk back up the road to Portree, praying for headlights on the horizon.

Mercifully, a man in a white Ford Escort pulls over, opens the door, looks strangely at the clock on his dashboard and then at me, barefoot.

"Some weird ones today. Had another kid in here before supper. On about elves and ogres he was."

YOU have to question the rationale of a boy that tries to strangle himself manually. Did Lox really think he would succeed?

After the time I encountered him choking in the kitchen, it was revealed my son was regularly cutting off his breathing with a variety of apparatus. He had some sort of challenge going to see what colour and what length of time he could achieve. Even in morbidity, he was competitive. Loxton told Kim that if he died, he wanted Steve to have to carry his body around and explain why his stepson had suicided. For someone so young, his ability to be vindictive was disturbing.

While I held many concerns about Lox's social aptitude and behaviour, his marks at school remained consistently high. At the halfway point of Grade Three he was achieving straight As well as performing well in athletics. That kept my attitude towards him somewhat subdued, but it mattered little to Steve, who held scant regard for academics or sportsmen. My partner placed more emphasis on the comments section of Loxton's report card, which regularly contained remarks like "requires constant monitoring for self-control". Once, when Loxton had achieved 100% on several exams in the space of a week, I took him out to a pizza parlour for a special dinner, where Steve subsequently chastised the boy for messy handwriting.

"You won't amount to anything if nobody can read what you're on about," Steve chided.

"If I had pencil right now, I'd stab him in the heart," Loxton said when his stepfather excused himself to the toilet.

From being initially happy to accept a new Dad and a new surname, Lox developed an unforgiving, mirrored dislike. His ability to hold a grudge matched the tenacity with which he approached most other tasks. Spiteful messages were left on hand-scrawled posters around the house and he would concoct stories of psychopathic disfigurements he wished upon Steve.

As time wore on, I reconsidered my own blind love for Steve. Perceptive as ever, the children seized upon my misgivings and our frequent arguments.

Poolhall—Jail—Library

"When are you leaving Steve?" was a favourite question, though never answered to their satisfaction.

At this juncture, the announced expansion of Lutwyche Shopping Centre meant several neighbouring houses in our street needed to be demolished. During the activity which surrounded, a mop-haired workman in his early thirties would appear sporadically. His rugged physique was such that my sister and my teenage niece visited much more regularly. Gathered on the back stairs, we'd exchange oohs and aahs as we ogled the tanned Adonis over the fence. Somehow from these schoolgirl shenanigans, Loxton became thoroughly convinced I would exchange Steve for this unnamed tradesman. He didn't even try to hide his disappointment when the fantasy failed to eventuate, eye-balling me as I told him it was all in his head. I wonder to this day what fortune has dealt an aging gentleman approaching 60, maybe still in the building industry, completely unaware he was once the subject of a strange child's vivid hopes and imagination.

Loxton's dismay was doubled when we received news that our house had now been included in a revised land resumption by the shopping centre. After so many shifts of home, we had started to settle and develop an affection for our Lutwyche abode. But this time circumstance was completely beyond our control and we were squeezed out without a choice. The only saving grace was that my name was now at the head of the government list for subsidised Housing Commission accommodation.

Via the Commission we paid barely half the rent of what we had to elsewhere, though the amenities were basic in their construction. West Stafford was an area built out of a bygone tannery era, now dominated by unsophisticated army housing for the nearby Enoggera Barracks – the same barracks where Marty had sold smut magazines for pocket money in his youth. But our new home on Bertram Street stood a good five kilometres from the Nichols' family house and I no longer felt threatened by them regardless.

We found Bertram Street right at the boundary with Everton Park and Stafford Heights, in a hilly corner far removed from the shopping precinct and different to the old cottage-style houses nearer the brook. Instead we were surrounded by mostly identical white, timber fronted houses with a standard two windows on the roadside, fibreboard walls inside and sloping, un-landscaped gardens. Houses were positioned dead-centre on each allotment, without driveways, gardens, verandahs or anything else distinguishable. Each clone was raised off the ground, separated from the earth by cheap slatted wood panels on three sides. Underneath was not sealed, nor large enough to renovate, so each time it rained it became a mudslide and breeding ground for mosquitoes, lion ants and click beetles. The unfinished guttering and weak joinings meant possums delighted in soiling and nesting in the roof.

To this day, it is the very same house that I spend my days.

During the first five years at Bertram Street, I was deeply concerned Loxton wouldn't make it to adolescence. As well as the threat he presented to himself, he was mercilessly bullied at his new school, while the relationship with Steve became increasingly volatile and violent.

Before my own eyes, I saw my new partner gradually allow his inner nature to unravel as we headed to a one-year anniversary. Whether formed by his years at the farm and smelter, he embodied bigotry, rejecting anything that was foreign or unconventional. Pride, to him, equated with being overtly argumentative. Steve became so disagreeable that it was tempting to change your tune to suit his, simply so the day could proceed. Yet even if you were to pander to his views, it was not beyond Steve to perform a befuddling backflip, contradicting himself so he could persevere with being confrontational. He revelled in melodrama, and molehills inevitably became mountains. An atmosphere of gloom and negativity was created *around the house, where the slightest actions were magnified and dissected. When we watched quiz shows, I wanted his every answer to be right. When dinner was served, I made sure his portion looked at least 50 per cent bigger than anybody else's. Out shopping, I willed the closest carpark to the door to be available. Anything, anything at all that assuaged his temper and critical commentary.*

My brothers Howard and Craig noted Steve's domineering and they would offer snide remarks and encourage the children to be purposefully disobedient. Whenever Lox and Kim visited their grandparents, Steve banned them from eating lollies or playing video games, complaining how spoilt they were. On one particular occasion when we returned from the drive-in cinema to discover the kids tucking into barley sugars, Steve completely flipped his lid.

"Right...," he bellowed, reefing Lox and Kim by the arms towards the car. It was his standard statement of machismo whenever he lost his temper. But this time he complained of a conspiracy by my parents, declaring it would be the last time we visited any of my relatives for the foreseeable future. Back home, he belted the children with a special cricket bat he had fashioned for such a moment.

While hate is an incredibly strong word, I knew the kids grew to hate Steve. And I knew I hated myself. Yet I could never bring myself to walk away from a second marriage so soon.

Unable to fathom the ongoing vindictiveness of his stepfather, Loxton eventually started blaming himself for the disharmony in the family. It fostered itself in a deepening self-loathing. He told me that he thought of his soul as "evil" and of feeling "alien" to other kids his age. No matter how obscure Steve's moods or rationale became, Loxton believed part of the weight rested on his own shoulders, resigned that he somehow deserved to be punished. Even when his eyes visibly burnt deep with anger, Lox would beat himself up for being too sensitive.

The need for my son to attend remedial therapy became even more vital at his new school, Stafford Heights Primary. On top of what was occurring behind closed doors, Lox had to split himself from what few friends he had made at Wooloowin. Only after we moved did I discover that he had formed a 'gang' at Wooloowin with two of his friends, fighting most lunchtimes against a group of New Zealand boys. His initial reasons for being in the gang were vague, but then I also uncovered that Loxton had a substantial crush on a girl called Lichelle, a half-Maori lass with striking facial features. Her cousin, whom she did not see eye-to-eye with, was the leader of the Kiwi rivals. It was revealed Lox stole his first kiss from Lichelle just before he switched schools, taken in the concrete tunnels near the sandpit while he gifted her his favourite Spiderman comic.

I questioned the seriousness of Loxton's 'gang' until I heard the house of his friend had been set on fire by their rivals. Consequently, I was forced to make him cut all ties with his old pals and start afresh. Contrary to my intent however, Loxton transferred that same rage to his new school, except at Stafford Heights he had no allies.

Word spread quickly around the small school community of a fiery ginger-haired newcomer. At first there was a degree of trepidation towards him, because my boy would often initiate conflict. But then he became a target for ridicule – the 'Red-Headed Rat Rooter' who blew his temper over the smallest matter and who nobody would play with or talk to. Despite being a strong runner, he was excluded from sports groups by the popular clique and, more often than not, spent his lunchtimes in the library. Loxton's frame of mind dropped further when, at his first athletics day at Stafford Heights he was beaten to second. That had not happened at Wooloowin. Within six months his school marks followed suit and plummeted to a level far below what we had come to expect.

To attempt to list all of Lox's trials and tribulations until he graduated from primary school would be an exercise in *futility.* From having a window smashed in front of his face by a frustrated teacher, to telling another teacher to *'Fuck off'* and pelting watermelon at him, his issues with discipline and authority rode an unnervingly familiar track. His next love interest Sarah, a girl he pursued eagerly for some six months, agreed to be his girlfriend for only half a day, on account of him punching another boy so hard he hit his head on a cupboard.

"*I don't like violent boys,*" nine-year-old Sarah told Lox in a statement of enviable maturity.

Rubbing salt into the wound, Steve's brother – my brother-in-law – Aaron was arrested the next year in a manslaughter case which brought widespread media coverage. Known as the most gentle and reflective of the Reimann brothers, Aaron beat his flatmate to death over a drunken incident which involved two other people. The details were murky, but the only part not to completely shock me was that a girl was somehow at the centre of it all.

Aaron's house was flashed all over the news bulletins and initially, when he was not known as the killer, the children were greatly concerned for his safety and their own. Loxton created a scenario in his head of a vendetta being carried out against all Reimanns by an unknown assailant. For nights on end he swore he heard someone on the front landing, rattling his window.

Yet when Aaron was finally convicted and publicly named, the distinctive surname was instantly picked up on by Lox's classmates. Around the playground he became known as 'The Murderer' and chastised even more than usual. I was forced to lodge a formal complaint when Loxton's fifth grade teacher also snapped at his ill-discipline one day.

"*Don't grow up to be a criminal like the rest of your family son,*" the thickly-browed Irishman instructed. This premeditated the aforementioned incident with the watermelon.

From the earliest portents, Loxton became fully-blown suicidal by 10. It was not something I feel I handled well, and perhaps a difficulty I chose to ignore largely. In therapy sessions throughout his teens, he claimed to have thought of killing himself every day from that age. To me that seemed preposterous, exaggerated. Aside from choking, he romanticised the notion of self-inflicted gunshots to the temple and submitted a school essay at age 11 about being 'vapourised, crushed and numbed' by the steel bumper of a truck.

"Infinite hopelessness can never be imagined. Explaining what it feels like is a waste of time. Waiting to die via an act of nature seems weak and a fate of extraordinary bland proportions," an extract from his essay read.

The written diatribe not only exposed a surprisingly vocabulary, but revealed a kid more sensitive to his surrounds than I previously suspected Loxton to be. His class had been invited to write a story about a challenge they faced, but his particular focus was on the tedium and pointlessness of dealing with Steve each day. The school, concerned by Loxton's state of mind, handed me a photocopy of his writing assignment, which I kept folded deep in my bedside drawer.

"Dinner time is an unavoidable period of the day which draws our family together," Loxton penned.

"As is the usual, Kim and I wash, rinse and wipe the dishes and cutlery after finishing our meals, sweep the floor and clean the bench tops and stove. If this takes any longer than 20 minutes Steve will roar at us from the lounge room.

"What the fuck are you two doing? You better not be stuffing around."

Alternately, if we don't clean everything spotlessly and pack the items away neatly, we will be dragged back into the kitchen and humiliated.

"How dumb are you hey?" he will yell. "I tell you, you're fucking useless. Might as well do it myself."

Of course, Steve never does do it himself.

Poolhall—Jail—Library

Over time his behaviour has become like static in the background. A gripe, a put-down, a random prod in the chest or whack to the head. It is boring above anything. Occasionally, as if to maximise the hatred between us, Steve will create a totally incomprehensible argument. One recent night springs to mind. I had finished the usual chores and retreated to my room, lying under the covers in pyjamas, reading a thick book about fighter planes. I could hear Steve rummaging in the fridge, most likely for kabana and cheese to have as an after-dinner snack.

"For fuck's sake. I'll bounce you kids one day, I swear."

This kind of muttering is to be expected when Steve is pottering about the place. His anger grew as he walked up the hallway and straight into my room. He hauled me from the bed and led me by the neck into the kitchen.

"What's this?" he said, pushing my head down towards the shelves of the open fridge.

I stared nervously ahead, twinging as the muscles in my neck began to hurt. Immediately I suspected I had done something terribly stupid. Perhaps the lid was off the beetroot tin and the red juice was leaking everywhere? Maybe I had forgotten to wrap the cheese and it had gone stale. Whatever the case, I acknowledged that I was capable of great stupidity.

"Well...?" my stepfather demanded as I peered around the fridge. I had no idea what he was on about. Then he reached down, snarling through his small rotten teeth, and grabbed a jar of honey from the door shelf. He forced the jar towards my head as if he were about to smash it over my face. I resisted and broke free, running around to the opposite side of the table, aware I would be too quick for him to chase.

"Right then, little shit. If you're going to be a cry-baby, you can sit at the table without moving until you figure out what I'm talking about."

I did what I was told, slinking to the chair Steve pointed towards. I thought to myself, "Who knows what his problem is *anytime?"*. As if reading my mind telepathically, Steve walked back behind me, giving me a trademark slap to the head on the way past. Sitting and pondering the situation, I became incredibly frustrated. I hated myself for not knowing the answer to the issue. Also, I very much hated not being able to move or do something productive with my time. The situation reminded me that my life is being controlled in every way and, as a kid, I have no way of changing that.

Twenty minutes of contemplation passed before I realised the source of Steve's ire. It was simple enough to make me want to punch myself.

"I know," I said, having given an extra minute of thought, just to annoy Steve. "I put the honey in the fridge, not the cupboard."

"Finally," Steve replied sarcastically, staring at me through squinted eyes. I motioned to move off the chair, with my legs and bottom cramped from remaining dead-still. "Actually, you can stay there. Ten minutes for trying to run away, ten for moving your leg before and ten for wasting the honey. Oh, and another ten because I feel like it."

He thought he was so damn clever. I imagined I was much bigger, so I could waltz straight into that lounge room, place my palm on his forehead and smash his head backward through the wall. The only problem was that fibreplast would be too soft for his head. I wanted something that would damage him beyond repair. Maybe I could have used the thick wood around the window sill to catch his scalp as I blasted him with all my strength. It would penetrate just above his forehead and splinter through all his facial features if I could get enough horizontal momentum.

Alas, I looked down at my scrawny features and realised my arms would do well just to open up the chilled jar of honey. Gazing deep into the yellow wall ahead, I cried to myself."

After that essay was submitted to his teacher, more tears were to come for Loxton.

DUBLIN // GALWAY

TOUCHDOWN at Dublin International Airport. After a near faultless run with transport and weather, I have for the past two days been at the mercy of Murphy's Law, Sod's Law and many other narcissistic creators of rules and regulations.

Coach and ferry timetables officially switched to the winter schedule on my last morning in Skye, a point I did not discover until arriving at the bus stop. Instead of the short ride to Armadale and eagerly anticipated cruise across the water to Malaig, I was instead forced into a much longer, later and more expensive inland trip via Fort William to Glasgow. Though my new route cast me glimpses of Ben Nevis – mightiest mountain of all in the British Isles – it was through the onset of thick horizontal rain, an onslaught which has continued unabated since.

Penny-pinching then led to a night spent sleeping upstairs at Prestwick Airport, a better alternative (on paper) to a paid hotel room in Glasgow, the likelihood of being stabbed and a long cab ride in the wee hours. I bunked down in the airport lounge with four fellow travellers – two Frenchmen, a Swedish girl and a gargantuan Russian who looked uncannily like Zangief from *Street Fighter*. Through his coarse goatee and barreled chest, he elicited occasional grunts whilst reading from a weighty novel, yet did not utter a full word to anybody until he disappeared at dawn with his luggage.

Alongside Brisbane Botanical Gardens, a cupboard, a hockey net and the carpark of the James Street Markets, Prestwick Airport is one of the strangest locations I have chosen to sleep for a night.

Taxiing the runway in the morning takes longer than to leap the slender Irish Sea from Glasgow to Dublin. The plane climbs briefly, only to subsequently drop, like a portly old lady hopping a small stream. None of my preconceived notions have readied me for the introduction to the Emerald Isle.

Bus is the most affordable way into Dublin's city heart. It carries the unprepared man on a confronting route of derelict estate housing, block after block of rectangles devoid of character. The degree of fade in the curtains and the number of clothes strung on the balcony are the only ways to distinguish one unit from the next. I wonder what pleasures the children inside experience. As the rain continues to pelt down a dark fist is ripping at my gut and returning me to a place I don't often like to visit these days. Abuse of all varieties is possibly rife in these outskirts, but here I am, a tourist who will not be stopping to help.

I try to imagine an Irish backpacker passing through my old neighbourhood or some of the other places in Brisbane where I still feel awkward trespassing. Nothing though, can convince me that us Aussies have it worse than here. At the very least, we have sun. Even in the poverty-stricken Indigenous communities of North Queensland, I've still experienced sensations of beauty and spirit. In these particular suburbs of Dublin there seems nothing dynastic or creative, no means for expression.

Blessed by my destinations to date, I cannot shake the somber twist in mood, not even after arrival to the much kinder surrounds of the city centre.

Ireland was supposed to be bright and merry; leprechauns cavorting with overflowing jugs of beer and a sly wink of the eye.

As soon as the hostel allows me to my room, I dump my bags and change from three layers of clothing to a jogging singlet and shorts. Unearthing a roll of electrical tape, a remnant from the last football season, I perform a makeshift operation on my muddy and torn runners, embalming them around my feet. Troubled enough to push out the front doors and jog through the narrow streets of the capital at great pace, I frequently turn heads as I bound the pavement. Indefatigable, I rush down Grafton Street and take a zig-zagging course that

Poolhall—Jail—Library

passes Trinity College, the Bank of Ireland, the bronzed image of big-breasted Molly Malone and the Guinness Brewery.

I run like I did on Christmas Day in 1990, the first of many times I ran from home, lasting five kilometres without looking back. That rare stamina that comes only with deep-seated anger and fear fuels my energy until my right shoe is entirely destroyed.

I stagger for a short distance with sole flapping tenuously until it becomes obvious I must discard the footwear for purposes of sanity. In finding a bin, I come under the shadow of a curious statue; a haggard looking rabbit embracing a large conniving rat of similar proportions. Gazing upwards in confusion at what appears a mid-arsenic-binge creation of Lewis Carroll, I realise I am the one who is out of place. Who is this interloper in lurid beachwear, puffing and rosy-cheeked in the middle of the day – strutting around in socks as office workers scurry well-dressed beneath the seven shades of grey which the sky has gifted them?

The footpath is like the cool shelf of a refrigerator and finding new sneakers becomes an immediate priority. In my soiled anklets I elect to run back to the city, navigating the glass-strewn streets of Temple Bar where professionals come to drink, before dodging the shattered bottles on the opposite side of River Liffey where the homeless prefer to imbibe.

A shop called Burton's springs out at me from a distance. This is the same clothing chain of which my grandfather has spoken repeatedly. It was at a Burton's outlet in Hull in 1945 that he bought the pants and shoes in which he married Mary Kirby. He was so nervous on his wedding day he took three showers and caught the bus to St James' Parish, forgetting his best man had organised him a chauffeur.

Outfitted as though I am incapable of dressing myself, I stuff my arms with a thin-fibred jacket, edges fashionably frayed, a three-pack of short white socks and an uber-cool striped scarf. This, I promise, is the only circumstance in my life in which I will consider paying good money for a neck adornment. To me, scarves still represent that gaggle of girls at 17 who thought Country Road clothing, high tea and calling each other 'darl' was the path to righteousness.

Underneath the counter is a black leather wallet, with the Burton name branded clearly in the corner. I add it to my purchases and depart, soon realising I remain unsuitably shod. Yet just around the corner is a cheap shoe store and, not far past that again, I spy a boxing gym.

Treated to just over 100 Euros of new garments, I indulge my body in another hour of torturous penance on the punching bag. Until I left Brisbane, I was regularly training for 12 rounds or more at Valhalla Muay Thai. Exactly a fortnight later, the pints, the sides of hot chips, the constant snacks of Hobknobs; they have me struggling for breath in five minutes. However, the self-loathing and insecurity is as strong within as ever. I push through the pain until I am fully spent, buckled over and panting between my spread legs on the matted floor.

Another day of similar physical punishment follows, until I have finally exorcised the nagging demons and convinced myself I am worthy and capable of holding people's attention. That night the flashy jacket comes out, as too does the poncey scarf, complementing my favourite jeans, which have the dotted artwork of a lady's face strewn down the outside left leg. I am feeling like someone with at least a few redeeming qualities – battening away the useless, ugly, poor, unfit, stupid kid to an evening in the cupboard. First stop is upmarket Q Bar, then the Auld Dubliner in Temple and then finally at the cosy Messrs Maguires. It is a warmer and more relaxed atmosphere than the others, capped off by the flavoursome Rusty, a red ale produced in-house with a micro-brewery.

Three or four hours pass without a word spoken to anyone, until Damien and Patrick strike up conversation. Damien is a social worker, while Patrick is studying politics. For reasons known only to themselves, they take me under their wing.

Another hour drinking and they are promoting me to a group of female acquaintances as if they were my best friends.

"He's a smart guy eh? What a big fit bastard he is eh? Bloody travelling the world, half his luck."

Hanging out with the Aussie has become their novelty for the evening. One girl in particular is growing progressively amorous. But for every kind word after midnight, every sip of beer, the sense of suspicion, paranoia and torment rises. I excuse myself, try to block out their questioning expressions and disappear home in a swirling, drunken flux. Everything is back to square one.

I hate who I am.

A little kid in a grown man's body awakens in the morning, barely lucid as he lugs his baggage to Busarus, Dublin's transit centre.

Four hours of tight and bumpy road separate us from the western frontier town of Galway, positioned alongside the Atlantic Ocean. I sneak to the very back corner of the coach and, not for the first time in my life, twist my neck sideward, resting temple on palm to alleviate a crunching headache. It's a technique I first discovered when I was 23 and struggling to report on a very important game of football. Thinking back to that day, I was wearing a skin-tight purple shirt with a dragon motif, hair coloured electric blue and eyes as wide as an opossum. I must have been a fool to convince myself that none of my colleagues knew what was going on.

Today, just as then, I feel awfully remorseful for an awful lot of things. As is wont to happen, my mind returns again and again to one person. To Jen. I have never made amends. She has not spoken to me in almost five years.

Every time I have told myself I no longer care, I've at least thought of her 10 times in between. Her departure is at the root of any unhappiness and failure. On this chosen day though, skull throbbing with lament, words come to mind that I've been unable to conceive in my brightest moments.

There's no point telling Jen that I love her and want her back. More than the comfort of any girl, it's my own sense of decency and dignity which I am chasing. Above all, I need to apologise from the heart; make peace with the Earth. That is the only way forward. I rummage through the daypack for my thick blue notepad.

Totally absorbed, I seldom glance up to appreciate the rustic wonders of Ireland's inner heart. Ignore the money I have spent in getting here, the catharsis which my pen is delivering has far greater value. If only this clarity had arrived much earlier and saved the repetition inflicted on the pained ears of my best friends as I bemoaned my woes.

When the bus creaks to a halt by Galway's main square I am at an anxious apex. Part of me wants to find the nearest post office straight away, but another part knows how big a gamble it is reopen the wound. If I mail the letter off and the police become involved again, this elation will surely plummet.

I decide to run the contents past my sister first. For all our ups and downs, Kim will tell me better than anyone how the letter will be received. Hurrying to the hostel – which I am pleased to say surpasses all others thus far – I hastily type out a copy of the intended letter and email it home. Pressing the 'send' button triggers another rush of adrenaline. I've left myself wide open for attack, yet at the same time freed my chest of a gargantuan weight. The greatest thrills in life come from vulnerability.

A wide, clean and warm room greets me upstairs at the hostel. The dorm is all mine – the other two mattresses completely empty. From the top bunk, I can reach a sky roof. In delightful solitude I raise myself up, squeeze through and take position on a ledge of the roof, gazing towards a crisp pink horizon. The sunset is gob-smacking, like layers of brightly coloured birthday cake squeezed onto the mysterious Atlantic. My father could have painted this. It's late on a Saturday afternoon and the hum of chilled wind against bristling trees and the odd squawk of a tern are the only sounds to disturb harmony.

Galway has a reputation for being lively, famed for music in cloistered bars and an effervescent student population. It's also surrounded by the unspeakably beautiful Connemara National Park, the Cliffs of Mohr and, half an hour off the coast at nearby Rossaveal, is the ancient settlement of the Aran Islands. My gloved hands tuck under my armpits, firm to my chest, and I lay back day-dreaming of the adventures ahead until the sun has completely vanished.

Later, dressed to the nines, I ignore the lessons of a night before and hit the winding laneways for several exploratory drinks. It leads to a bar on Eglinton Street called GPO, coincidentally the name of my least-favourite nightclub in Brisbane. Yet there is none of the same pretension. The locals strike up conversation and invite you to dance frequently. It must be said the lasses of Galway are collectively the most beautiful bunch of people I've ever witnessed. Their skin unblemished, accents twirling in the air like Catherine wheels, playfully prodding and giggling as they engage you with meaningless jokes and deeply meaningful eyes. Still, somehow it comes to pass that I find myself sharing alcoholic communion with two German boys from a small town in Bavaria.

We go shout-for-shout at least twice over on heavy pints of Smithwick's as we intercept new arrivals to the bar and give them a full social interview. It transpires that a large expedition of law students from Trinity College has embarked on a three-day sojourn to Galway for the Halloween weekend. The concept of celebrating Halloween is so foreign to me, that I had not taken any notice of its arrival, even if thinking back over the last few days, there were numerous shop windows and newspaper articles to assist my meek powers of realisation. As the crowd swells, the majority of passing girls gravitate towards A.J., the taller of the two Bavarians. He has stylish jet-black hair and enviable dress sense, exuding a confidence that borders on cockiness the further we escape from daylight.

Audrey is among those girls drawn by this magnetism. I recognise her face instantly, though she is much more preened than when I saw her last. She had been sitting two seats in front of me on the bus from Dublin, looking rather down-hearted. Notable on that journey for her long, brown, athletic legs, she is tonight wearing a flowing dress, sweeping her chestnut fringe to the left of her face, framing saucer eyes and thick pouting lips.

An Irish boy called Ciaran introduces Audrey to our group. Informs us all that she has recently broken up with her boyfriend and is looking for a cute guy to cheer her up. A.J. seizes on the opportunity without hesitation and holds her cheek with one hand as he talks directly into her ear above the nightclub music. They are laughing and joking while I maintain a distant air, pretending I am otherwise preoccupied and largely disinterested. When A.J. is pulled away by another girl to go dance on the floor, Audrey looks to me and the smaller, balder Bavarian – Joel – for attention. Initially I resist and keep my head turned towards the crowd, for there is nothing worse or more powerful than a girl who knows she is the centerpiece of a room.

But then Audrey leans right over to my shoulder and lets out a surprising American drawl.

"Hey, you're the scary guy from the bus, aren't you?" she says, smiling as though she has no comprehension of her insult.

I've always detested the brashness of Americans. My face shows it.

"Aww don't be so sensitive Mr Talkative. I'm only joking. You were on the bus, though right? I was actually going to chat with you, but you, uh...did look kind of foreboding yeah."

"Oh, and why is that?"

"Well, let me start off by saying tonight you don't look half as scary, so it's all good. But yes, you were scribbling away in a book and you had that big jacket on and you hadn't shaved."

"I don't suppose I looked obviously hungover?"

"I was going to say that, but I'm apparently rude enough hey?"

The banter continues back and forth with the kind of dry sarcasm I reserve for a special few. Most regrettably, I find this woman unshakably engaging. Refraining from any flattery or outward praise, I keep baiting her with snide comments at regular intervals, exhausting every last ounce of wit I can summon. My calm face is concealing a constantly scrambling mind. When I next take a break and glance at my watch, we have talked for two hours straight.

A vixen with a powerful air of independence and assuredness, Audrey also has the telltale intelligence of someone who was not always so cool. Feigning disinterest towards her becomes increasingly difficult. Amongst the bluff and bravado, she lets slip a few personal gems. She comes from a small island near Boston and is currently studying abroad in the historic Austrian city of Salzburg. Her ambition is to become a leading geologist, but for now she is completing a double degree in journalism and archaeology, spending her spare time learning German and hiking the Alps. None of it explains what she is doing in Galway.

"Look I'm kind of bored of this wretched talking," I say, "Can't I just kiss you and get you to shut up?"

It's a cheeky gamble. By this stage of the night we have slumped side-by-side on a darkened couch, our shoulders and heads already touching. It would take us only a 45 degree turn each to lock lips. Instead, Audrey reels away, a startled and disapproving look washing over her face.

It's all part of the rouse. Audrey watches my downcast response and then cracks an enormous smile. Placing a hand to my chest, she leans above me until her flowing mane shrouds us both from prying eyes. We brush lips softly with a chill down the spine that feels like I've been returned to adolescence. Lingering, she stays staring at me from mere centimetres apart, her right index finger tracing my stubbled jaw.

"Hmm, that was okay I guess," I chirp, salvaging my respiratory pattern. "One last drink?"

But by the time I return from the bar, Audrey is laughing hysterically with Joel, playfully slapping him on the shoulder. Great. Just what I needed. Another incorrigible flirt. Even if this is just a one-night liaison, I detest that familiar feeling that I mean nothing more than the next guy.

"Heya!" Audrey yells overly-dramatically, punching me in the stomach at the same time as I hand across her drink. "Joel was just telling me that he is the fourth-best pool player in all of Bavaria. How awesome is that?"

Before I have time to respond she grabs me, kisses me and whispers in my ear: "We have to leave. Joel asked me to go home with him. I didn't know what to say, so I started laughing stupidly instead."

I am forced not to blurt out laughter as Audrey slyly crosses her jugular in cut-throat fashion. We excuse ourselves to dance, but do so only momentarily before leaving via a side door.

It turns out that Ciaran – the Irish boy that first introduced us – is also hosting Audrey at his house. The story is complex; until recently Ciaran was dating Audrey's childhood friend Lauren, but it had all fallen apart at the worst time possible, just after Audrey booked a ticket to Ireland. Presumably angst-ridden, Lauren had disappeared back to America. Ciaran though, stuck true to his word and said the offer of the spare bed still stood, particularly as Audrey had already set a wider itinerary of tours and travels that intersected with Galway. I am assured many times there are no shenanigans going on between Ciaran and the geology fox.

Poolhall—Jail—Library

This is all of importance, to explain why we have eventuated at a nondescript cottage driveway some three miles out of town, gripped together and exchanging saliva madly on the bonnet of a car. We have been waiting almost two hours for Ciaran to return from GPO with the front door key, fearing both frostbite and the harsh reality of an encroaching dawn. Maintaining our furious passion in subzero temperatures and with tremulous bladders takes every ounce of concentration and energy.

When Ciaran does languidly amble by, his own arm draped around a pretty young girl, Audrey and I race inside for the toilet. We then lay embraced on a wide couch in the lounge room, falling asleep with our hair in each other's faces as we chat to the point of exhaustion.

Despite the anticipatory tension and our immediate physical presence, there is no frivolity that night or in the morning that follows. However, there is later down the track – the culmination of three straight days in each other's presence, a period spent kissing under hooded jackets on a rainy Galway Bay, boating around the historic offshore islands, meeting strange local characters and spending far too much time gazing pathetically into our mutual, constantly fawning eyes.

Without exaggeration there is one point, in a lively cellar bar, where we sit opposite each other, unable to speak or finish our meals for at least a whole hour as our coloured irises dart side-to-side and we exchange dopey, contented, disbelieving smiles. This same ritual is recreated at dinner at Al Muretto's and then later at the plush Victoria Hotel on our last night together.

Audrey is by far the smartest and best-looking girl I have ever shared a bed with. It's tempting to shield myself and concede she is out of my league. But in a mere handful of days, on an extended, expensive and blessed stopover in an isolated Irish town, I have discarded many depressive misgivings about my own past and future potential.

A PURELY horrid phone call came on the morning of April 12, 1989, my 31st birthday. As usual Steve was up early readying himself for work, but avoided the ringing telephone. At this point I was four months pregnant. Taking shallow, staccato breaths, I listened to my distressed mother on the other end of the phone.

"What? Why? When?" My questions followed like train carriages unable to brake. There was an aching in Mum's moans that made me tense up and almost lose my footing.

I immediately presumed that my father had died. He worked tirelessly for not only his employers, but also in keeping the house shipshape for my mother's demands. He suffered bad circulation, a strain of emphysema and would frequently nod asleep mid-conversation. We would joke when he started dozing off in the middle of a family gathering, breathing heavily and drooling. Yet underneath, I'm sure we all held a secret fear he wouldn't wake up one day.

As Mum detailed to me the exact occurrences of the previous hours, I became aware of my face bristling, my eyes shot wide with light, only anger and injustice withholding the tears. My upper body hunched until a means of physical support was required. Propped up by the wonky telephone stand, I heard that it was not my father at all who had forced such hysterics.

It was my brother Howard.

By now, my elevated voice had brought the children to the hallway. Steve quickly shooed them back to bed and grabbed me a seat. When I finally hung up the handset, I chatted with him briefly and we agreed that nothing would be said to the kids. As Steve departed for work, I locked myself alone in the lounge room and left Loxton and Kim to serve out their own breakfasts. Normally they would walk to school around 8am, but by half-eight they were still milling around.

"Mum," I heard Loxton yell, as his shadow slid under the door, "We just wanted to wish you happy birthday."

Poolhall—Jail—Library

I could stifle the waterworks no more. And in truth, I wanted the kids to stay home with me that day more than anything. Unbolting the entrance, I prepared myself for the expected onslaught of questioning.

"You're not going to like this Lox. It's to do with Howard."

By this age my son had already mastered the art of patronising my emotions. In fact, I would have considered it a favourite pastime of his. But in this instance the mere mention of Howard's name, meant he treated my words with the utmost seriousness.

"Is he okay?"

"Well he's not dead. He's in hospital."

"Why? What's happened?" *he said, slamming his fist on the sofa at the same time.*

"He's slashed his own throat. Grandad found him this morning...oh it's just..."

I broke down as I watched Loxton's face melt into a sea of angry tears. His response was to grab his school port, sling it over his shoulder and storm off towards the front landing. Given Loxton's disposition of late, I now had two people to be deeply concerned about.

As he reached the front door Lox turned back, clumsily trying to wipe his watery eyes across his uniform sleeve at the same time.

"Mum?"

"What?" *I replied, my attempt to feign ignorance admittedly poor. He wanted the rest of the story and I had the utmost reluctance to bring it to either of my children's ears. I compromised by sending Kim to hang the washing and calming myself with a cup of tea.*

"It's not a good story Lox. You can't repeat any of this. Not to your friends, not to anybody. It's not something we should ever talk about again. Howard's been thinking funny for a while now. Nanny and Grandad found out he's been seeing a lady...

one he pays money to be his friend. He thinks he loves her and he told his doctor that she likes him too."

Loxton looked confounded. He thought his uncle having a girlfriend was exciting, not a cause for being upset.

"Anyhow this lady...well it turns out she already has a boyfriend; a nasty gangster, drug-dealer type of person. When Howard told the lady he loved her, the other man didn't like it and told your uncle that neither he nor the lady wanted to see him again. He said a few things to make Howard very upset; that he was a loser and that everyone was laughing behind his back, and the lady had been throwing away his presents. You know Howard. He isn't a fighter, but I think the man got him pretty angry and he may have said some things which weren't nice in return. So, this other man ends up by telling him he is going to break into Nanny and Grandad's house and kill all his family. That's made Howard very, very scared."

I became aware of how much I was baby-talking to Loxton, but he took the content of the story so far to heart that he did not even consider the manner in which it had been delivered. He was entirely devastated and infuriated, even beyond my expectations.

"You see," I continued, trying to divert the story elsewhere, "The last few weeks Howard has been going back to the mental hospital. Grandad has been trying to get him help, but one day Howard is happy to stay there and then the next day he begs to be checked out. Nobody knows what parts of his stories are real and whether Howard has just convinced himself of the whole thing. And then, well...he's hurt himself. This is what happened because he got too upset."

I didn't know where to go from there. I felt Loxton deserved the truth, but hadn't considered how he would cope with it. My son's perception of his uncle had been largely idealistic until then. He had never considered him as needy, afraid or susceptible to love's torment. But suddenly Howard was all of these things and was lying in a secure ward, stitched almost a *hundred times around the neck. It was a significant fall from grace in Loxton's eyes and, although concerned for Howard's life, it made him reevaluate how well he knew anybody. For some time, he had become sharply sensitive to how insincere and hurtful the world could be in general.*

Needless to say, I was also shattered by the news. To hear that on my birthday, and to become the intermediary in a family full of emotion, placed a large strain on my health, to the point it threatened my pregnancy. In the weeks that followed my blood pressure rose to critical levels and I too no longer felt I was coping psychologically. Briefly, I was assigned my own bed in hospital until a better handle on my well-being could be achieved. Howard however, lasted near to 12 months in the psychiatric compound after his surgery. Loxton visited him most weeks, undistracted by the arrival of his first and only brother.

After a 10-hour labour, Bobby eased his way into the world 5lb heavier than any of my other babies. By the time I gave birth, I was a full fortnight overdue and resembled a dangerously inflated beachball. Indeed, the latest arrival was large and boisterous in every way from the moment the doctor slapped his behind. Steve could not withhold his delight at having a son of his own making and I too felt proud to have irreversibly unified our bloodlines. Though often resentful at the attention Bobby received, both Lox and Kim treated him always as a full brother and nothing less. Still, with 11 years between the two boys and nine years between the two youngest, they shared more of a mentor and minder role than as playground accomplices. To me, the most pleasing development was that the kids finally abandoned their undisguised wish that one day I would walk out on Steve.

As Loxton graduated from primary school and took on his next great institutional challenge – Everton Park State High – the onset of testosterone was like an accelerant drizzled onto naked flames. The combustible relationship between him and Steve entered newer and more dangerous territory. Emptying nappies, baby-sitting, scrubbing the bath and lavatory; they were all new tasks added to the children's chores at a time when Lox was grappling with his uncle's fallibility and greater scholastic expectations. In class, Loxton had even fewer friends than primary school, and went through a heart-breaking period where two of his only pals began to avoid him because he was considered so unpopular. They feared his reputation would rub off on them. Outbursts of unfathomable rage left me concerned for what direction Loxton was headed toward, and fearful in a manner that I never expected motherhood to bring.

At home, Loxton and Steve hardly ever spoke and when conflict occurred, it heightened to the point where the elder would physically push the younger into tight corners – against walls, benches, the stove – and then invite him to fight his way out. Loxton never did. He merely submitted and took the force of Steve's chest against his face. Eventually Steve would grow tired of trying to rile him and elect to either smack him in the head or strap him on the behind. Loxton often accepted the full imposition of blame upon himself. He was totally devoid of confidence and yearned for discipline, convinced all punishment was deserved. As a rule, Steve never apologised or appeared regretful, so there was no other way for situations to de-escalate aside from the other person admitting full fault.

Then Loxton went and made it all worse by falling for a girl.

I likened the young Wendy Wilson to a monkey, first time that I laid eyes on a picture of her. She admittedly had some cuteness to her, though when I told Loxton she looked like a skinny chimp, he didn't see the funny side. As a mother, I don't know you can look at any undeveloped 12-year-old girl and realistically think of her as a long-term prospect for your son. Saying that, she was an athletics and softball star for the school, and also the top of almost every class. Plenty of boys took a shine to her because she remained approachable, despite her lengthy list of achievements. At the time The Wonder Years was all the rage on television and Wendy was known by the nickname 'Winnie', on account of the wholesome brunette heroine, blessed with a round face, bright smile and thin frame.

At the beginning of high school, Loxton only attended school discos to avoid castigation from classmates. Even if we offered to pick him up later, he would walk home by 9pm in a foul mood and shut himself in his room. Over time however, he began to break later and later curfews. We would find him smuggling bottles of home brewed beer from underneath the house, borrowing clothes supposedly more fashionable than those inhabiting his own closet and eliciting phrases which sounded like they belonged to another language altogether. Lox's attempts to grab Wendy's attention brought himself to the point of being unbearable.

"Could you believe Mrs Matthews?" I heard him moan one day in the presence of Wendy. "Why the fuck did she send me outside the class? What a bitch."

Wendy hardly paused in her step. "Well you were being an idiot," she said, continuing up the street as Lox stood deflated on the front landing.

It appeared my son's powers of seduction were yet to reach full bloom.

From playing the tough guy to playing the bleeding heart, Loxton finally formed a closer relationship with Wendy by confiding about our troubles at home. Seeking love from sympathy was not something I would have recommended, based on my own experiences. It seemed as though it may have been a tactic handed from father to son. Yet my opinion held no sway at this point, neither on the object of his affections nor the manner in which he undertook himself.

The pair bonded when Wendy was herself spurned by the older Timothy Hartman, the clean-cut swimming star of the school, on the verge of graduation and with the looks of a young Ryan Phillipe.

As Lox retold it, he caught Wendy one day as she left class with her books held high and covering her face. As he stopped to chat, he noticed her tiny brown eyes fluttering with tears, her cheeks puffed and drained. It was the moment of weakness for which he had been waiting in anticipation.

"Oh hey, ummm....is this about Tim?"

Wendy's face didn't budge an inch from that of melancholy, but this in itself gave my son his answer.

"Do you want me to walk you to maths?"

"Uh yeah, okay. Hey let's get going. Tim's sister and her friends are coming this way."

For most of the trek between the two buildings, neither said a word; Wendy in mournful reflection and Loxton in guilty contentment. As they cleared away from the other children she began to cry more freely.

"I bet there's plenty more people who think you are wonderful. Plenty more fish in the sea and all that." It wasn't going well for Loxton at this point until he changed tack. "If you're feeling down you might want to go speak to Doug the chaplain. I've talked to him. He's good."

Wendy brightened a fraction, grateful for the advice and concern.

From then it was almost a fortnight until they spoke heart-to-heart again at an early Wednesday swim class.

"You know what you were saying about Doug...what have you been seeing him for?" Wendy asked.

Loxton knew he wasn't going to impress with talk of being mentally unbalanced, so he sent the conversation on a meandering journey.

"Just general stuff that gets me down from time to time. I can give you his extension number if you like."

Though the topic was avoided temporarily, Wendy again pressed Loxton for information that afternoon. Encouraged by her interest – mistaking teenage curiosity for affection – and equally encouraged by her appearance in bathers, he agreed to confide in her prior to science class.

Wendy began the saunter down to the laboratories with anticipation, but was left ultimately disturbed. Lox told her that he thought of death constantly; that he was intimidated daily by his stepfather. He detailed a spiteful vision of a doomed world that would one day implode amid greed and falsity. More pressing for Wendy however, was the desperation with which Loxton seemed to want to share his burden. He wasn't just affected by his sadness, he was obsessed and convinced of it.

The thought processes behind his negativity held neither reason nor appeal for a girl from the double-storey brick houses of McDowall, where streets were named after famed entertainers and set back against bushland; where parents had careers, not jobs; an environment that laid the platform for achievement and dreams which appeared within arm's reach.

Wendy's ultimate flaw was not immediately telling Lox how she truly felt.

Instead, twisting his dark confession into some fantastical romance, my besotted boy decided that the following week would be the perfect time to declare his undying love for Wendy. Although wary of Loxton's fervour, I spoke with him when he sought my opinion about how to best handle the situation. If he was going to place his heart on the line, I wanted him to do so in a chivalrous manner which would uphold his dignity.

A poem and accompanying letter were to be placed in Wendy's school port the next swimming lesson. We had pored over its contents endlessly to ensure the warmest reception possible. However, prior to planting the artefacts, Loxton was supposed to engage his object of affection in witty conversation to help grease the wheels. That he failed to do so sent him into a fluster and instead he held onto the note and poem. For the remainder of the day he moped about in a depressing air, full of self-pity and praying divine intervention would bring him Wendy's heart without any action on his behalf.

As he trudged to class that afternoon, another group of children moved to join him. Loxton spotted Wendy among them and started walking faster, the discomfort of his clandestine plan leading him to try and create distance.

"Loxton!" Wendy yelled, anchoring herself behind the group and waiting for him to turn. Loxton skulked back. "What is up with you today? You've been so miserable and difficult."

Unable to control a cacophony of internal machinations, he whipped out the folded poem and letter from his pocket and thrust them towards her.

"Here. Here's why," he snapped, again turning his back and walking off.

Wendy entered class five minutes later, refusing any eye contact and stepping straight to her desk. Not once in the final hour-and-a-half of the school day did she gaze in Loxton's direction. Initially he felt his heart being wrenched, but then felt a strange relief. He was convinced, even before handing over the letters, that Wendy would reject him. Yet he felt compelled to do it nevertheless. At least now he had some confirmation of his standing.

Lox had not lost Wendy. For he had never possessed her. But what he stood to lose most was the reputation among his classmates, and this is what he suddenly became most fearful of. Unable to conceal the turmoil, he confided his actions in his best friend of the time, Milton, who sat at the next desk. Milton shot back a disapproving look, shook his head and mouthed 'Why?'

That spiraled Loxton into a greater state of anguish where his only source of comfort was that Wendy was a decent person, not prone to gossip or likely to reveal his embarrassing declaration. I remember him arriving home livid in the extreme, convinced I had sabotaged a blossoming affair with my recommendation of poetry. As much as his attitude angered me, I took pity, for I saw how unsettled the experience left him, and the unease with which he tried to sleep. It reminded me incredibly of my own pursuits in passion which terminated in smoldering wrecks.

Loxton arrived at school the following day determined to appear unfazed by Wendy's rejection. He sweated up a storm playing touch rugby on the concrete by the tuckshop, his habitual preparation for a day of study. As the hours ticked by, he became convinced he had escaped any fallout from his diabolical foray into romance.

That was until the lunch break, when Wendy emerged from her accounting class onto a verandah which overlooked the packed playground and queue for the lunch line.

"Loxton Berg," she yelled at the top of her lungs over quickly turning heads, "I HATE YOU!"

LIMERICK // CORK

AFTER a marvelous stay in Galway all I can think about on the bus ride to Cork are the two emails lodged in my inbox and the one email I am convinced I will never receive.

My sister Kim has replied to my earlier letter about Jen and given her approval for it to be sent. She has solid judgment, although I suspect Kim does view my eligibility and writing skill through rose-coloured glasses. There's also an email from Mum; one that has got my goat.

Then there is the third email – the email that Audrey has promised. At our parting she said she would like to catch up with me in London. Yet this came after a lengthy discussion about serendipitous encounters and their majestic aura. We both know that to force a second meeting will be at risk of tainting the very basis of our whirlwind dalliance.

It's an overcast day as the bus heads through Shannon and then Limerick, headed south to Cork. A dull half-hour stopover in Limerick convinces me I made the right decision to skip through it at haste.

Jostling uneasily at the back of my mind are the words Mum has seen fit to send halfway around the world. Where she draws the motivation and justification from, I'll never know. Usually there is an understanding between us that I'll never venture any information about my love life and she will never ask or even feign interest. But on this occasion, she has chosen to ignore protocol in a major way. I suspect it may have been prompted by my message to Kim, because between them they have an utter incapability to keep secrets.

Anyway, Mum has written how 'funny' her memories of my doomed teenage relationships now seem in reflection. In particular, she has been reminiscing of late about my first serious crush, Wendy. 'Winnie' and I are actually quite civilised friends these days and I plan on bumping into her now she resides in England. But while I may have externally conquered the demons of her courtship, that general period of my life is one that still drives a chisel to the kidneys.

Mum can freely bring herself to recount the 'cute awkwardness' and the stomach-churning romanticism which I produced in bundles. Oddly enough, she never talks about the beatings or the self-hate that drove the desperate, continual search for affection. She doesn't recall, let alone recognise, how she stood around when certain things happened.

Ask me what I remember about falling for Wendy and one of the first moments that jumps to my conscience came in our lounge room on a Saturday night. Mum and Steve had cottoned on that I was keen on a girl and they were pecking away at me like vultures.

"So, does she have oranges, mangoes or melons?" Steve confronted me in an absurd state of intoxication, cupping his hands before his saggy chest, as if imitating varying breast sizes.

I was almost ready to leave the house and pretended I hadn't heard his lurid question, offering only a look of bewilderment.

"You know what I'm talking about," Steve barked.

Repulsed, I moved for the door. "I dunno." My cheeks involuntarily pushed towards the corner of my eyes as disbelief and contempt rose. He made me cringe in such an inescapable way. I attempted to disguise my reaction, but was unable to do so.

"She's probably just some slut anyhow," Steve retorted.

Wheeling around, full of youthful chivalry, I gritted my teeth: "She is not a slut!"

"Slut, slut, slut, slut," he replied, measured and looking straight into my eyes.

I stood shaking my head at Steve. The challenge had been laid down, our mutual stares unblinking and focused firmly on each other. Years of mutual hatred come to the fore. Looking into his pickled pupils, there was one thought that stood alone. "Get fucked."

"What did you say boy?"

Slowly I repeated. "Go and get fucked."

Steve slammed down his jug of beer and cast aside his packet of chips. Seemingly intent on setting a land-speed record for fat, inebriated men, he dropped his feet from where they rested on the pouf and hopped up at me. I took the ill-conceived option of trying to lock myself in the bedroom, rather than heading straight for the back door. We staged a tug-of-war briefly at the doorway, but my short, sharp bursts of strength failed to counter his persistent pressure. Flinging open the door, he wrestled me onto the ground and locked his arm around my throat. I was almost taller than him by this stage, but as he lifted my body and frog-marched me back towards the lounge room, I could feel myself choking with feet barely touching the ground. Mum was screaming and crying by now.

"Both of you stop it!" she yelled. Steve dropped me in a heap on the floor and told me to stay put, then went and unlocked his workshop downstairs, where he always retreated after a fight. Mum was crying so hard I thought mucus might bubble out of her mouth. She flicked her eyelashes and gazed harshly at me.

"Why? Why do YOU do this?"

Totally unable to comprehend her accusation, I allowed my own tears to escape. There was no sanity or objectivity at all in that house. It was hopelessness all around.

The sound of blubbering was all that permeated the airwaves. That was until I heard a heavy foot on the bottom of the back steps and the screen door being ripped open. Steve had come back with a plank of thick timber. As if invoking some redneck spirit, he usually referred to it as a piece of 4B2.

"No don't," Mum shouted.

"He needs to be taught a lesson Karen. If he's so big, let's see how he handles this. Huh, how do you like that King Shit?"

With that he threw me down and left me staring at the distasteful red and yellow carpet while he blistered my legs and posterior with the timber. After he rolled off and cast a proud eye on his doing, I limped into the bedroom to suffer alone. I would now be too late to walk with Wendy to the disco as promised and too wound up to enjoy myself anyway. Selfishly, I hoped she would ring to see if I was okay. But the silent phone assured I was never an integral part of her evening.

When morning descended, I felt sick in the stomach and sore all along my back. I rolled over tentatively and craned my neck to inspect the damage. Thick browny-purple bruises stained my flesh. Once again, I was left to wear long trousers to school.

Shorts were the standard among our social circle and those who donned trousers were open to both ridicule and torrential sweating. Body image was vital at this stage, with all the boys gradually starting to take more care with their appearance. No lie, I would look around the classroom daily and rank everyone in terms of attractiveness. Without fail, I placed last. Even on days where I didn't have hideous bruises and was feeling my best, I still couldn't rationalise sitting anywhere but at the bottom. This wasn't a case of feeling sorry for myself, just a harsh acceptance of what I considered reality.

It was time to face up to a lot of things. I was shit. What I wanted to be, the way I was, I was shit. I looked shit, I felt shit and everywhere around me there was shit. All this posturing and introspection about suicide was tiresome. I needed to do something and stop moaning.

Poised to explode, I only needed something small to set it off. Steve obliged, chastising me when I arrived home the next afternoon for putting my feet on another seat as I studied. I lowered them down, but then he started complaining about the house not being clean enough.

He wanted me to do this and that, but then I knew if I left the table to satisfy him, he would only complain I wasn't doing my homework. If I allocated time for both, and cleaned and studied until bedtime, I would get into trouble for not spending enough time with the family. If I asked to stay up later, I would get yelled at.

There were no correct answers. Frustration was overpowering. My spirit had been totally exhausted. It felt as though any life or fight that I started with was now utterly depleted.

I bit into my pencil.

"What are you shaking your head at me for? I'll give you a reason to shake it." With that, Steve whacked me across the back of the crown. I hadn't even realised I was shaking my head. What I really wanted to do was rip his head off and shake it. I imagined severing it with a fishing knife, in a jagged motion and then starting to pull at his vocal chords and veins before standing back and kicking the loathsome skull from his malevolent corpse. That way I could locate whatever tormented soul resided inside him and allow it to escape from the hole in his neck.

I was sent to my room, so I exited by ramming my chair against the table, pulling my door shut and turning up my pathetically tiny stereo until it blasted through the house. Nirvana's *Territorial Pissings* was my weapon of assault, an inspired purchase following on from when Howard and I had bought *Nevermind* after its first review on JJJ. The opening riff was all I managed to get out, as Steve stormed in, grabbed the cassette and threw it against the wall, sending shards of plastic across the room.

"Do you wan' another fucking one?" He waved his fist high in the air, his eyes boggling white and red. I was on the edge of my bunk, so I pulled my thick doona across my torso and legs while he tried to swipe. Only one of his hits connected. I probably looked scared on the outside, but a part of me was laughing at the feeble fool. When Steve left the room, I crawled across to my tape. Some of the plastic around the heads had broken off, but it could still play I thought. I put it back in the cassette player, packed my bedding into the cupboard so it looked as though I was hiding there and then hit the play button, with the volume all the way up.

Quickly I jumped from my window, dropping two metres to the front lawn and then scampering over the fence and to the corner of the street. Inviting Steve to chase me, I slowed down. He knew from previous incidents that I could outrun him in a footrace, but clouded with anger, I thought surely he would try. It would be immensely satisfying to see him left short-breathed and flailing. A wicked grin stretched across my face and I sat, crossing my legs, waiting for his burly frame to come puffing down the street.

However, as clever as I thought I was, that notion disappeared the instant I heard the car engine start up. Steve screamed out of the driveway in the car and down towards where I was. I feigned towards a laneway I knew he could not access, but once he took the bait and hopped out to chase on foot, I ran up the sidewalk of lengthy Kidgell Street until I was over a small hill. Knowing I was unsighted, I then stepped sharply to my left and doubled back around houses to the original laneway. I ran in the opposite direction to which I had first intended, appearing as if I was going home. The next street over, I could hear Steve back in the car and driving up and down, looking to see if I was hiding. With him distracted, I took the chance to put some distance between us. Pleading for my stomach and legs to hold up, I sprinted as fast as I could in a straight line until I was almost at the main road. Finding more laneways to cut through, I changed direction again slightly. There was no way he could find me. Not even I had thought it possible for me to cover that much distance in a short amount of time. Struck for what to do next, I walked to the newsagents and started browsing through magazines. When that was done, I wasted time looking around various other shops and went to walk past friends' houses. It was dinner time and I felt too rude to knock on anybody's door, so eventually I grew bored enough that I decided to face the music. Sneaking around the back way to suss out the situation, I saw Steve and the car were still gone. Pretending as if nothing had happened, I walked straight in through the screen door and calmly headed towards my room. Mum stood infuriated before me and tried to herd me into the lounge room for a lecture.

"Don't say anything!" I yelled before she could get her words out.

"Steve is at Nanna and Grandad's. He thought you ran there like last time. Do you have any idea how bad this makes us look? Do you know how bad it makes ME look?"

I shrugged her hand from my arm angrily. Clearly it was time to do something. I never wanted to physically hurt my mother like I'd seen Marty and Steve do, but right then it was hard. Out of everything that was happening under our roof, what she cared about most was other people's impressions.

Battening down in the bedroom, I skipped my Nirvana cassette forward to *Something In The Way*. Then I grabbed scissors from my desk and went to work on the cables attached to my alarm clock. I sliced through them and peeled the insulation back so that the electricity could surge straight from the wire and into my skin. Laying down, I held the two main cables above my chest, either side of the sternum. Tingling and then numbness came over me as I nervously lowered the electrical current onto the tiny hairs jutting from my torso. For a fraction of a second I let it touch my skin, zapping my body and pulling the air from my lungs. Scared, I flicked the wires away. I could hear Bobby bathing in the next room.

My selfish sense of pride fought hard against overwhelming fear and stupidity. "Go on. You'll only regret being here. No one can punish you when you die. There's no continuation." Believing it was what I MUST do, I eased the cables back towards me. Looking down I could see scarring marks from where I had last touched.

"Hey, hey Lox!" Bobby was pushing against the door, making comical animal noises as he tried. I had blocked the way with my mattress, but he was jimmying his way in. Clearly, he was in a happy mood, laughing and enjoying the challenge. It momentarily distracted me, but I knew that outside of that moment, there would only be interminable unhappiness. I firmly believed that destiny prescribed I should die at my own hands. That was something I was convinced of with religious zeal.

I arched the cables up towards my head, taking what seemed like an eternity until they were right in front of my eyes. "Straight to the brain," I thought, remembering our science teacher's advice that the eye was the only external part of the central nervous system. I stared at them for a good few minutes, but waned in my enthusiasm. I couldn't do it, especially not with Bobby about to burst in.

Yanking the cords by the insulation, I pulled them clear from the wall socket and removed the danger. An avalanche of guilt crippled me. Why was I always weak? Just do it and stop fucking around. Then again, what if Bobby had found me? How would that affect his life? What would happen if he inadvertently electrocuted himself too? There were no answers, just a total feeling of failure with every direction my mind took. The most positive thing I could think was that at least I had tried. I could come back and do it again soon enough.

*** *** ***

I'VE spent a whole day mulling this horse effluent over in my head. Come on, it's just a bloody email. It's 15 years down the track and you're traipsing around a new and foreign city like a mopey bastard. Just get on with it you big sook.

Cork is the 'rebel' city of Ireland's south, only beaten in size by Dublin and incredibly proud of its local culture. Street performers, sidewalk artists, dizzying alleyways, hand-knits and a rich underbelly of artisans vie for attention with nearby

Blarney Castle, where kissing one particular stone is said to deliver the gift of eloquence. Tonight is also the finale of the Jazz Festival, and cafes are buzzing with brass notes and boisterous exchanges.

I walk the streets for a half-hour, cross a lit bridge astride the River Lee and decide, of all places, I'm going to spend my night at the bowling alley on the north bank. It's a relic from a bygone era. Wooden pins, thickly-striped brown and orange walls and knowing glances between long-time combatants. Already well over budget, I order an ungodly dinner of rock-hard potato gems and grizzly chicken wings, drowned in HP sauce. For a moment I am returned to the age of five, sitting in my grandparent's warm and dimly-lit lounge room.

Extending my delightfully new and revolutionary hobby of frivolously wasting time, I bask in the glow of an engorged stomach and alternate between reading a pamphlet for a concert that has already passed and watching the eager competition amid the lanes. By the time I hit the internet kiosk across the road, I've distracted myself enough to forget completely about my mother and her selective version of history.

And there in my inbox is a one sentence memo from Audrey.

"Keep saying dingo my friend...so, so sexy."

It elevates my spirits ever so slightly. I always attract the mentally askew girls.

SADLY, the relationship between Loxton and Kim was tenuous at best throughout their formative years. They were not close siblings in many respects. You could even say Loxton despised his sister in infancy and then grew to merely tolerate her in adolescence. About the only thing holding them together was their shared experience of living under their stepfather. Even Loxton's sense of kinship with Bobby was somewhat flimsy. After the initial enchantment of having a brother began to fade, a resentment formed on Loxton's behalf. He not only harboured misgivings for the amount of time he spent supervising Bobby, but also for the way that Steve considered our first shared offspring to be perfect in every way. Now and then Kim would express similar sentiments, but she did not possess Lox's infinite ability to maintain a grudge.

Kim was far more loyal and supportive towards me. So as much as she disliked Steve, she fell in line when I made it clear my future was with him. As a girl, she also had the gift of placating Steve's moods more successfully than the boys. This would in turn only infuriate Loxton even more, leaving him to remonstrate loudly about her 'softer' treatment. In any case, Kim had very few memories of her real father and saw Steve as her natural guardian.

Her behavior did admittedly cause me a level of concern when she reached puberty. Attempts at avoiding Steve's belligerent side bordered on flirtatious, though entirely innocently from her perspective. I had been around enough men in the past to know that it takes a certain level of maturity and esteem on the part of the male to recognise these exchanges for what they really are.

In Kim's instance, I was especially protective, because her first father had already crossed certain boundaries, before she could even speak. Steve knew of this and had given me every assurance he was not a similar type of man.

He'd chosen a time when I was in hospital for two days for surgery to betray that trust.

I'd considered leaving the children with my sister while I faced the scalpel, but felt it would be a positive experience for Steve and the two eldest to bond instead. My husband complained that the sole reason for him being portrayed as gruff and over-bearing was because he could not spend enough 'alone time' with the children outside of his work commitments. To him, it was necessary on weeknights to play the role of the enforcer and disciplinarian, because the children lacked a strong and guiding hand. Steve said he resented being typecast in this role, for it meant the children never confided in him and avoided contact as much as possible.

When I returned home from hospital, it was Loxton who was most fidgety and distant. This lasted for several days. As individualistic as he perceived himself to be, when it came to taking a course of action with potentially drastic consequences, he would usually seek me out for advice. That he couldn't do so on this occasion was perhaps what ate away at his stomach the most, denying his usually rampant hunger. Teenage boys are strange at the best of times, but Lox was behaving in an unavoidably tetchy manner. It sent all my motherly senses into overdrive.

"Loxton, what on Earth is up with you? You've barely looked me in the eyes or said a word since I came back from hospital?" I ventured.

"Have you ever wondered if you were trapped in a burning building, like 20 stories from the ground, what would you do?" he said. "Would you jump out the window or try and run through the flames down the fire escape? Because either way you are probably going to die."

Great, I thought, we're going to do the death thing again. I'd told Loxton a million times over that I would be there for him whenever he was feeling low, but his morbidity seemingly knew no bounds.

"Well, I'd probably jump," I offered, *"Then they could organise one of those big blankets and try and catch me. Mind you, they'd need some damn strong firefighters to break my fall."*

My attempt at humour failed and Loxton sharply slapped the side of the kitchen bench in frustration.

"No! I don't mean that. I mean what would you do in a situation where you had no idea what the right answer is or what you should do? You might pick one option and die even though everything you've ever been taught tells you that's the smart and correct thing. And what is right may be completely wrong the next day. Sometimes things in life are not like exams. How can anyone ever be certain they are doing the right thing?"

"Well that's not really the question you asked me before. You can't be angry at me for saying I'd jump."

"I'm not angry at you. I just need to know what you do when nobody has ever given you the answer to something before and it's not obvious. I like to be right Mum."

"Is this to do with a girl?"

"Kind of, but it's not what you think."

"What should I think then?" I asked, opening my arms to comfort Loxton.

He rebuffed my approach and reversed back towards the far side of the room, tension and anxiety teeming through his body, from his furrowed brow to his tightly clenched hands.

"Ok. I'm only going to say this because I think it's the right thing to do. I could be wrong, but at least I don't think I am. It's something Kim has told me. I don't want you getting angry at me."

All mothers know that a child's plea for you 'not to get angry' usually pre-empts the type of revelation that either boils the blood or crushes the heart.

I motioned with my hands for him to continue his story.

"Kim said not to tell you, but I think the other day Steve might have touched her...you know...down there," he blurted.

"In what way?"

"He asked her where Marty had touched her when she was small. Like, he asked her to show him the spot."

"Why would he do that?"

"I really don't know Mum. Kim was very upset when she told me. I don't think it's a lie. She said he slipped her knickers aside and said 'Is that the spot?'. Then he kinda' rubbed her."

"He did fucking what? Why have you two not said anything earlier?"

"Steve told Kim not to tell anybody; that nobody would understand and that he needed to know he could trust her if she was going to be his daughter. If you say anything Mum, he is going to know Kim told me and then I told you. We will all be in trouble."

"Nobody is going to be in trouble aside from Steve," I assured him firmly. A feeling of utter betrayal and disgust overwhelmed me. Were there no decent men at all on this planet?

I called Kim in from outside where she was playing on the swings and moved quickly with her to the bedroom. My girl threw an evil stare towards Loxton as we passed, but behind closed doors she only confirmed what her brother had felt urged to reveal.

Kim's eyelashes gripped onto crystalline tears and my own face was a parched red as we then returned to the kitchen.

"What Loxton did was right. If anything like this happens again you have to tell me straight away next time," I urged.

The kids looked at me for a sign that would indicate the consequences of their tale. But I could not give them one, for I'd had so little time to digest it all myself. I ran to the bathroom to be sick.

When Steve arrived home, I again took the conversation behind closed doors. I conveyed to him from the moment his boots touched the front steps that I was angrier with him than at any other point in our relationship. Our conversation ended with Steve walking out past the children, avoiding eye contact and collecting a handful of belongings before driving away. The kids stood agape and with a slight hint of pride. Both stopped peeling the vegetables for dinner as they ran to me and held me as I cried.

Initially there were no words at all, just sobs, until the question that lingered overhead proved too heavy to stay suspended.

"Is Daddy going for good?" Kim squeaked timidly.

"Yep," I said, regaining my composure and turning away from them to attend to dinner. I took the carrots, potatoes and squash they had prepared, filled the pots with water, lit the gas burners and went to sit by myself in the lounge.

Again, I had failed. No matter how much I had justified Steve's temper and intolerances, I could not push his predatory nature to the back of my mind. That was the one thing I simply couldn't overlook or excuse in the name of a settled and financially stable future.

And there was to be no sympathy or comfort in the eyes and arms of my children. Though they understood how deeply this had cut me – a second marriage disintegrated – we all knew that at least a small part of them had always willed it to be this way. They wanted a life free of Steve. They wanted me on my own, perhaps forever.

That, I certainly did not want.

LONDON // AMSTERDAM

"OYY who ya be tryin' to be scarin' boy?" comes the voice from the other side of the door.

After prolonged knocking, I hear the sound of a rusted metal hinge. The letterbox flap halfway down the door pokes open. An old Caribbean man is staring through the thin slot straight at my crotch.

"Tell me what ya sellin'."

"Sorry to bother you. I'm not selling anything. I just noticed this is 20 Kilburn Road and…"

"If ya not sellin' anything, then ya gots to be trouble. Nobody bothers me this time of day."

"I apologise sir. I wonder, then, if you know where to find 20a Kilburn Road?"

"I not be lettin' ya in okay? There be no 20a," he says, dragging the final letter through four bars of suspicious inflection.

That's strange, I think. I spoke to Jerome this morning and double-checked his address. He didn't sound too stoned at the time and my map-reading skills border on legendary.

But before I have the chance to verbalise my doubt, the old man has already muttered something gruffly under his voice and slammed the flap closed. I try yelling louder at my adversary, but he continues bolting a second door inside before disappearing.

This is my welcome to London.

I ring Jerome three times until he finally picks up.

"Ha, I'm at my place now, I'll just look out the window and see if you're downstairs," he says before resuming. "No mate you must be lost. Wait down the tube station for me and I'll grab you from there."

Before I know it, that big handshake of his is jolting my arm out of the socket.

"Foxy Loxie. Good to see you brother," he chirps. Jerome calls me Loxie primarily because he knows I hate it.

As we make it back to his abode, I tell him of my final hours in Ireland, running to the Blarney Stone in the morning so I could be the first person that day to press my lips to it, avoiding sharing saliva with a thousand other tourists. I tell him about the adjacent Rock Close, a garden which I found far more fascinating than the stone itself. There, thick tree roots morphed themselves over moss-covered rocks while dense fog cloaked itself around my ankles. Not far from an ancient sacrificial altar stood a singular crimson-leafed tree and 'wishing steps'. The atmosphere amid the thicket was akin to some fantastically macabre Tim Burton dreamscape.

I then talk of flying into London and a strange nervousness which I haven't experienced on the rest of the trip. Typically, I am deterred by any city much bigger than a million people. Sydney has three million and I don't care much for it at all. So how I handle a metropolis of 12 million remains to be seen.

London does have a certain aura to it though; like a jury that must be faced, or a signpost that must be passed at least once in your life. The city judges where you stand at that precise moment in the modern world. It tells you if you have made the grade or are still treading the path to becoming somebody. Londoninium – a melting pot for the ambitious, adventurous and mischievous.

While I blab away, Jerome reaches the top of the street and points to a perpendicular sign that reads 'Kilburn High Road', a thoroughfare we now begin to follow.

"Was this what you were looking for?" asks my friend, cigarette dangling from his lip.

"You said Kilburn Road. Not Kilburn High Road. It's your crap directions that were at fault."

"Shit, you mean there is another Kilburn Road? My bad. You learn something new every day. We all know the High Street as Kilburn Road."

Jerome shrugs nonchalantly, sucks the last remaining life out of his menthol cancer stick and tosses it underfoot as we pace out the few blocks to his apartment. We pass a Polish tailor, a Nigerian watermelon vendor and a quintessentially English pub called The Famous Cock.

Both Jerome and his partner Joanna work as journalists in the English capital. A trash addict at heart, Jerome earns a living by sub-editing the gossip columns of a national tabloid. Among his tasks have been dressing up as a Dalek and having his own breasts signed by Katie Price, aka uber-plastic model Jordan. Meanwhile Jo has found herself stuck in the hell of suburban reportage on the city's Eastern outskirts. When we walk into the apartment, she tells of her prize article that afternoon – about a local retiree who travelled to India to marry a dolphin.

For Joanne, at least, the day has necessitated a glass of vino, so after a quick debrief we make our way back to the tube station and into Leicester Square. A cavalcade of world-famous sights pass us by as we traipse our way to the Thames. The theatre district, with its footpath handprints of Sean Connery and Arnold Schwarzenegger, quickly turns into the neon billboards of Piccadilly Circus and the Eros statue.

We double back through Trafalgar Square, past the monolithic lions and Nelson's Column before ambling by the Queen's Guard and the Prime Minister house on Downing Street. At least a dozen cherry-red double-decker buses fly by before we reach the intersection facing Westminster Abbey, the Houses of Parliament and Big Ben. Crossing to the other side of the river, we stop for photos by the Salvador Dali museum and the London Eye, then grab warm chestnuts from a street vendor on our way to completing a full loop to Charing Cross. There we opt to warm down with a few reasonably priced bottles at underground Gordon's Wine Bar. With its low-hanging ceilings, candlelit rooms and laidback ambience it is justifiably popular, despite its obscured location.

Poolhall—Jail—Library

This weekend marks Jerome's 28th birthday and while we have two years' worth of catching up to do, there's also the promise of adventure in the morning. Despite an already stretched budget, I've only a few days ago agreed to alter my plans and join my friends in a whirlwind visit to Amsterdam to mark the special occasion. Our flight leaves at 6am.

We're not even there yet and Jerome has the same mischievous glow to his face which has pre-empted so many of our odysseys.

***   ***   ***

JEROME is reclined – nay slumped – with his head dangling over the far side of the bed. He is laying the wrong way, side-to-side rather than head-to-foot, and his eyes are fixed at the pattern on the wall behind him.

His right arm slowly rises upwards like a dazed cobra alighting from a charmer's basket and rotates several times before forming a fist. Sharply Jerome stabs out his index finger in the direction he assumes I am in.

"You...," he begins between muffled chuckles, "You Foxy Loxie. Yes you. You have to try this."

"Oh really?" I reply. I'm laughing so hard at Jerome that I cannot sit up straight.

"Yes man. This...this is fucking delicious." He breaks delicious down into syllables as if to emphasise his point. DEEE-LISH-EE-USS. It verges on orgasmic.

At this point in time I have nothing in my bloodstream aside from Heineken. It's fair to say Jerome has a few more foreign particles mingling amongst his red and white cells.

When we hopped off the plane this morning the first thing we did was catch a two-tiered train from Schiphol Airport to the centre of Amsterdam. The second thing we did, at Jerome's behest, was walk hurriedly from the station in the direction of the nearest koffieshop which sold weed. A fistful of Euros was then exchanged for two bags, a new lighter, a pipe and a whopping big plate of pancakes. Ever the enthusiast, Jerome condensed a phenomenal amount of ganja into his first cone piece and, within 10 minutes of arriving, had stupefied himself to the point of being mute. The pancakes went untouched for at least an hour.

Joanna and I sat twiddling our thumbs, slowly sipping beer at 10am while waiting for Jerome's sister Donelle to arrive and bring the party to its full complement. When she did so, it at least sparked the birthday boy to awake from his coma. His first reaction was to pack two more gargantuan cones, blitz one himself and then watch on proudly as his nearest of kin followed in his footsteps.

Left with two members of the walking dead, Jo then excused herself to go on a boat tour of the canals. Similarly, I made off in the direction of the Van Gogh museum, not ever having been tempted to smoke tobacco in my life, let alone pot. It's something about smoke in my lungs that I just can't abide.

When it came time to reconvene some three hours later, we found Jerome tripped out of his skull on magic mushrooms in our darkened hotel room. Donelle was nowhere to be seen, last sighted somewhere near the plaza staring aimlessly into a shop window. So, off Joanna toddled to try and find her, while I found myself stranded with an award-winning journalist intent on describing to me just how very 'deee-lish-ee-uss' his exotic fungi were.

"How much have you had man?" I ask the supine corpse from the opposite side of the room.

"Just half a packet. I shared it with Donelle. Unbelievable brother. Fan-fucking-tastic. I'm going to get myself a whole packet tomorrow."

Sometimes when you look at somebody under the influence of an illicit substance it looks like they are in a whole heap of pain, or that life and energy have been completely devoured from within. That's another reason I never do pot. If I want to do drugs, I want something that heightens my being, fills me with vigour, stamina and joy. Pot makes you sleepy, makes you antisocial, makes you retreat within your own shell and flip out at the slightest thing. At least that's what I've gathered from many years watching friends toke away.

But in this room, a hotel room we have rented privately off the internet, which looks like a cross between a brothel and an Alice in Wonderland backdrop, Jerome certainly doesn't look pained in any way. The only time he doesn't seem completely at peace is when he is laughing. The way he says 'deee-lish-ee-uss', it sounds as if it has been shot from the bow of an angel. His whole body ripples with vitality. I've never heard anyone describe a drug as delicious before. From what I'm observing it certainly does seem fan-fucking-tastic. Face it, I'm sold.

"Mate you reckon when you get that other packet tomorrow, that I could come with you?" I chance.

"Are you serious man? That would be fucking ace. Awesome. You will not regret this one bit."

For a brief second, Jerome returns to normality, sits up, stares at me and smiles like a father who has just seen his child through to graduation. Then he curls into a ball, crosses his arms over his stomach and begins to titter hysterically, rolling from one end of the bed to the other.

Eventually Jo returns with Donelle in tow. As the mushrooms slowly exit the siblings' metabolism, we head just a few streets to the west to the Anne Frank Museum by the sides of yet another canal. The museum fronts the house where little Anne and her family members hid in secrecy during the Second World War as Holland was overrun by Nazis. We read the plaques fitted around the house, sneak through the creaking rabbit warren of rooms which kept the former occupiers oblivious to the outside world and stop to read excerpts from Anne's famous diary.

The diary, discovered after her death, reveals a rapidly maturing, highly observant teenager who understood and analysed her surroundings more than one would ever suspect.

Her father's musings are pinned on the wall near the exit and they resonate loudest, for he was the only survivor. Upon returning from Auschwitz concentration camp he discovered his entire family gone, many family friends murdered and tortured. Suddenly his greatest link to the past became the diarised words a daughter had elected never to share with him while she was alive. Perhaps worse than being left with nobody, he was now left forever more with the tainted reminder that even those you care for the greatest rarely ever reveal their true self. Had he ever known anybody?

It makes me think again of Mum; what I am doing now, what she is doing now. What has happened between us in the past. I think of all the things I will never tell her. I wonder what she has never told me. And I wonder which parts of what she has told me are true.

The next morning I awake in our garish hotel room, its tiles checkered black and white, with two double beds positioned side-by-side and covered in love heart duvets. I've had to share my bed with Donelle, but despite her being of a suitable age and gender, nothing untoward has happened in the night, or even been considered for that matter. Aside from respect for my friend, I still have Audrey fresh in my mind. Besides, my thoughts are predominantly fixated on what will happen that afternoon. Ignoring Jerome's rollicking performance the previous day, I've only knowingly witnessed people feast on mushrooms once before. It was at a house party in my teens, where more than 30 kids waited around a friend's kitchen as if it were a homeless shelter. On the stove were two giant vats; the type of large silver cylinders you see in school cafeterias. Inside each of the vats were approximately 20 litres of chocolate milk and an impressive collection of wild mushrooms, picked from the dairy farm adjoining our school. It was stewed together for hours while the eager masses gathered.

When the cook – a scrawny, freckle-faced 16-year-old with a ponytail – finally licked at the ladle and gave his thumbs up, everyone jostled in with an empty milk bottle and filled it to the brim. Everyone that was, except for me. I had a rugby league game scheduled for the next day and the threat of letting my teammates down weighed just as heavily as the possibility of a random drug test.

What transpired in the next few hours was nothing short of total mayhem.

At first, I sat next to one friend on the couch, asking him for updates with annoying regularity.

"What's it like man? Is it a good feeling?"

He just kept smiling back and saying 'yeah' until he reached a point where he couldn't speak, threw his hands out like a robbery victim and walked off into the dark night air. We found him hours later, hunched over in a freezing cold telephone booth three suburbs away, with no idea what planet he resided on.

Another good friend, a prolific drug-taker called 'The Doctor' by our classmates, ended the night strewn out over the neighbours' front yard, convinced he had lost all movement from the neck down.

"I'm just a head. I'm just a head!" he cried until ambulance officers arrived.

The flashing sirens were a trigger for mass paranoia among the remaining party guests, some of whom had sat cross-legged in a circle, staring at a reflective disco ball for hours. The tenants of the house and the ponytailed cook totally freaked out, ordered everyone outside, bolted the doors and then ran off into nearby parkland. I didn't know whether to laugh, call for more help or take flight myself.

It transpired that I spent the remainder of the night either driving locked-out guests back home or cruising the streets picking up bewildered stragglers.

With that occasion still singed into my memory, I'm not approaching my first experience of mushroom consumption entirely blinded by Jerome's glowing recommendation. After all, he has told me previously of a night where he ate them alone in his lounge room, then felt ringed clouds of evil descending and smothering him until he walked shirtless to the top of a cliff and threw all the remaining shrooms into the wind.

Regardless, this is no time to play chicken. As we head up the stairs to street level, I'm cloaked by a veil of machismo, hiding any nervousness deep within. I WILL eat these mushrooms, even if it kills me.

In just two days we've made solid friends with the transsexual Thai window dancer who lives next door to our hotel. We have to walk right past the window to unlock the gate to the street, tip-toeing by a backdrop of purple strobe lights and a six-foot Asian in high heels thrusting a bulging crotch in rhythmic fashion.

"I reckon we should name him…err her, Anne Frank," I say to Jerome. "You know, as in she's called Anne now, used to be called Frank."

We both wave through the glass and bid the hard-working ladyboy good morning. If she's up dancing this close to breakfast, business must be in a downturn. In any case, I might as well be courteous now, because lord knows she'll probably be laughing through the window back at me come nightfall.

Poolhall—Jail—Library

THE prospect of a return to our days as a penniless triumvirate sat fine with the kids. Indeed, between them there was excitement at what lay ahead without Steve in our lives. Loxton could not help but tell his classmates that his much-despised stepfather had moved out, although he thankful spared the details in respect to what was inflicted upon Kim.

It was to be expected that he should erupt when, the following week, he returned from school to find me sitting hand-in-hand with Steve on the lounge, watching afternoon sitcoms.

Lox did not even acknowledge his stepfather, instead fixing a burning stare in my direction.

"This is absolute bullshit you know," he said, pausing momentarily before carrying his bag out to the hall and yelling over his shoulder. "I wish I had AIDS or cancer. That way I could get rid of this whole fucking situation. Never have to see any of you ever again."

"Loxton, your language!" I yelled scornfully.

"No listen Mum. This time, you shut up. This is all a big game to you. I don't know if it is some fucked-up plan or test of yours, but what on Earth are you doing? What is it going to take for you to leave him?"

"Hey!" Steve barked, "Are you going to say hello to me or not?"

Steve knew Loxton had ratted him out and Lox knew his stepdad had extended his control over my life to an almost unshakable extent. Before the night was out, I forced them to hug and declare an uneasy truce.

One of the concessions made to placate Loxton was allowing him to finally play sport for a club. At a minimum, he had nagged us every year since he began primary school. As neither Steve nor I were fans of sport in any way, we actively discouraged him for a long time. Many an argument was had about us prohibiting Loxton from watching sport on television or telling him to return books he had borrowed about inconsequential athletes. He took to hiding in his room under the sheets with a little red transistor radio whenever a big event like the Olympics or Wimbledon or State of Origin was played. Steve heard the crackle of the radio one night, stormed in and busted it to pieces. We both agreed that Loxton had to be diverted away from sport for his own good, lest his grades at school suffer.

But at almost 15 and with a temper that knew no bounds, we figured perhaps it was best to relent. Besides, we needed a substantial sweetener to convince him to keep quiet about what Steve had done. Over the course of Steve's absence, it emerged my husband had also committed something similar towards Kim a few years beforehand, and there had been an additional incident at the hands of a man who lived briefly across the road. The issue was much bigger than originally thought.

Lox had two friends – Milton and Matty – who both played rugby league for a nearby club at Mitchelton. Since he first stumbled on a game as an infant in Toowoomba, Lox was fascinated by the speed and aggression, two things he possessed in verifiable amounts. What he lacked for a long time to make him competitive in the playground however, was any notion of skill and size.

Just before the major incident between his stepfather and Kim, two things had been occurring which conspired to seal Loxton's course of fate. One was that he underwent a substantial growth spurt at 14, suddenly becoming one of the tallest boys in his class and filling out marginally more across the shoulders. The other thing to happen was that Doug, the school chaplain – a figure Lox had become particularly close to – began running an after-school club called 7.17 that dealt in activities designed to encourage group participation and foster self-discovery. It also ventured into the realms of religion, though by this point Loxton had already told me he didn't believe any God – of any faith – existed. He paid little attention to anything that sounded like bible-bashing.

Poolhall—Jail—Library

What he did find himself drawn to was a game played at the start of every 7.17 meeting. It was much like rugby league, but played inside with a tennis ball instead of a football and no defined try lines. Instead, the participants ran from one end of a long room to the other, grappling with each other on carpet until they were brought to a standstill and forced to pass the ball to somebody else. The chaplain had introduced the game under the rule that it only took a double-handed grab on the shirt to signify a gentle turnover of possession. But the game quickly grew out of control, with ripped shirts, full-blooded collisions and tussles that lasted a full minute at times. Unwittingly Doug had created a monster. In fact, not one, but a whole room of monsters. And one of the biggest monsters was my son.

Drawing on untold reserves of anger, Loxton found himself rejoicing at a newfound ability to intimidate and dominate other classmates. He would find himself unable to stop short of flinging them into the walls, body-slamming them on the ground or crushing their limbs as they struggled to break free. Conversely, when he was on the receiving end of such punishment, Lox would laugh and encourage the other combatants to hit him harder. Those 10-minute exchanges prior to each 7.17 assembly developed in him the knowledge he could finally turn the tables on those who tormented him. Now he had size, power and – most importantly – confidence to balance his existing rage and fleetness of foot. Any apprehensions he'd had about stepping onto a rugby field disappeared in the blink of an eye.

For the first time, Loxton had other kids asking for him to join their side, rather than pushing him in the opposite direction. When the New Year came around and the rugby league season drew close to beginning, he was being invited to parties every weekend, by children we'd never even heard of before. At least it was taking him out of our hair.

The Mitchelton team was known as the Panthers and wore red and black. They were not a big, flashy club like neighbouring

Arana Hills, but offered cheap playing fees and a family atmosphere, which we were thankful for. Players typically came from single-income households with ties to the army and physical trades. Among the past graduates of the club was Australian and Queensland representative Paul 'Fatty' Vautin, the same one who worked as a television commentator for many years.

"Is that what you want to look like?" Steve would often say to Loxton. "An old fat redhead with a face like a smashed crab? If you play rugby league you'll end up with a head like him or Artie Beetson."

Loxton was growing better and better at brushing aside Steve's comments as he became more assured of himself. He realised that laughing at his stepfather had a much better effect than biting and responding. Still, true to their ceaseless conflict, Steve never stopped trying to stir the pot and Loxton never forgot a single word.

It took almost two months of the season before Lox scored his first try for Mitchelton, but once that hurdle was overcome, he scored in close to every game. Indeed, twice he scored four tries in a single match. His elation was countered by the fact that Steve had taken on the job of team manager when nobody else applied. On nights when the club was unmanned, Steve also filled in as barman. Not for one second did Loxton perceive these actions as a step in an ongoing peace process. Much to my dismay, he elected to view them as Steve infringing on his turf; of him shadowing and taking credit for the one activity where Lox earnt admiration from his peers. Loxton said he hated the way Steve was praised for developing his talents and the fake manner a rosy father-son relationship was painted throughout the club.

"I wish they all knew he was such a cunt," Loxton blurted in one outburst.

"He will never be able to do anything right by you, will he?" I asked despairingly.

Even to me it was suspicious that whenever Loxton trained for an hour, Steve would manage the bar for three hours. Some nights, when Loxton wasn't playing or training, Steve would say he had been called to the bar to fill in at short notice. On the nights when this happened, the rest of us would order in pizza and watch the television shows we weren't allowed to watch on days Steve was home.

Still, the first few months that Loxton started playing football were easily the most settled time in our history as a family. It took the combative edge off of the boys and allowed them to focus their legendary tempers on complete strangers, rather than each other. All five of us would pile into the van on weekends to travel and watch games together. Only recently a teenager, Kim took a shine to several of Robert's teammates and needed little coercing to attend. Similarly, Bobby made friends with some of the other toddlers we saw each week.

All this lasted until about halfway through the season, when I was excited to discover I'd received the gift of motherhood for the fourth time. Unlike my experiences with Loxton, Kim or Bobby, the onset of tiredness, irritability and heightened hunger was almost instantaneous. I began to wait at home instead of going to football, often requesting Kim stay by for company and to assist with chores. My daughter and I enjoyed the time and space together in any case. Perhaps we enjoyed it a little too much.

From the occasional pizza night, we grew to snacking on a handful of 'treat' meals each week when Steve was absent. Sometimes it was a couple of iced buns. Sometimes it was a burger and large chips. Other times it was a whole cheesecake between the two of us. I noticed Kim putting on weight, but rationalised my own heaviness by way of the pregnancy. When a later scan revealed I was carrying twins, it only served to justify my burgeoning belly. By the end of the year I had grown from a steady 105kg to just under 140kg, still shy of the 155kg at which I would eventually give birth.

By the end of the year, things were also going pear-shaped between Loxton and Steve again.

Given $10 a week in pocket money, Loxton was made to pay $20 a fortnight to his stepdad for being driven to football. In any stand-off or when Steve wanted something doing, he would always revert to withdrawing Loxton's rugby league privileges as his main threat. At first this sent Loxton into a blind, uncontrollable rage. But after a handful of similar admonishments, he nonchalantly dared his stepfather to do so. I could see in my son's eyes that he was increasingly willing to take his skills at physical confrontation from the rugby league field and into the home.

At one stage, after several weeks of sustained performances, Loxton was invited to attend try-outs for the Brisbane Under 15 representative team. My son attached a certain amount of prestige to the squad. Only four boys from Mitchelton were asked along.

From where Loxton's sense of self-image had been positioned six months beforehand, it was a dramatic turnaround. He shunned parties, social occasions and new clothes so he could train and save money for his football fees. On lunch breaks he started lifting weights in the school gym rather than playing outside with friends. Rugby league had initially provided Loxton an avenue to avoid segregation at school, but now he was actively courting it as he poured everything into a new-found ambition.

I didn't have the heart to tell him that we wouldn't be allowing him to go to the trials.

"He won't make that squad. Besides, does he expect me to drive all the way over the southside in peak traffic?" Steve reasoned.

AMSTERDAM

CATATONIC and severely under-dressed, the Japanese girl sits on a bench by the canal. She assesses oblivion with unblinking eyes. This is exactly what people mean when they refer to those 'lost' in Amsterdam. Young, bright things with designs of expanding their minds, stopping en route to even grander destinations, yet never managing to shake the revelations which the city brings. They come as wandering souls, check in for a weekend, stay for a lifetime.

Jerome and I shuffle the icy pavement, waving to the girl who does not flinch at all, let alone acknowledge our presence. While she delves deeper into hypnosis, we keep on the lookout for a suitable venue to consume our freshly-purchased punnets of mushrooms. Given a choice of four different varieties at the Smart Shop on Spuistraat, I opted for the Amazonians. The menu at the counter rated each species on a number of criteria: energy, hallucinations, brainwaves and laughter. The Amazonians tipped the top end of the scale for each. Perfect.

Iggy Pop is glaring down at us from the wall when we ease into a dimly lit café not far from the laundromat. His emaciated frame, in all of its vein-carved glory, has been painted onto the walls in 500 per cent scale. From the darkened booths, the floor gives way to a well-worn pool table, adorned with fluorescent balls. I observe two fidgety, self-conscious figures pot the last remaining orbs as Jerome orders half steins of Schneider Weisse. In this bar, it seems the only way to look at others is through the corners of strained eyes.

"These go down best with a really airy beer. Quite nice," Jerome says, patting the mushrooms through the thickly fleeced lining of his jacket. He sends me a wink that would do Sid James proud.

Spreading his hallucinogenic fungus across the counter like a packet of crisps, he begins to peck away, encouraging me to do the same. Casual as anything. Ambivalent to any judgment. As if we were playing cards to pass the time on a laborious journey.

It's not immediately 'deee-lish-ee-uss', at least not to the taste buds. It's a little dry, not quite sickly, each mouthful filled with the promise of magnified sensations in a matter of moments.

"Just you wait Foxy Loxie," my perverted mentor chirps.

The alcohol, when washing down the shrooms, delivers a cleansing sensation. Indeed, the beer somehow feels like the healthiest part of the equation.

I try to distract myself by sizing up Iggy Pop's spindly limbs, stretched across the café, strangling the four walls closer together. Think of anything but what lies ahead. Act calm – and more importantly – look calm.

Then the first dip of the rollercoaster arrives. My stomach drops and rises in the blink of an eye and my line of thought is smudged under a heavy thumb. What have I done?

Panic nudges its way in, but tapping my fingers lightly is as much as I will allow myself to display this on the outside. I've pushed off on this journey and suddenly realised the current is too strong to negotiate. Not even vomiting at this point will avail me of the toxins which have begun to seep from synapse to synapse. Like the first time I dumped a pill, I have no idea what happens next. And how much of the uneasiness is actually attributable to the mushrooms and how much to my own nervous expectations?

The pool table becomes vacant and we uneasily tread the bowed floorboards to set ourselves a frame. Hit by the shards of luminescence from above, the balls take on transmorphic properties. Little pink, yellow and orange globules, shifting like the contents of a lava lamp, somehow sticking to the green felt as if drawn together through an innate dependence. I can feel myself slipping into deep existential contemplation about the presence of gravity when my train of thought is brought to a screeching halt through a loud CRACK!

Jerome has taken his first shot of the frame and sent two balls sailing into the café. One hits the front window at pace. The second drops lower to hit a skirting board and bounces back at our feet as if mocking us. Bending over to pick the ball up without toppling off balance is a mission in itself. Co-ordination flickers in and out at unpredictable intervals.

The pretense of playing a game of pool is hard to substantiate. In 45 minutes we barely clear five balls from the table. Essentially, we are enjoying swinging a stick and watching the pretty colours ricochet from side to side.

Giving up the ghost, we walk back past the frozen-in-time Japanese girl and head through Dam Square to a pastry shop.

Transfixed by the assortment of goodies, I stand close enough to the glassed display window that I can touch it with my hand still in my pockets. Apparently, I am there for well over five minutes, ignoring the repeated approaches of bakery staff as I gawk blankly. In this same interval, Jerome has been drawn down an alleyway by a dread-headed Yardie with a tale of despair. By the time I am awoken from my stupor and shooed away from the bakery, my friend is walking away with the Yardie's arm wrapped firmly around his shoulders.

"I'm tellin' you mon, I left my car fa two minutes and somebody gone and smash my window right in. Can ya please just stand here and look after it until I get tha police?" the stranger pleads.

Now, I've read *Mr Nasty* before. I've heard how shit goes down in Amsterdam. As Jerome gets led towards a secluded dead end, the alarm bells are going mental. It's one of those 'act now or forever live with regret' moments, so I swallow heavily and run up behind the pair, reefing Jerome free in one fell swoop.

"Hey...what the fuck mon?" the Yardie spurts.

"C'mon Jerome. Bloody hell. What are you thinking?" I chastise.

"So, you two are not gonna' help me? Not help a man when he needs it?" the shyster lays it on.

I do my best to ignore the imposing figure beside us and continue berating Jerome. He's grinning back at me in a haze.

"Yeh Foxy Loxie, what if he does need our help?"

"Shut the fuck up and get going. You'll get yourself killed or robbed or molested."

It's a feature of being under the influence that I am decidedly more headstrong and blunt. Normally I'm the guy that's happy to go with the flow; not cause any ripples. But at this precise moment, something is twigging in my head. We should not be here.

I angrily dismiss the Yardie's pleas as he follows us back up to the main street, where we turn left past the hydroponics shop and the Pink Elephant sex theatre. Five minutes on and we find ourselves by the Oude Kerk, a centuries-old church that stands at the heart of the red-light district. We veer along the row of lit windows, where girls of every creed contort their bodies and beckon to come hither. The odd one or two are attractive, but in the main, you would not wish to touch any of them with a ten-foot pole.

To me, finding love in the arms a complete stranger for the purposes of a monetary exchange is demeaning, not solely to the girl, but entirely to your own sense of self-worth and to the concept of affection. I theorise that once you pay money for it, you could never again imagine love with the innocence and wonder of a true romantic. Essentially what you are giving away is far more valuable than what you are receiving, whether it comes at $10 or $2000 a pop.

Saying that, it's hard to pretend you are standing on a pulpit of righteousness and intellect when you are being carried along by the fuel of toxic mushrooms. You put these in your mouth Mr High-and-Mighty, knowing it would poison your brain. Don't get too caught up in your own supposed moral superiority.

Every 10 metres is a new drug dealer, whispering under his breath "You want coke, hashish, speed, ecstasy?" We don't stop or even look up until we find ourselves back at the Freedom Café, the very same place Jerome came to straight from the train station on Day One. It seems much jauntier now that I have imbibed.

Indeed, the paintings of aliens on the walls are jumping out at me. They are not in 3D or haunting in any way. Rather they are like an old 60s cartoon, jumping back and forth across a singular plane with simple movements, bopping about as they enjoy a jolly good time. I cannot feel any weight in my feet, and my fingers and toes are numb to touch. Before I become conscious of it, I am doubling over with uncontrollable laughter, needing to push away from the table to give me room. I look briefly back up at Jerome. He smirks and it sets me off again, roaring from deep within my stomach. I'm trying to gauge how irrational I am being, so I glance at the barista, who must have seen my type a thousand times before. Even his deadpan face gives me the giggles. So, I concentrate on the walls once more, its colours and details now sharp and shining with even more lustre than before. I'm biting my lip as hard as I can to keep from laughing like a madman, trying to internalise the amusement.

Jerome stands up and excuses himself for a minute, assuring me he is just going to the other koffieshop across the lane, bearing the glorious title 'Double Reggae'. Of course, this makes me laugh, but I convince myself a business name as preposterous as Double Reggae would tickle the funny bone even if I wasn't as high as a kite.

Within five minutes my friend has returned, holding a hard, plastic novelty monkey that stands just over a foot tall. Jerome turns the cog at the monkey's feet and when he releases it, the monkey furiously masturbates itself.

"I saw this yesterday," he says between heaving guffaws. "I've always wanted a wanking monkey."

There is no way I am going to regain any form of composure this afternoon. Not at this rate. Not with a polymer primate before my eyes that has no qualms about administering self-pleasure in public.

The laughter of lunacy continues for a good two hours more, even when Jo and Donelle return to sit with us. Jo's presence instills in me a paranoia about how ridiculous I am being and gradually my thinking shifts to be more contemplative. I want to go and sit in nature, among bushes and trees and, with a stiff wind to my back, think about all that ever was and all that could ever be. I want to use this time on mushrooms, this opportunity, to delve further into my thoughts on disassociation of the brain and body. The concept that the world we see is only a game of our imagination is something that intrigues me greatly. Who are my friends then and what recess of my mind have I imagined them from? What about the sports and physical pursuits I enjoy? Are they just concepts my brain has developed, where the exertion is purely perceived?

Several times I try and persuade the others that I would like to be alone, but they will not let me go wandering. We start walking as a group instead, grabbing a steak dinner at Uncle Coco's – which trumpets 'warm beer and lousy food' as its slogan – and visiting several koffieshops we have somehow missed thus far. Among them is the infamous Bulldog, a dark and overtly commercial franchise filled mostly with men, wearing thick parkers and exchanging unspoken judgments. It has none of the bonhomie of our earlier destinations.

While in Bulldog my vision begins reversing. Somehow, I can see what is behind me, but not what is in front of me. When I move left, my vision has me turning right. It takes me a few moments to realise why I am tripping over my feet. To make sure, I scurry outside and look at the neon writing, which now has flipped 180 degrees. The others follow closely behind and I again state my case that I should return to the hotel room to ride out the biggest peaks alone, lest I ruin everybody's night. They say it is of no concern, but after prolonged pleas I convince them I will be fine and ready to rejoin them later.

Once the door to the apartment locks I am sent on a mind-dissolving journey. Laying fully dressed, under the sheets of the bed nearest the window, I am attached to the outside world only by the honking of evening traffic. Every other observation plunges deeply inwards at the basis of everything I consider life. The number 12 – my favourite number – keeps repeating over and over. Twelve months to the year, 12 hands on the clock, 12 disciples in the bible. Are not these the very markers by which we measure what we consider existence? A higher power must have implanted the number in my subconscious for me to one day unravel this secret. And now I come to think of it, why do my friends all have names similar to the disciples. There's Thomas, Matthew and erm, Jay and Rocky. Oh, and Eddie. They were all disciples, right? Holy fuck I've just stumbled on something monumental!

When I glance back at the digital clock beside the bed, only two minutes have passed. Real time is moving glacially in comparison to the speed at which I am making new discoveries.

I can't keep from thinking about nature and I imagine my neural impulses as the root of a giant tree, joining at the trunk of what we describe as everyday reality. But if the mind does imagine the world around us, then do the branches at the top of the tree represent parallel dimensions, where we can exist simultaneously in time? I totally believe in this. Fuck yeah, I'm onto something. These mushrooms have acted as a kind of open-sided elevator inside the tree, rising from the trunk of arbitrary life to the uppermost levels, where I can step out in any direction at the floor of my choosing to another, completely different existence. The mushrooms are merely a vehicle, man. Yes, that's it! Just like the aeroplane that supposedly 'flew' me from one side of the planet to the other and began this whole expedition. How does anyone really believe that happens? The plane was merely a plot device, as are the people you have met along the way. They transport you from one dimension to another.

Glancing back at the clock, only another minute has passed.

Aside from the number 12 and trees, the other thing that's dominating my thinking now is doors. Every person, every conversation, every location, every obstacle, every opportunity; they're all just effectively doors. You either walk by, or you stop, turn the knob and step into a different existence. Does any part of you stay behind once you enter that door? Will it be possible to one day, perhaps at the moment of death, see yourself cloned across a vast number of possible outcomes and identify the points of divergence which made a difference?

Right now, I'm looking at the toilet door. It's tiny. Something is beckoning me to it. I must find out what is past the checkered tiles and slapdash Wonderland paint job. The toilet is built into a crevice; what looks like a former cupboard between the stairs and the equally miniature shower. It's clearly a recent addition to appease the subdivision of a three-story house into separate hotel rooms. The door is not even rectangular. It's shortened and angled on one side to fit the irregular space.

As I squeeze inside, the hood of my jacket catches on the door. I have to use my weight to free it, because not enough room exists to turn around. How on earth do people get their pants down in this cramped space? I hear the door latch behind me as I struggle to sit. Then, I look back up and it's a sliding bolt. Did I slide the bolt shut, imagine the latching sound and then forget about it altogether? This wasn't a good idea. Maybe it's a trap. Why hadn't I considered that mushrooms could also be a vehicle for my downfall, and not just for enlightenment?

I feverishly try to slide the bolt open, but my spindly, weakened fingers will not grip properly. They slip off the bolt like elongated raindrops. I'm stuck. Slapping at the inside of the door and the thin walls, I feel no strength. Do I yell and scream for help and risk looking like a lunatic? Perhaps I am a lunatic and have always been, dreaming up a world outside where I had a job, had friends, enjoyed things. Is this what being truly crazy is? My vision is filled with an image of a haggard, aged Loxton, laying in rags on the side of the road, cursing and convulsing in an imagined cage while passing pedestrians shake their heads. Soon I have convinced myself this is the reality of it.

You never had any friends. They won't be coming back. The mushrooms are merely opening your eyes to the destitute vagabond you have always been. The next person to break into your psychosis will be a mental health worker telling you it's better you go with them. Best not shriek and attract attention then.

Without that digital clock beside me, I have no idea how long it's been since my imaginary friends left me here.

LOXTON was crushed. Steve's refusal to take him to representative trials was another moment to lodge in his file of discretions eternally unforgiven. Kids asked Lox whether he was too scared to show up or whether he was just not up to standard. Even after Loxton was made captain of the high school's Grade 10 team, he still harked back to the missed opportunity as a blight against his name.

Shortly after there were two incidents (at least of which I am aware) when Loxton let slip his disciplined approach to sport and fitness. Both happened around camping trips.

The first concerned a geography and history excursion into the Queensland outback. In the days leading up to the class departure, Kim alerted me that Loxton would be attempting to steal a substantial amount of Steve's beer. I kept a close watch over my son's activities, but nothing seemed out of the ordinary. On the morning he was due to leave, I even searched and patted down his luggage, finding nothing. It was only as I watched him out the driveway that I saw him stop next to a bush, burrow through the foliage and collect four tall bottles, before running off into the distance. He could get expelled if the teachers caught him. And he would have his arse tanned if Steve found out. I decided to cover his tracks and say nothing of the whole incident.

His second alcoholic escapade was an end-of-season football trip to Moreton Island. However, on this occasion the drinking was actually being encouraged by those adults leading the jaunt. I knew well in advance what Lox would be up to and, with the fathers of the players also invited, I saw it as a 'male experience' for Steve and Loxton to share. They split the cost of three cartons of XXXX and were gone early on a Friday. On Sunday afternoon they returned red-eyed, sunburnt and disheveled, almost immediately turning in for bed.

It eventuated that they had drank non-stop, with Loxton vomiting two days in succession, taking part in a jousting competition where he wore a metal biscuit tin on his head and almost being run over by a four-wheel-drive as he slept on the beach. Meanwhile the bigger revelation was that Steve had made a fool of himself in front of the other parents on the Sunday. Hit with a tomato in a jovial food fight, he became enraged, quit on the spot as team manager and openly cried before chasing one of the fathers with a link of sausages, using them like nun chucks. The other kids baited him in his drunken stupor by holding up barbecued meat, sucking on it and repeating "Stevie, I've got your sausage" with a lisp in their voices.

Citing embarrassment at his own actions and the behavior of his stepfather, Lox vowed not to touch alcohol again. It was to be a promise he would keep for two years, right up until he completed high school.

"I don't want to turn out anything like him," he would say in reference to Steve. "When people drink they say things and do things they don't mean. What's the point of being somebody you aren't and hurting people along the way?"

As well as his dedication to football and schoolwork, Loxton also entertained himself with what I would consider immature pursuits for a teenager. He was obsessed with basketball cards, jigsaw puzzles and word games. Together they provided a distraction while his classmates occupied themselves with girlfriends and parties.

More in keeping with other teenagers however, was his devotion to rock music. Forever loyal to Triple J radio, he saved his pocket money once the rugby league season was over and bought a Sony CD player with Bass XPander. His Uncle Howard had the same model and the main reason they were both fixated by it was due to a singular opening riff – the 'dum, dum, dum' opening strains of Nirvana's Come as You Are. Indeed, ever since he had heard Nevermind in Grade 9, Loxton recorded and kept any interviews or magazine stories he could find which referred to the band. He drew portraits of Nirvana's *band members on the covers of his books and learnt the lyrics to their songs by heart.*

Several tough decisions had to be made by Loxton over the holiday break before he began Grade 11. One concerned a future career. It was senior school and still he maintained a stubborn belief that he wouldn't live long enough for it to concern him. However, he had already completed a compulsory week of teacher-organised work experience with a map publishing company and his exam results were high enough to work towards a career in cartography. Passing from junior to senior meant each student had to specify six subjects to study over the next two years. Lox chose geography, modern history, accounting and physics for electives and then enrolled in the most difficult mathematics and English courses offered. If he wanted to do cartography, teachers highly recommended completing graphic design instead of physics. But ego got the better of him and he refused, partly because physics was regarded as the toughest subject and partly because the graphic design teacher had once lifted him by his throat and struck him with a wooden ruler for perceived mischief.

Another difficult decision to make was whether my son would confess his feelings for a new love, Macy. After his previous failings in romance, Loxton tried hard to keep his latest interest under his hat. But over time he let slip a few morsels when we were talking one-on-one. The girl had come across mid-year from another school. She was a bit of a hippy, loved grunge bands and had long, matted blonde hair. She was supposedly the reason behind him smuggling beer on the geography trip. Unlike his past fixations, he'd actually worked at building a solid friendship with this one and was mortified at the thought of ruining it.

One potential sniper that stood on the sideline was Kim's friend Jen. Jen was next door neighbor to Macy and caught a lift with her to school each day. She was also of the gossipy type. Certainly, I never really trusted her and I gathered my daughter didn't either, as she told tales that often made her accomplice seem spoilt and self-obsessed. I believe Kim was drawn to her through a weird idolisation that bordered on jealousy. Jen was tall and slender, had a face like a young starlet and was always dating the kind of boys that Kim fancied herself. Loxton knew that anything he said about Macy in his sister's presence would travel at embarrassing speed via Jen and up the chain of adolescent rumour-mongering, straight to his interest's ears. It made him even more stand-offish and blunt with Kim than normal.

***   ***   ***

THERE were more important matters due for family consideration at this time however. I discovered my father, who I had grown much closer to in adulthood, had started developing cancerous cells in his leg. It shocked me that our time may be coming to an end at such a relatively young age. The severity at which I initially took the news rendered me bed-bound for most of the day. It also struck the children, who ferociously adored their grandfather. When Steve arrived home, he flew into a rage about the messy state of the house and the fact nobody was speaking to him. He never stopped to ask what was the matter. Instead he disappeared downstairs to his makeshift cellar, reemerging with the familiar clank of a handful of long-neck beer bottles as he scaled the wooden steps to the lounge room. I lay still, sobbing at more than one circumstance.

It was a full hour later before I decided it was best to get up. I found Loxton and Kim cutting vegetables in the kitchen as I passed by to explain the situation to Steve. Barely a word left my lips before I started to cry again, a display of unbearable weakness which riled my husband. He had consumed two litres of beer already and it erupted from his throat in a foul-mouthed tirade. Without any concept of why we were so grim, he insulted us all mercilessly before rising to physically stand over the top of me.

Kim was surprisingly the first to stand up, putting her short frame in between us and telling Steve to back off. Steve reeled his arm back and went to take a swing at Kim. Before he could do so, Loxton barreled through, forcing Kim to the ground and removing her from harm's way just as she was about to be struck. In the same motion he clipped Steve with his shoulder and knocked him off balance. His stepfather's wild punch landed against the wall, opening a hole in the plasterboard centimetres from where Kim's head had been

Enraged by the interference, Steve shot an open-palmed jolt to Loxton's chin, grabbed him, twisted him around and locked his elbow around his throat. Initially Loxton panicked, but then offered a curious submission. He relaxed and went limp in Steve's arms. As if offended by the lack of fight, Steve smacked my son across the head two or three times.

Loxton began laughing maniacally, like the way he had enjoyed being whipped with a kettle cord by his uncle in his youth; like the way he found it hilarious that his face should bleed when diving face first into bitumen.

"Go on. Hahahah. Fucking kill me," Loxton yelled. "I sooo want this."

Steve dragged Loxton's dead weight from the carpet of the lounge room through to the linoleum of the kitchen, where it was easier to throw him about. He forced him up against the steel buffer at the front of the stove. Three of the burners were lit and dinner was boiling.

"No, you hit me. Go on," Steve beckoned, opening his arms wide, while keeping Loxton pinned with the weight of his chest.

Loxton wasn't falling for it. We all knew what would follow if he decided to fight. Instead he looked deep into Steve's eyes.

"Why? Why the fuck do you have to do this? Why can't we be a normal family? It's not our fault your work sucked or somebody spoke to you the wrong way and you came home and got drunk again. This is stupid. I hate living here. Go on, just kill me. If you touch anyone else though, I swear I will call the police this time."

Stepping back slightly, Steve poked Lox sharply in the sternum, repeating the action every few seconds to hold him in place.

"Call the cops? Oh, will you now? Go on then mister. If you're so tough get past me and grab the phone. Show me how strong you are."

Moving to the side a little, Loxton tried to edge past, but with little momentum or confidence he was unsuccessful. Steve grabbed his arm and pulled it behind Loxton's back with brute force. He was pushing Lox closer and closer to the burners when it became my turn to snap.

I shot across and grabbed Steve by the shoulders. He moved around and shrugged me off violently, at which point Loxton escaped and ran to the far side of table. Steve berated me for sticking up for my son, but I fired back crossly.

"You can't do that Steve. Not anymore. That's enough. Stop the fighting. When will it end?"

My mind was racing, jumping from thought to thought, simply seeking a way to end the conflict, but with no clear method to achieve it.

"Steve, my Dad has got cancer."

Wiping the froth from his moustache – two parts beer and two parts vitriol – Steve dropped his arms by his side and leant towards me snarling: "Well if somebody had let me know..."

That was his way of opening up for discussion. He twisted his head to Loxton and pointed as if to signal there would be a second installment of brutality, then he went and sat down in the lounge room. We closed the door behind us as I attempted to strive for peace. I couldn't believe my Dad's health had become secondary to yet another tempestuous drama.

Finally, after more than an hour of to-ing and fro-ing, Steve decided he would offer us all an apology. He invited Kim and Loxton back into the room. The children noticed he *had been crying drunken tears and were visibly startled by his appearance. They entered ready to hear him out.*

Yet, just five minutes into the reconciliation he started back up, detailing how he would "fucking kill us all" and telling us that if he left, we would have no money. Loxton got up and walked away.

"This is the ultimate disrespect you know? All we care about is Grandad and you are making this all about yourself."

More violence and shouting ensued, with nothing resolved or gained.

NOTTINGHAM // LINCOLN // HULL

CALLUM freaks me the hell out. He sits at the end of the spare room where my thin camp bed is located, polishing rifles salvaged from World War Two.

It's only a few days since I returned from Amsterdam and descended from the great mushroom cloud. In that space of time, I've managed to be subjected to watching both *Saw* and *Resident Evil* at Jerome's house, caught Agatha Christie's *And Then There Were None* at the Gielgud Theatre and now find myself in the proclaimed 'gun crime capital of England', Nottingham.

My body is enjoying this holiday, but my anxiety levels have been subjected to a rigorous workout.

In fact, just before lobbing in Nottingham, I went and visited the city where my Uncle Howard was born – Luton. I thought it would make for a nice homage and piece together a few more sections of the jumbled puzzle that is my family. It was similar to why, the day beforehand, I'd walked from Wembley to Sudbury see the house my Grandad grew up in. Let's just say Sudbury was a fulfilling experience and Luton... well it was something entirely different. Anywhere that has a marketplace selling 'I Hate This City' badges is clearly not too worried about its outward image.

But that is all by-the-by and now I'm half-awake in the rear room of a Nottingham apartment, while a chubby teenager in an SS helmet cleans antique weapons in the doorway. I was always a little skeptical of making this visit to the Rodd family, but Mum insisted. She's been pen-friends with Bernice Rodd since they were 10.

Bernice emailed me in advance of my arrival and said to be on the lookout at the train station for 'A short fat woman with brown hair and a sequined bag, a tall man with greying hair and a teenage boy with a beard in a death metal shirt'. Her descriptive skills could not have been more precise.

I expected it to be a long first night in town, as Callum was celebrating his 18th birthday and it fortuitously happened to be a Saturday. However, it became evident early that Callum was not spoilt for social options. Instead he chose to spend his coming of age with me in the Rodd's tiny front lounge, eating pork pies and drinking beer in silence, aside from the occasional guffaw at *Little Britain*.

In the miniscule shards of breaking dawn, Callum has now decided it is the optimum time to sort through his armory in the room where my makeshift bed is assembled.

"We've got a show next week in Suffolk," he explains, churning toast in his mouth like a cement mixer. "I'm lieutenant for the Midlands military re-enactment group. Oh, and I'm also the photographer."

It's important that Callum primes his weapons now, as we have a packed itinerary today and then he'll be busy working before the next weekend rolls around. Either that, or he is simply looking for an excuse to show off his impressive arsenal.

"Did you want to see my grenades?" he asks just as his father, Allen, comes in to fetch us.

"We should be off soon. It's a bit of driving to get to see what we want," says his Dad.

With that, we are in the family station wagon, leaving a lovingly restored green army jeep to sit by itself in the driveway. Allen it seems, is just as much the military enthusiast, though his passion is with the vehicles, not so much the guns. The first place he drives us to is a friend's farm where his Alvis Stalwart is parked. A six-wheeled amphibious truck first used by the British in the 1960s, the Stalwart sits amid a graveyard of tank recovery vehicles and armored personnel carriers. I'm told the family pride boasts an impressively monstrous 6.1 litre V8 Rolls Royce engine, but it is not until we are up the road in the village of Blidworth that I am truly impressed. This is the graveyard where Will Scarlet was buried, Bernice informs me.

Pure nonsense and fantasy. Now we're talking!

It's on from there to Sherwood Forest, to the Major Oak, the broad, hollow tree where Robin Hood and his merry men were purported to have taken refuge. A trio of American tourists in front of us complain loudly that they are not allowed to "take a piece of the tree home". I feel an overwhelming urge to drag my knuckles across their foreheads.

At the gift shop I buy a misprinted coffee mug that has Maid Marian adorned with a moustache, then we walk onwards to Edwinstowe and past the church where Marian supposedly wed Robin. Bernice kindly pays for me to try my hand at long bow archery in a small clearing, where a stocky, bald man points towards a mobile target. Contrary to my complete lack of accuracy with a cricket ball, I drill three arrows into the side of a plastic brown bear, being pulled along on all fours by a rope. How such a creature came to be in Sherwood Forest, I do not question. I simply walk away chuffed that my weeks on the road (and on the drink) have not entirely absolved me of all dexterity.

Callum, the weapons expert, follows us back to the family car in somewhat of a huff.

We depart for a looping trip in the car that takes us past castles in Newark and Belvoir (cryptically pronounced *Beaver*) and then back to Nottingham's newly unveiled watersports centre.

"We're not much for sports ourselves, but we thought you'd enjoy it," says Bernice as we stand collectively by the banks, ensconced in multiple layers of clothing, staring otherwise silently and blankly at Arctic water flowing over the man-made rapids.

That evening we set off for an ale at Ye Olde Trip to Jerusalem, built into the sandstone footings of Nottingham Castle. The Trip is among a contentious dozen establishments claiming to be the oldest pub in all Britain. With hand-dug caves at the back constituting at least three rooms, it does appear to have genuine credentials. A date of 1189 has been placed on the opening of the inn, and it sits right near a location known as Mortimer's Hole, making it central to several historic events. The aforementioned hole presents an opening in the sandstone that leads to a series of interconnected tunnels and leads up to the heart of the castle. When Richard I, the Lionheart, returned from the crusades, it is alleged his treasonous brother Prince John used Mortimer's Hole to flee. But Allen, showing his breadth of knowledge, hastens to warn me about the romanticism associated with King Richard.

"He only spoke French and was away overseas for most of his rule. Do you really think he was as popular as legend has it?" he muses.

I've grown fond of Allen and find him much warmer than his son, who by this time has excused himself and gone home. Callum it seems, can only handle so much fun in a specified timeframe.

In two days, I have also developed an affinity for Bernice, who reminds me of my mother in so many ways. I can see why they have been friends for close to four decades. She is knowledgeable but self-conscious, socially awkward but full of good intentions. The three of us get on famously well into the night, until we inevitably touch on the many letters Mum and Bernice have exchanged throughout the years. The lady has, in essence, known me since before I was born. She can tell me much more about Mum's relationship with my real father than what I remember myself. She can recall an ambitious little girl, an angsty teen and a struggling young mother that I rarely get to hear about.

"But you know with Steve, she's found someone that finally treats her how she should be," Bernice drops.

There's a silent pause at the table.

"You'll have to excuse me if I disagree," I say through gnashed teeth, before providing an edited, clean-for-publication summary of the last 15 years.

"I don't know. Your mother seems very happy with Steve. I think he's good for her," Bernice responds.

It's a pity to end my stay on a downer. As much as I try to hide my disappointment, I'm gutted to think this is how the history of our family is perceived among friends. Of all the injustices I feel at my childhood, it's this continuing perception – not the lack of anyone's intervention – that will hurt the most for the rest of my days.

Our walk home is a sullen, wordless one, past the Notts County ground, past the Nottingham Forest stadium and Trent Bridge cricket oval. I don't want to seem ungrateful for the Rodds' hospitality, for the genuine, open-hearted people they are, or appear thankless for the new light they've been able to shed on some of the missing years. It's simply that this subject is the one topic for which I don't have a poker face practiced and prepared.

Even in the morning, when the tiredness and alcohol are no longer mitigating factors, things are still uncomfortable as Bernice and Allen scratch together a cooked breakfast and see me off at that station.

My next stop, Lincoln, is only an hour by the train and is essentially a layover on my way to my intended destination, Hull. I spend most of my day there moping; about the years I'll never get back, about the lack of contact from any friends back home, about the fact I haven't organised a hostel room in Lincoln in advance. After unsuccessfully walking around the 'new town' looking for accommodation down by the River Withern, I drag my two bulging backpacks up the aptly named Steep Hill. It's a cobbled Roman street that takes an almighty gradient up through a hotchpotch of independent tearooms, pubs, giftshops and book stores, arriving at the entrance to Lincoln Cathedral and Lincoln Castle. Both look grand atop the hill and are visible for miles across the otherwise flat Lincolnshire countryside. The cathedral, used as a backdrop in filming of The Da Vinci Code, is a glorious gothic monstrosity dating back to around 1000AD.

The setting piques my spirits and I am reminded once more I am the only one who shapes my destiny today. As luck would have it, the King Edward House – a regal lodge only metres from the cathedral – is offering rooms for a discounted price. It's still a fare double what I have been paying elsewhere, but I treat myself to a room with a vista. At night I find a restaurant in Silver Street that charges £3.99 for all-you-can-eat. By the time I leave I am engorged, in higher spirits, and feeling a touch sympathetic for the proprietors.

*** *** ***

HULL is not a destination to visit unless you have burning reason. Each time I have mentioned I am travelling to Hull, the sole response has been 'Why?'. It's famed predominantly for its crime rate, grim industrial landscape, an abundance of neck tattoos and shaved heads. It's also the city where my grandparents met in the Second World War, starting the most enduring (and perhaps only) love story in our family. The city is where my mother was born, delivered by a midwife at 299 Anlaby Road. It's the port where my Nan lost her closest childhood friend and several neighbours in the German bombing raids.

I accept I may be mentally unhinged, but it's one of the locations I've most looked forward to visiting since I left Australia. Hence why I have booked five days here.

Something as simple as the railway skirting the River Humber and passing under the Humber Bridge is a gift to appreciate. I've heard so many stories about both landmarks and how my mother never had a chance to walk the bridge before she emigrated. Instead, Nan and she would catch the ferry to visit Nan's family just a few miles away in Grimsby and Cleethorpes.

I arrive into Paragon bus and rail terminal, another oft-spoken place name I can now attach a mental image to. My hotel is quite a walk away up Spring Bank, but pleasingly it is located close to KC Stadium, where I will be spending Saturday night. I've got two tickets to see Australia play New Zealand in the Tri Nations rugby league and one of my old McDonald's co-workers, Ferris, is making the trip up from London to join me.

First though, I have a long list of peculiar family-related sites to visit. My first day of missions has me seeking my maternal great-grandparents' graves in Chants Hill Cemetery. Or at least that's the name of the cemetery given to me by Mum. I soon find out, after several dumbstruck looks at the council office, that it's the Northern Cemetery on Chanterlands Avenue that I seek. Such are the challenges of tracing family history through anecdotes, nicknames and fading memories.

An elderly, slender, goateed employee on a bicycle guides me around the graveyard to a plot in the far western corner. It says "Richard Towse Kirby, died 1951. Also, Alice Kirby, died 1971." Buried together, 20 years apart. I can't remember if Richard was the one killed by a kick to the head from a horse, or whether he was the one that died sitting upright in a chair, so stiff from rigor mortis on his discovery that he had to have both legs broken before he could be laid to rest. Either way, I remember he was one particular ancestor that met a grizzly end.

Neither of my grandparents speak openly of their parents. Nan doesn't mention her parents because she was so fond of them – particularly her father. Grandad doesn't speak of his because he is too proud. All I know is that his father walked out on him as a child, saying he was simply off to the shops. It's such a cliché that I can barely believe it.

I take a photo of Richard and Alice's grave and head off towards Anlaby Road, a confusing section of bitumen that starts near the city centre and changes name at indeterminate points. To make reading street numbers even more difficult, a newly-built overpass, a church and a bus depot all throw the ordering of houses out of whack. I turn back over my course at least three times before feeling confident I have found 299.

A man, who in hastened judgment I deduce to be on the down-and-out, stands between a rusted gate and a flight of stairs, leading up to an open doorway. On this chilly weekday he is frozen in both expression and pose, wearing a ragged camel coat and puffing on a thin cigarette.

"Sorry mate, but I don't suppose this is 299?" I volley across the gate.

"Are you looking for apartment A, B or C?" he responds in monotone.

"Ah I'm not too sure. You see – and this will sound strange I know – but my Mum was born in the front room of this house in 1958. I've travelled from Australia to see where she grew up."

"Well it's been divided into three apartments, one for each level, since some time back I believe," he says, his voice thawing word-by-word.

"Ah okay then. Not what I expected, but everything changes in time doesn't it?" I say, standing on tiptoes to peek through a lit room over the man's left shoulder.

"Look I'd invite you to come up, but I don't keep much of a home. Besides I don't really have a front room as such. I think you'll find your Mum was born in the bottom apartment and the owner for that is out of town. Down south I believe. She's a young thing, not a bad looker. Picked up the place for £33,000 or something ridiculous on account of the damp and rot…"

Something stops me in my tracks. I've come all this way and still, I relent at his flimsy reasoning. I could easily argue my way to a look inside his apartment, but there's a politeness or perhaps fear of disappointment that nails me to the spot.

"It doesn't really matter mate. Look as long as you don't mind me taking a few pictures from the outside, I'm sure that will keep the old lady happy."

Poolhall—Jail—Library

"Not a problem at all. Did you want me to pose out here or go inside?" he asks with an unexpected flurry of excitement.

"Umm, I might just get the one of you outside and then a couple of the house on its own if that's okay."

When I finally settle down at the computer in the lifeless Hull library, I have photos not only of my great-grandparents' graves, my Mum's birth home and a pastiche of other locations legendary in family folklore – I also have several pictures of the church where my grandparents married. St James' in Sutton, North Hull, was in full regalia when the local bus dropped me off. A modern-day wedding was in progress, featuring a beautiful couple amid a blooming garden, behind a procession of cream-coloured Rolls Royces. I was hit by a surge of pride as I closed the shutter on the camera.

I attach the photographic essay of Hull to an email addressed to Mum and re-read a suburban newspaper clipping from the internet:

A couple from Gordon Park are reflecting on 60 years together as they celebrate their wedding anniversary today.

Ted, 78, and Mary Berg, 80, first crossed paths by chance in wartime Hull in 1944.

Grandson Loxton Berg said: "Granddad met Nan when she was looking in a shop window with two friends. He asked for directions back to where his ship was docked, as he was serving in the Royal Navy.

"Once she'd walked him back to his ship, he memorised the route and offered to walk her and her friends home, because it was almost nightfall.

"When they arrived at my Nan's family home, she gave my Granddad a pocket calendar with a rose on the front. He still keeps the same pocket calendar in his wallet to this day."

After this chance meeting it didn't take Ted long to realise that Mary was the woman for him.

Ted, who served in the North Sea convoys to Russia and patrolled the English Channel during the D Day landings, says: "When the ship left port, we kept in correspondence. One day I wrote to Mary telling her I intended to marry her and two weeks after she responded that's exactly what we did."

The couple married at St James' Church, Hull, on September 21, 1945 with three bridesmaids, close friends and family.

Mary added: "When I saw Ted on the day I was dumbstruck. He was so handsome and I have never regretted marrying him."

The couple went on to have seven children (one deceased at birth) in England, before moving the family to Australia in 1967.

Since then they have been gifted 13 grandchildren, 13 great grandchildren and two great-great grandsons.

Ted said: "In all our time together we have never argued. We have had our differences of opinion, but I just walk away. Couples should always share, be honest and there shouldn't be one boss."

Ted is now a full-time carer to Mary as she is blind and unable to walk.

Ted said: "I love Mary and always will. Wherever she is, I am never far away."

Poolhall—Jail—Library

FOR my generation it was the day that Elvis died, the day that John Lennon was assassinated, when Bon Scott was found unconscious in his car or Jim Morrison chose to 'break on through to the other side' for good. At first, that was how I treated Loxton's reaction to the day Kurt Cobain loaded up on heroin and blasted his brains out; an acute melancholy, the first death of someone for whom he felt admiration and influence – and above all – a sense of connection. I guess from Loxton's previous behavior I should have recognised the path it would lead him down.

I remember the week they discovered Cobain's body in April 1994, because the following week was my birthday and then, a fortnight later, I gave birth to wonderful twin girls – Pip and Alyce. Loxton was morose through it all. He cared of nothing else than some stupid singer he had never met who had lived on the other side of the planet. His school results dropped markedly over the next two terms, he barely talked around home, and was prone to giving up tasks in a hopeless huff. I found and disposed of an alarm clock in his room where the electrical supply had been severed and pruned back to expose the wires. Loxton carried the weight of his body around like it was a burden to his own shoulders, his eyes focused at the floor two steps ahead, his mouth dependably downturned.

The two people Loxton would confide in at this time were his Uncle Howard and that girl – Macy – that he had chosen to latch onto. Together, they only seemed to reflect his despondency at the world and provide further darkness to his hate-filled eyes. As well as listening to Nirvana every single afternoon, Loxton would now lock himself in his room and launch into track-after-track of various grunge and metal bands they had copied for him. Soundgarden, Pearl Jam, Stone Temple Pilots, Rage Against the Machine, and the soundtrack to the skinhead film *Romper Stomper*. These I could stomach to a certain degree, but when Lox really wanted to up the confrontational ante at home, he would resort to one tape that I couldn't stand. It was by a bunch of no-hopers who called themselves Alice In Chains.

'I want to take dirty, a stinging pistol, in my mouth on my tongue. I want you to scrape me from the walls and go crazy like you've made me' was the verse he would choose to elevate to the highest volume ad nauseam. After I grew sick of it and banned it, Loxton then reverted to another song that featured the line 'All this time I swore I'd never be like my old man, but what the hay, it's time to face exactly what I am'.

Within a few months though, my son had moved onto another band that, in some ways, made me wish he had stuck with the depressing grunge diatribe. It came time for his 16th birthday party and I promised him he could have a small gathering at home, hoping it would extricate him, at least momentarily, from his wallowing. Concerned Loxton's self-enforced sobriety was isolating him from his friends, I even suggested that Steve buy him a six-pack of beers for the night. Lox accepted the offer.

Later however, Steve grew drunk and sleepy on his home brew and totally forgot the pledge about the six-pack. As normal Loxton got his back up, gave us all the silent treatment and retreated out back to greet his guests and blare the stereo. That was when I first heard of Cypress Hill. Their music was all about gangsters, violence, and above all else, the smoking of marijuana. Loxton played the tape at least four or five times during the night, started a game of basketball with a pineapple stolen from the kitchen and chipped his teeth doing push-ups on the driveway. He had two friends that stayed past the others, shirtless and clinging to buckets on the cold winter grass, relieving the contents of their stomachs as Loxton stood by soberly and blasted them with the yard hose.

When the morning came and we found two bongs in Bobby's cubbyhouse, the question had to be asked: Was Loxton doing drugs? He swore black and blue that he couldn't stand the stuff; that he hadn't even touched a drop of alcohol. He said *the pineapple ballgame and the push-up incident were merely through boredom, to impress others.*

"Sure, my friends do pot, but I never have and never want to. And you just have to trust me on that," he protested.

Then Loxton started dying his hair all colours of the rainbow, reading up on psychotherapy and saying he intended to become a writer (while barely passing his English grades).

Approximately 90 per cent of his stories from school and parties revolved around two tubby stoner kids, Wes and Jabba. Like Loxton, they had mostly existed on the outer fringes of social cliques. But they were suddenly flourishing as pranksters extraordinaire, ascending through the ranks with a drug-delivered ability to impress and humour new friends.

"You should have seen Wes on Saturday, he took some LSD, went wandering around the streets and came back swearing he had talked to red aliens who were going to gatecrash the party," Loxton once revealed.

"He disappeared later again and we found him passed out on the main green of the lawn bowls club where his grandfather works. He'd broken into the gardening shed and used lime powder to spell out a huge tribute to Ice-T. Ice-T is a rapper, by the way Mum. Man, the greenskeeper spends so much time preparing that lawn, you can imagine their face when they found out.

"Anyways that's not the best bit. Wes's grandfather gave him a call just last night and says 'Holy Christ, Wes would you believe it? Some knucklehead's gone and burnt the letters E.T. into the bowling green. Haha, His grandfather thought Ice-T was E.T."

With that Loxton began chuckling uncontrollably. Maybe a decade earlier I could have seen the humour in confusing a black singer for a wrinkly, homesick alien, but I was gobsmacked at once by the immaturity, irresponsibility and the boys' disregard for their bodies.

It mattered not, because the next week Loxton would come rolling through the doors with an equally absurd story.

One week, Wes stole all the hosepipes from his neighbourhood to stockpile a lifetime's supply of bongs. Another time, when an international cricket star moved in directly across the street from his house, Wes relocated a bus stop in the dead of night – seats, signs and all – so that it obscured the cricketer's driveway and left him trapped inside. Some other smoke-filled day of the week, Wes brazenly told his teacher his ambition post-school was *"To live off your taxes"*.

I had no time for Wes at all, but Jabba I had known since we moved to Stafford, when he went by the much more sensible name of Thomas. When Loxton first met him at primary school, he was a cute, blonde, cherubic thing that said he wanted to grow up to be a politician. In fact, if I recall rightly his very precise ambition was to be the next conservative prime minister. He'd always struck me as a kid of great ambition, but somewhere along the way the wheels began to fall off.

"Oh boy Mum, we went to a party up at Sparkes Hill reservoir the other night and, well, nothing great was happening, aside from Wes trying to pee off the top of the water tower and holding a beer at the same time. Then Rocky, Jabba and I decided we'd go for a walk to the corner store on Trouts Road. The others were drinking bourbon and smoking reefer, so they wanted some munchy food and more cola. And I just wanted to buy a pack of basketball cards. As it happens, we got there and walked around for what seemed like an eternity. The others were so smashed I tell you. I chose a pack of cards from the box, Rocky eventually grabbed a hot dog and we left Jabba deciding which ice block to buy. We paid, were out past the register and practically on the street when the shopkeeper screamed at us: 'Hey you boys! I don't know what you've been doing, but kindly remove your friend from my freezer' Hahaha. Jabba must have been leaning over, staring at all the ice creams through the glass and clean passed out. He had his *arms stretched out and was snoring loudly. We physically had to lift him from the freezer, but then he woke up and told us to fuck off."*

Loxton was chortling and play-acting and his demeanour was so removed from the gloomy, angsty norm that it utterly confounded me. He was unapproachable for all but a few minutes of the week, but then would spring to life with stories that revolved around drugs, over-indulgence and the new-found popularity of those that hit it hardest. I could see him slipping away from me. Not only him, but I could see all the other kids in this circle slipping away from their own parents. I sorely wanted to believe my son wasn't mixed up in the worst of it, but the evidence was mounting.

I became more and more confused about what I wanted for my son. Above everything, I wanted him to go to university. I had made that promise at the family court when I was granted custody. Whatever Loxton chose to study was up to him. I didn't care if he was going to be a doctor or an engineer or a scientist. And I didn't particularly mind if Loxton was going to run the usual gamut of girls and alcohol while finding his way. But what I really couldn't abide by was drugs in any way, shape or form. I didn't really like smoking either, so for him to seemingly choose weed went completely against the grain. Then again, I dearly wanted my boy to feel popular and to resolve some of his anger issues. Within my own head, I knew the list of expectations – the game plan – wasn't clear at all. I guess what I really wanted to do was snap my fingers and take things forward two years. Take us all to a situation where Loxton and Steve were no longer under the same roof, no longer at each other's throats, and where Loxton would have a girlfriend, a part-time job, some stability in his temperament and be on his way to bringing the first piece of university parchment into our family.

HULL

NOBODY has inspired this whole trip more than Ferris. When I first met Ferris at 17, we were two skinny kids being paid $4 an hour to flip burger patties and carry buckets of gherkins. Working overnight shifts at an inner-city takeaway store, both of us would be threatened weekly with the sack for failing to shave our pathetic goatee beards. I've looked back many times since and wondered whether the greaseball manager knew one of the kids he was berating had been taught, at the age of four, to use an automatic weapon concealed under his pillow.

A Palestinian by birth, Australian at heart and, these days, an effervescent life-force that resides in Golders Green, a largely strict orthodox Jewish area of northern London; Ferris is all sorts of paradoxes and adventurous tales compressed into a bundle of enthusiasm and endless possibilities. You suggest something to Ferris and he's out the door before you know it. Nothing is ever too inconvenient. There's always a way and a means.

He has ridden a motorbike across northern Africa, drank homemade wine with strangers in remote caves in Eastern Europe, abandoned a car to walk the cliff villages of the Cinque Terra, dove backwards into the cavity of an immense coral shelf deep under the Red Sea.

A project manager for a major British organization, he is just back from taking his Mum around the Mediterranean. A month before that he drove a black Mustang through the American desert. Maybe two months ago he was skiing in Bulgaria. His legs are still sore from a charity run to the top of London's tallest building.

I could forgive him for not being overly enthusiastic about a hurried trip to Yorkshire's East Riding to watch a game of rugby league. But you know what? He has still made the distance. And now we are sat in The Eagle, the closest pub to where my Mum was born, somewhere around our fourth or fifth pint.

Poolhall—Jail—Library

"You know I reckon my Grandad would have come to this pub for sure back in the day," I say, the bubbling amber eliciting fermented sentimentality.

"Oh yeah, for sure. What a town hey? Ah Hull. I had to come and see for myself," Ferris replies.

Drinking has filled a void. By the time Ferris arrived here I'd spent the intervening days not only researching places of our family's past, but also exhausting the local 'sights'. I'd been to the Street Life Museum, Wilberforce House (dedicated to the abolition of slavery), Prince's Quay, the Maritime Museum and an old, mud-encrusted icebreaker preserved for posterity on the waterfront.

Ferris doesn't particularly want to drag me through any of these a second time, and says he can appreciate the gritty beauty of Hull nonetheless. It's a right proper community, for better and for worse. For a man that senses with his soul, that is enough.

In London, Ferris has a pokey little room in a flat he shares with four other people. Or is that five others? Possibly six? I can never quite work it out. They seem to come and go, occupying whatever floor space or room is available at the time. Other guys of his age and professional standing are spending their weekends hunting the urban jungle for those last evasive, minimalistic, stainless steel, onyx-lined accoutrements that will complete their lives. Instead Ferris reserves his life for living. His domain is adorned by two posters he stole from work, a calendar that came free in TNT magazine and a whole load of postcards, photos and letters rounded up from far corners of the globe.

There's a history of us sharing a few beers that stretches back to a McDonald's Christmas party in 1996. By guile we found a way to receive unlimited drinks at the bar, a heady achievement for anyone at age 18. Hazy memories exist of an awards ceremony that night where one of our colleagues received a stuffed Ronald McDonald doll for his many hours of toil. Ferris and I began playing football with it on the mezzanine level, kicking it side-to-side above the assembled crowd of company dignitaries. Eventually the doll burst, coming apart at the neck. Its innards spilled down an internal stairwell through the heart of the party and we were revoked our drinking privileges.

Outside, with rain falling lightly as the party ended, we sat bedraggled in the sheltered entrance to a neighbouring café that had been closed and abandoned. For the first time I started talking openly about my paralysing existential fears. I'd been reading a lot at this time, drilling down to the minutest detail of reality and perception and not handling it at all well. I grew up a kid so focused on achievement that it blew my mind entirely to begin thinking that none of it counted for anything. All those landmark indicators like exam results, sporting accolades, career and marriage prospects; they were all that my one-dimensional mind had considered until I left school. I had been the general public's 100 per cent successful test subject of indoctrination through popular education and a strict upbringing. But suddenly, I had been struck by the rather crippling revelation that it was all bullshit.

Lately in particular, I'd become convinced that the world was infinitely tiny, smaller than the size of an ant, that we were ultimately insignificant and the playthings of some wicked, devilish creature. And it was completely doing my head in.

I sighed into the midnight air: "It's fucked Ferris. We don't have the power to change jack shit. Why bring us into this world? That's if birth really does happen and it's not part of this whole make-believe scenario implanted into our brains. What if these buildings aren't real? What if you aren't real? What if……*I…am…not…real?*"

With defences down, I cried more than I had at any time in front of another man. Big, viscous sobbing and slobbering. Tortured, I looked into Ferris's eyes for the slightest sign that he had considered all this himself and that I was not completely alone, completely bonkers.

"Woah, steady man," he said. "For sure I've thought about this and, you know, we can't change a single thing, so why send yourself crazy?"

And with that Ferris punched me as hard as he could in the meat of my arm, got up and started walking away. I dried my eyes and followed after him, convinced forever more that he was a demigod, a philosophical giant who had contemplated the entire anatomy of the universe well before me. And somehow, he found reason, balance and equilibrium without breaking a sweat.

I always suspected he saw right through me as a charity case, an unnerving but ultimately harmless one who was a product of his broken home. But he humoured me that night and he has forever since, right up to this surreal reunion on the other side of the globe.

*** *** ***

AS IT eventuates, Australia wins the Hull Test 24-12 over New Zealand and once more Ferris and I find a way to complementary drinks. In recent times I've been utilising Ferris as a consultant for a work project and this has allowed us not only free entry to the Test match, but also an invitation to an exclusive post-game shindig in the bowels of the stadium. We've come a good distance – in all senses of the term – since our humble beginnings.

This time around we aren't rollicking drunk, and there are definitely no tears. But we still have enough reverie in the veins to want to hit the town after the function is over. Our first port of call is the Tiger's Lair, the official clubhouse of Hull's soccer team. The Tigers have won promotion twice in successive years to come from what is effectively fourth division to the cusp of Premier League entry. It's an exciting time for the club and I have followed them proudly from afar, but on this night there is very little happening at the clubhouse. It's mostly addled old men, backslapping and hee-hawing.

We walk onwards to the city centre and are struck at once by the armoured riot vehicle parked in the middle of the clubbing district. The police stand around on-edge, waiting for trouble to start, as if it were an inevitability. It sets an adversarial atmosphere from the outset. Young ladies and jack-the-lads start to arrive, fresh from a few warm-up bevvies at home, trotting quickly to the bar of their choice, every one of them holding tension in their eyes and shoulders.

A blonde-haired cartoon angel on a bed of clouds and a she-devil emanating from a pit of flames sit above the entrance to Heaven & Hell nightclub, tucked away down Anne Street. The thick 12-foot-high doors give the business almost as much of an intimidating presence as the head bouncer. He looks to be 140kg and verging on six-foot-eight; a Doberman on steroids. I've noticed security guards in England are not merely big like they are in Australia. They are generally gargantuan, kitted out with stab-proof vests and head-kicker boots.

As I approach the head of the line and fall into the shadow of the bouncer's giant latissimus dorsi, I feel his breath down the collar of my jacket. He grabs me roughly by the arm, opens a chain to the side exit and slings me out onto the pavement.

"No club colours!" he barks. No introductions. No explanations.

I'm wearing a retro Queensland jacket from the 1980s. It has three white stripes along the shoulder and the remainder is maroon. I've worn it out because it's the only long-sleeve in my pack that smells half-decent after two months on the road. Needless to say, I hadn't anticipated that a vintage zip-up from the other side of the world could potentially be seen as the spark to ignite wild violence.

We retreat around the corner and assess our options. Underneath the jacket I am wearing a green and gold shirt, but it is not expressly an Australian shirt. It has the name of an underground record label splashed across the front. I put my tee-shirt over the top of the jacket, obscuring any references to Queensland, but leaving the sleeves poking out from underneath.

Surely the bouncer could have no problem with that? Surely, he would recognise I have seen the error of my ways, atoned and returned with only peace and benevolence in my heart?

He eyes me as we reach fourth in the queue again, fixing his stare.

"I told you already. GET. THE. FUCK. OUT!"

People are so friendly in these parts.

*** *** ***

WESTERN ENGLAND

After weeks upon weeks of playing the conscientious tourist, immersing myself in historical readings and artefacts, retracing the steps of my forefathers and being drawn to locales of inherent spiritual attraction, it is now time to lose myself in pure, indulgent stupidity.

The adventures to come on these next few days carry a disclaimer. To anyone who hasn't seen the movie *Human Traffic*, my usual babble will perhaps seem even more incongruous than normal.

On paper the immediate itinerary looks like your typical western railway trip. Having left Ferris back in London, I'm now scooting solo through Reading to Bristol, then onward to Cardiff.

Aside from catching up with my great-uncle Jim, the premise of the week is wholly moronic. For instance, Jim – my grandfather's youngest brother – will only host me for a brief few hours in his mobile home on the outskirts of Reading before driving me to a tiny village called Mapledurham. A speck on the map, rested against the northern bank of the Thames, Mapledurham is the filming location for the favourite wartime film of my childhood, *The Eagle Has Landed*. Save aside from visiting the church and windmill where Michael Caine's troops went down with guns blazing, there is no other reason to visit the rural parish.

From Mapledurham I will travel to Bristol and attempt to dig my hands into a musical sub-culture which in the last 15 years has given birth to Portishead, Massive Attack and Tricky. But let's face it, hitting Bristol in 2005 to chase the trip-hop vibe is about as useful as trying to surf the Balearic wave in Ibiza or hanging out in Seattle to catch a sniff of the latest grunge sensation. I'm at least a decade too late.

Of course, I realise all this and, if truth be known, the days intervening Monday and Friday are merely biding me time for a monster night on the lash. Ever since I watched *Human Traffic* for the first time five years ago, I've desired a completely crazy end to the working week in the seedy bowels of Cardiff, reaching for the lasers and banging out to hardcore drum'n'bass.

To tap the lyrical vein of main character Jip: "I'm gonna blow steam out my head like a screaming kettle, I'm gonna talk cod shit to strangers all night, I'm gonna lose the plot on the dancefloor.

"We're gonna get more spaced out than Neil Armstrong ever did. Anything could happen you know? This could be the best night of my life."

MY SUSPICION of Steve having an affair was, I guess in reflection, linked to post-natal depression. Initially I became convinced he was secretly liaising with Carmel, a divorcee who lived across the road. Steve had warmly embraced her at the last New Year's Eve party and planted a kiss on her cheek while I sat inside, engorged with the as-yet unborn twins. That tidbit of saucy gossip spread quickly around the neighbourhood and it was as much a cause for humiliation as it was anger. I forbade him from visiting Carmel or performing any odd jobs at her house, as he had done in the past. Still, this did not allay my fears.

Steve was arriving home from work later and later each week it seemed. When I discovered a new girl had started at his depot – long brunette hair, tanned, shorts barely covering her nether regions – she became the prime suspect. We had barely made love since the previous year and, though it wasn't unusual for him to be emotionally disconnected, he seemed absent from the relationship physically, emotionally and literally. The task of catering to new-born twins was multiplied in difficulty by the amount of time he spent outside the house.

I never had any proof to my claims however and was met with repeated denials. My closest friends insinuated it was all in my head. They told me to stop fretting and that the thoughts were the product of overworked hormones. Yet I felt I had to share my hunch with more people to ascertain if I was completely bonkers or justified even in the slightest. Unfortunately, I made the mistake of confiding in my son about this notion.

Steve and Loxton were already proceeding along the path to all-out war. My partner had completely withdrawn from Lox's football commitments, other than to ban him for a second year from attending representative trials. Whatever thin strain of mutual tolerance they had achieved when Steve was manager of the team was now entirely gone. To reveal to Loxton that I thought his step-dad was cheating was like lighter fluid to the bonfire. Through a flattering, but not-often displayed sense of loyalty to me, Loxton began taking on more chores and organising activities to keep my mind occupied. At the same time, he shut Steve out of his daily existence with an aggression that had noticeably escalated. My son was growing into a man's body and instead of playing the wounded soul to Steve's barbs, he now stood chisel-faced and unflinching, exchanging deep stares whenever an accusatory missive was cast in his direction.

One of the main diversions Loxton organised was for us to complete large jigsaw puzzles together on a Sunday, as this was Steve's usual day for watching car racing in the lounge with a few beers under his belt. For several weeks we worked on a Swiss landscape, wooden chateaus with flags draped from their eaves, set against the snow-capped Alps. The more time I spent on the puzzle, the more I was gradually drawn into Loxton's depressing world view and, as we jiggled the pieces of this blissful landscape into order, I found myself agreeing more and more that the whole home situation 'sucked'.

It was close to Christmas when we approached finalisation of the jigsaw. Without fail that time of year was always steeped with intensity at Bertram Street. It could have even been the last Sunday before the yule – my memory eludes me now – that Loxton returned from his nightly shower to see the 10,000 puzzle pieces broken up and strewn across the floor.

He automatically suspected Bobby, who occupied the bottom bunk in their room. Loxton grabbed him and shook him roughly.

"Hey! Did you do this? I'll kick your arse."

Bobby opened his eyes, curled his little mouth and turned his head side-to-side.

"Daddy did it."

Loxton took off down the hall infuriated, marching back towards the lounge room.

"What the hell did you do that for? There was absolutely no need."

Steve was on his third jug of beer by this stage and had an air of self-contentment. He crossed his arms and half-smiled.

"Well it was a stupid place to put the puzzle wasn't it? You want to leave things on the floor, expect them to get stood on."

I was in the middle, looking from side-to-side, watching the space close between the two of them. Loxton's arm was twitching at his side and he had pure menace in his eyes

"How come it was on the other side of the room then? You kicked it. You didn't stand on it. You know you're a tosser don't you?"

Steve twisted his head, keeping a mocking grin firmly in place. Slowly he lowered his beer glass down and stood up. Loxton baulked and turned.

We all knew it was the usual scenario of cat and mouse, where the cat likes to paw at its prey before devouring it. Steve chased Loxton to the hallway.

"Don't you two dare fight in there while Bobby is trying to sleep," *I screamed after them.*

Loxton stopped dead, propped, allowed Steve to catch him, then for the first time lifted and straightened his arm, delivering a strike to his stepfather's forehead that sent him reeling into the linen cupboard.

***   ***   ***

DIRECTLY *after the punch, Loxton ran toward the back door, kneeing Steve in the groin for good measure as he grappled past. With Steve in shock and pausing to collect his thoughts, I had the chance to intercept him. But even with my full bodyweight leant against my husband, I couldn't prevent him from retaliation. As I clung to one arm, Steve steamed into the kitchen, cursing loudly as he dragged me through every step. When he reached the knife drawer and grabbed for a long fishing blade, I instinctively let go.*

Bursting out the screen door, Steve held the knife threateningly aloft.

"You are mental. I'll call the fucking cops on you," Loxton yelled, standing only 20m away beneath the washing line.

"You'll call the fucking cops? I'll call the fucking cops about you boy."

Part of me was praying that none of the neighbours were ringing the police that very moment. Another part of me knew it would be the only solution should the situation deteriorate any further.

"You two just bloody stop it. I'm not asking you. I'm telling you. You are both as bad as each other. I've had enough. Enough, goddamn it!"

The boys remained at the same distance, chests puffed and staring intently. I continued to berate them as they stood statue-like. Eventually the adrenaline drained from the confrontation. Steve had a hesitancy in his eyes that hadn't existed previously. I seized upon it, placing my arm around his shoulder and convincing him to lower the knife and return inside. Loxton remained outside and somehow we achieved an uneasy truce so that everybody could sleep under the same roof that night.

The following day Loxton kept the door to his bedroom shut until after lunch. When he emerged, he totally ignored Steve. He didn't acknowledge his words or his presence. Naturally this infuriated Steve, escalating the situation to Code Red once more. When Lox returned to his room, upped the volume on his stereo and encouraged Steve to rant into my ear again, I ordered them both outside to the patio.

"Right, let's do this like adults. You want to be treated like an adult Loxton? Start acting like one. Everybody can have their say. We will all take turns. Steve and I have been talking for a while now about how we can make things better for you around home. We know this next year at school is important. We're going to buy you a caravan so you can have your own designated space in the back garden. It will be your own. You won't have to share a room with your brother and won't have anyone walking through. Your stepfather has also promised me he will cut back on his drinking. Isn't that right?"

"Yep," Steve replied glibly.

"So, what are you going to do to change things Loxton? How will you change your behavior?"

Lox was startled and suspicious.

"You are really going to get me a caravan? You mean that? Wow. Well, I guess I need to learn how to control my temper. I won't swear at you guys anymore, I promise. I'll keep trying to do well at school. I'm...I'm still going to be allowed in the house for dinner and stuff, aren't I?"

To be honest, I had no idea how we were going to afford the caravan. I just knew that the current situation couldn't stand.

"Yes, Loxton we are very serious. And of course, yes you will be allowed in the house. One thing I want us all to commit to is that we are going to see a family counsellor"

The boys shrugged a nonplussed approval as I excused myself to check on the twins inside. Climbing the stairs, I could hear Steve and Loxton engage in mumbled, meaningless conversation.

I was carried by an air of optimism. There seemed to be genuine give-and-take, a reasonable chance of accomplishing peace. A simple, civilised exchange of words between the two was a marked improvement on the past few months. There was no reason upon my return to believe things couldn't continue in a positive manner.

But then I found Loxton slumped in his chair, staring downward at his feet. Steve was looking sideward, pretending to be distracted by a sparrow in the bushes.

"Oh, what now?" I demanded.

Neither would reply. Loxton had the first makings of tears in his eyes. Steve was giving me a bewildered look.

"Look we've just had a real good chat about things, haven't we?" I probed. "How can all that turn to shit in a matter of *minutes? Tell me you buggers. You two are bloody hopeless. Now tell me what's been said."*

The air fell silent until Steve, pressured by my unimpressed gaze, broke first.

"I don't know what his problem is. He started going on at me again about how he was going to call the cops and..."

Loxton jumped up and exploded.

"Don't you fucking dare. You want to know Mum? Want to know what your dear husband said while you went inside? He said he was going to fucking kill me. His words, not mine. He waited for you to go and said 'I'll fucking kill you yet. Your Mum can think what she wants, but I'll get you at some point.' So hey, what do you think about that Mum? I suppose you still love him. I suppose nothing will change. Nothing ever fucking changes."

With that, he stormed back inside, slammed his bedroom room and antagonisingly brought the stereo to life again.

CARDIFF

HUMAN Traffic is as much a film about drugs as it isn't. Let me explain. My first viewing of *Human Traffic* at age 21 was a good six months before I'd ever touched any kind of narcotic, yet I felt a tingling in my skin, a tightness in my chest and a other whole level of joyous mind explosions. There was a remarkable subliminal connection, captured on acetate, linking people, music, ideas, places and time.

The film was about compulsion, magnetism, disconnection, a trust of instincts, burning sorrows, cynicism and the search for something or somebody to relate to.

This was at a time in life when I had plenty of friends but struggled for a true sense of connection with anybody. I was the sort of guy people would 'get' in dribs and drabs, but never feel expressly comfortable in knowing or understanding. The same applied in reverse. About the only person I felt connected to at that point was my partner, who I considered an absolute soulmate. And yes, in many ways, being exposed to *Human Traffic* was like that terrifically rare sensation of falling utterly and completely for someone. Even without a single engineered chemical in my system, I 'got' it. I sensed it. I knew what the characters felt in their heart of hearts.

Then not much later my girlfriend walked out on me. Or it could be argued I pushed her.

No, the break-up didn't make me jump headlong into a rabid ecstasy phase. In fact, the opposite happened. I retreated more than normal, became secretive and, for months on end, had no desire to be intoxicated. What did happen though, was that I become known as an extremely empathetic 'piller'. On the rare occasion I did go to a party, if one of my mates was on a good E, I could read their vibe and surf it with them, allay their fears, then go home and dissect the otherworldly sensations it aroused in me, completely sober. For me at the time that was enough. I felt like I was receiving a valuable lesson in spiritual insight without having to fork out for the goods myself. My buddies couldn't believe I was spending entire nights drinking water alone.

As night follows day however, there did come a time when I was finally lured to experiment myself. It was a huge decision at that point. I'd been vehemently anti-drugs for all my teenage years, then switched to merely ambivalent when my social circle was inundated with them. Despite what Mum thinks, I'd never even tried pot or cigarettes beforehand. Still haven't.

Aside from family pressures, rugby league was what made me so opposed to artificial substances. Since 15 I had been conducting a strict regime of exercises every night before bed and using as many school lunch breaks as possible to get stronger and fitter. In fact, at the point where I hated my stepdad the most, I made myself do a push-up for every word I spoke with him. That was my way of ensuring I never broke the icy atmosphere or made him ever think I had forgotten or forgiven everything he had done. With all that effort leading to this point, I didn't want to jeopardise everything, test positive to drugs and run my health into the ground.

But when the girl I expected to share the rest of my life with walked out the door, all those good intentions got tipped on their head. This came at a time where I was also losing my passion for football, leaving me with barely a shred of belief in any object or ideal. Reinvention was what I sought most. I wanted to be more flexible, less structured, more understanding of differing viewpoints.

Of all the places to reset my moral compass, it was Yatala Pie Shop where I decided to drop my first ecstasy tablet. A historic bakery situated amongst scrubland halfway between Brisbane and the Gold Coast, Yatala Pies is the type of place middle-aged day-trippers seek out on their way home from a mountain drive.

On this particular day though, there were hijinks afoot and, along with half-dozen of my best friends, we were on our way to the Big Day Out music festival at the Gold Coast Parklands. The other boys were in the bathroom, bottles of water in hand, dispensing the pills feverishly as I sat on the deck and chewed through two steak and kidney flans.

Jabba came out smiling ear-to-ear, wringing dry his hands as if absolving himself of all responsibility for what was to follow. All these guys had been into ecstasy for years and every single one of them was pumped for an afternoon and evening of mental mayhem. I made a snap call on the spot.

"Hey mate if there's a spare one going, I'd like to give it a try," I said, nonchalantly flinging my words in Jabba's direction.

"What? You? My gawwwd. Mr Anti-Drugs. Are you sure you don't mean you want another pie hunger-guts?"

"Serious mate, you know...only if it's not a hassle."

Jabba lit up like a lantern, slapping me profusely on the back.

"My pleasure mate. No problem at all. I only wish you'd spoken up earlier and we would have brought you a few extras. But don't worry, I'm sure we can rustle something up."

The next half-hour felt like it was spent stood before the highest tribunal in the land. Everyone in the car knew I was about to drop for the first time. Suddenly they had vindication after my many years of judgmental abstinence. And within myself, I was constantly fluctuating between deep regret and defiance. No matter what I had done beforehand, this seemed a concise point at which I could now be considered a kid who had gone off the rails.

I had to wait until we pulled into the carpark at Southport Sharks Football Club, next to the festival parklands, before we could split the pill. Jabba insisted it was best first time around to only take a half-a-pill, not a whole. We divided up on the centre console of his parents' Subaru and I swallowed without water, the chemical concoction of god-knows-what leaving its unmistakable taste against the back of my throat.

By no means was this my first festival at this venue. It would have been my fourth or fifth at least. So, by this stage I knew all about the oven-like conditions, where January heat torches down onto the dusty, dry trotting track ringed around centre stage. It combines with the total absence of shade and the constant clop-clop of 40,000 revellers to mimic the sensation of being stranded amidst a 12-hour Saharan dust storm.

We had a traditional meet-up spot at the base of the highest light tower, in case we got separated, disorientated and intoxicated. This was where I chose to head after just 20 minutes of the festival, having successfully lost all of our crew. Jabba was notorious for going walkabout, but I hadn't expected him to go gallivanting on such an auspicious occasion as my first E.

I must have stood waiting by that tower for the best part of an hour, which as any casual drug-taker will know, is smack bang in the time zone when the chemicals start to do their magic. That said, when the first member of our group arrived back – a string-bean mechanic called Brandon – I didn't consider myself much more than a little vague, perhaps a touch dehydrated.

"How long you been standing here? Don't tell me Jabba just left you? You're looking a little red man. How you feeling?"

"Feeling okay mate, pretty thirsty though."

"Haha, yeah rightyo. Your words are coming out a little funny. Let's get you some water."

I'd been on the one spot for so long that when I lifted my foot to walk away, I felt a cold sensation run all the way down my shins. A few trickles of sweat jostled free by the movement suddenly became a gushing icy river. With each step the light breeze caught the hair on my legs like a roaring trade wind billowing behind the sails, carrying me uphill towards the drinks stand.

Midway we were intercepted by an old university colleague who'd recognised me from afar. He was conversing enthusiastically about cricket, while I hid behind my sunglasses, mumbling inaudibly. Then it happened.

In one sudden shift everything – and I mean EVERYTHING – became separated into just two colours. They were either pure white or cornflower blue. There was no shade or detail, only silhouettes. All the blue slowly gravitated towards the sky and the mass of people walking past became nothing more than white waves reaching up from a white sea to fight the horizon.

Brandon saw the look of disassociated terror on my face, told me to sit down on the spot and raced off with a fistful of drink tokens. As for my university friend – well I slumped cross-legged and ignored him until he walked away confounded.

"Water. You have to drink water," said Brandon as he returned with two bottles.

Sure enough, I drained both bottles and my vision and general well-being swiftly returned. Now I had another savior in my life, Brandon.

"Holeee fuck, welcome to ecstasy my friend," he bellowed.

At the time I considered it nothing more than a bit too much sun. As a fair-skinned, ginger kid I'd experienced quite a few delirious, dizzy afternoons from running around in the backyard without a hat. But I guess looking back, it deserved some concern. I knew it was somehow related to the effects of the pill, but it didn't feel altogether different to the kinds of head-spins I would experience late at night on alcohol.

My next lesson in ecstasy survival came half-an-hour later when we found Jabba and the others, relocated to a shaded spot upon the hill. We were sat just outside a minor stage where Australian crooner Alex Lloyd was kicking off the mid-afternoon sets. This was right around his *Black The Sun* period, where Lloyd was lovesick, introspective and brooding. Everything he sang reminded me of my ex-girlfriend.

I went completely silent and sat there pretending to rock away to his melancholy vocals, but inside I felt completely hollow. Truth was that I loved Alex Lloyd's music, but at this point he was making me 100 per cent miserable. I was disappointed the ecstasy had done so little, I was disappointed

Jabba had left me to fend for myself. I was reliving every heartbreak I'd felt in the preceding months.

"You okay mate?" Jabba asked, staring straight into my eyes.

"Uh...I don't know what to say."

"What are you feeling? Is the eccy doing anything for you?"

"Mate I don't mean to kill the fun, but it hasn't done much at all. And I just feel sad. Really, really sad."

"Haha. Yeah fuck, I probably should have told you about that. When the pill wears off, you'll have a comedown. Everything will feel shit for a little while. Gee that's worn off quickly though. It's probably because you're a bit bigger than me. You might need a full pill to get a real kick hey. Wait until the end of this set and we'll go to the bathroom for some more."

That next period, sat pretending I couldn't wait for another hit, was absolutely torturous. I was trying to internalise my emotions so I didn't ruin everyone else's day, but all I wanted was to go home, lay in bed (or even underneath the bed), thinking about how much I hated the world. Did I really need another pill if this is what it did to me?

"Don't worry, the next one will be much better," Jabba said, reading my mind.

We slunk into the grotty toilets, Jabba dropped a small plastic wrap in my hand, and we squeezed into separate cubicles. When I unfurled the packaging I saw a speckled, dark green pill embossed with a question mark. I couldn't afford to hesitate, so I swallowed it down.

This time I made sure to grab myself a supply of $H2O$ in advance and we walked briefly across the apex of the hill before sprawling out and facing the second-largest stage. The slope of the ground formed a grassed amphitheater against which the afternoon breeze began to gather momentum. I felt much more relaxed now and began joking about with Jabba, who was flat on his back, slightly higher up the hill than me.

The hit didn't come immediately for me, but for Jabba – still riding the tail-end of his first pill – it was only a matter of minutes. I was moulding my body shape deeper and deeper into the turf when Jabba comically inched his way downhill next to me like a hyperactive worm. He was much closer physically than we would normally be seen in public.

"So, what do you reckon of Laura?" he quizzed without introduction, referring to his long-term girlfriend. "Truthfully, what do you say?"

I could tell he was riding high on the pill, but answered as honestly as I could anyhow. She seemed a good girl, good for him. I told him I appreciated he would converse in such an open way. It was just the beginning. He blurted out so many deep truths, in turn asking me about the most personal of subjects, all the while hanging off every word and ignoring the world surrounding us. Together we laid bare what 15 years of friendship had still managed to conceal. We were cutting behind the everyday bullshit, discarding the bravado and leaving ourselves open and vulnerable.

Rather than being unnerved, I felt totally exhilarated by it all. The wind began to gust harder and harder. I held the ground and held my breath, for fear both of them would be taken away. Thus, I discovered convection was my personal trigger for the onset of a pill 'rush'. For some people it is water or human touch, but for me nothing beats a flurry of wind.

Placebo, one of my favourite bands of all time, came on stage and the dreamlike state magnified. I wanted to stretch my arms as wide as they could reach and rejoice in the moment. Superimposed musical notes began to form against the skyline in my vision, brightly coloured bubblegum cartoons that would pop and disappear. It was bliss.

For the next eight hours Jabba and I would become immersed in the most intense conversation of our lives, sometimes standing in an open field, not looking at anything in particular other than ourselves. We were peaking out of our brains.

Poolhall—Jail—Library

"Far out Lox, I tell you I have never had anything this strong. They call them Riddlers. They're tripstasy, a mix of a trip and an E. You've been very lucky on your first day."

It felt like we were on a carnival ride that had shot off at the highest point of its normal trajectory, now floating around in unchartered territory.

That day totally changed my life – for the better. I opened up about innumerable topics, let the weight of 1000 issues drop to the floor. I discovered that elusive sense of connection.

***   ***   ***

SO that's a not-so-short way of explaining why I've waited impatiently for Cardiff to arrive on my travel schedule. For me, the backdrop to *Human Traffic* and the joyous, liberating sensation of my ecstasy honeymoon go hand-in-hand. One encouraged the other, which then encouraged more re-watchings and more re-indulging.

I don't in any way consider myself a pillhead. I've rarely done it more than five times a year and have a strict rule that I never drop on back-to-back weekends. I understand my job relies on me having a certain degree of clarity and alertness, which I won't sacrifice for the sake of a few laughs.

If I'm to be honest I'm probably at the stage, five years on from that Big Day Out, where I'm chasing the connection sensation again. Everyone is moving on, saving for houses, settling down with girls, allowing themselves to be content with a life serving the system. Conversely, I have this burning hunger for enlightenment and adventure that just won't subside, no matter how many hurdles it puts in the way of a nice, cosy lifestyle.

As much as I'm looking forward to going stark raving bonkers in the Welsh capital, I've been fastidious in my preparations. Via the wonder of the internet I have managed to track down a list of nightclubs and other locations used in the filming of *Human Traffic*. And despite the rain falling relentlessly when I arrive, I make it an immediate task to set out on foot and photograph them all. This little expedition will give me my bearings for the weekend to come.

My trek is met with immediate disappointment. Of the clubs I've researched, three are deleted straight away. Emporium is closed until further notice, Independence no longer exists and Vision has been turned into a budget clothing store. Thankfully, I find two of the others – the proudly Welsh Clwb Ifor Bach and Club X. The former is tucked away in a gritty part of the CBD, used mainly in *Human Traffic* for the alleyway scenes. The latter I discover is one of the biggest gay clubs in Wales.

Along the path I encounter two other interesting drink spots – a hip vodka joint named Moloko (a reference to the fictional drink in *A Clockwork Orange*) and the Prince of Wales Hotel. When I first enter the cavernous Prince of Wales, I am convinced it is the location where the *Human Traffic* characters chant a sarcastic, alternate national anthem reeking of despair. The pub has the same grand staircase and balustrades as in the movie. But when I order a ridiculously cheap pint and ask the barman for confirmation he replies in the negative.

"Nah, that scene was filmed at Gassy Jack's, up past the town."

Oh well, another treasure hunt failure for Berg. One location I cannot mistake or avoid however is Millennium Stadium. It dwarfs the city centre, towers over decaying Cardiff Castle and owns a healthy slice of the River Taff's banks. Along the boardwalk are shiny metal poles with silver dragons clinging to their sides. The Welsh passion for rugby union and its links to the national identity cannot be overstated.

My hostel is in the western shadows of the stadium, and it is there on the first night that I meet a quaint Welsh couple called Timmy and Tammy, along with a big-breasted, blue-eyed girl from Melbourne, Georgia. They invite me out for the night and I am only too keen to jump aboard. After spending the last few weeks catching up with friends and relatives, retracing history and getting whacked on mushrooms in Amsterdam, I have overlooked one of my main duties as a backpacker – pursuing attractive members of the opposite sex. Meeting Audrey in Galway now seems a distant memory.

Alas, it only takes an hour or so to realise Georgia is one of the most self-obsessed and moronic people I have encountered. She dominates conversation with her life's travails, her ditzy exclamations leaving me to seek an excuse to leave. I find an alibi when we switch to an expensive African-themed bar.

"Wow look at these prices. I'm sorry guys, that's me out. I've got a limited budget this weekend."

If there's one thing fellow backpackers understand, it's the importance of stretching your dollars thinly. They hardly question me as I disappear around the corner, not to the hostel, but back to the Prince of Wales where I enjoy a few cheap Brains bitters on tap. I sit alone, disappointed in myself that even on a Friday night without obligations, without any need for a social conscience, I cannot at least attempt to sleep with a girl I don't fancy.

What's the big problem? Everyone else is doing it. Georgia would have done for a mindless fuck. Why bugger around with social snobbery when you're after a blinder of a weekend and saying hell to consequences? I convince myself I will try much harder the following evening, returning home for a deliciously lengthy sleep, horizontal rain battering the window beside my bed.

After a late rise there is only enough time for an afternoon sandwich and an unsatisfying tour of the castle. I can't begin to explain how much I have grown to hate the 'no photo' rule at popular landmarks, particularly those where you aren't informed until after you pay. Of all the injustices in the world, in the shoes of a tourist I feel this is the most heinous.

Nothing shall dampen my spirits completely however, as tonight is the Big Kahuna, Judgment Day. I allow myself an extra hour for exercises in my dorm before I hit the town. The push-ups pump my esteem, as does the arrival of a busload of American girls. Before I know it, I'm dancing my way to the shower, pulling on my favourite lurid striped top like a footballer on his international debut, straightening my hair with guitar-string finesse. The free radicals are going ballistic.

A beer and a read of the local street press in the hostel bar gets me thinking about how to best flow with the night. I desire total symbiosis not only with the city, but the precise people sharing this glorious evening. I cotton onto the idea of a 'choose your own adventure' pub-crawl. I will monitor the assorted groups in the room, select a few that interest me, then subtly follow the first one to make a move. I will repeat this for at least two more venues until I find somewhere likeable and happening. The only condition is that I can never follow the same group in succession.

A group of three American girls and a guy hop up not five minutes later, making their way to the coat stand by the exit. It's my cue to drink up and, without making eye contact, I begin my surreptitious plan. Travelling solo makes you an undeniable loner at times, but tonight is the first time I've felt like a downright stalker. To ease my conscience, I add the additional proviso that I cannot approach any of my targeted groups for conversation. They are merely vessels to link me to new places and other faces.

There's a hiccup on the very first stage of the game when the Americans lead me directly back to the Prince of Wales Hotel. Yet within three more drinks and three more changes of venues the whole charade has worked a treat. I'm standing elated on the central dance floor of Creation, a huge club sprawled over several levels. Old-school Faithless and Underworld tunes are blasting over the speakers and I've been adopted by a bunch of maniacs from Swansea. They've travelled down together for a crazy weekend and they're doing their level best to complete the mission. Exactly the sort of crew I was after.

Poolhall—Jail—Library

Only one issue – while the alcohol is flowing smoothly and I've dispensed with most inhibitions, the avenues for chemical enhancement appear dried up.

"Fucking right, we've tried. If you get onto some be sure to let us know," one of the Swansea lads insists.

At 1am and with the wallet thinning, I decide if I am going to score ecstasy, I want it to be at one of the clubs featured in *Human Traffic*. That will complete the quest. Clwb Ifor Bach intrigued me when I passed it yesterday and was situated in an area where drug consumption seemed a fair-to-even bet. When I perform reconnaissance on the queue, there's a healthy number of 20-somethings, with a good portion of cute and alternate-looking females. Music is thumping out of the closed upstairs windows.

I'm hit with a £9 entry fee at the door, but it proves much more justified than the toll at Cardiff Castle. Two decent deejays – Zero Zero and Sumo – have the final sets of the night and they rip out tune after tune to a densely packed room sweating at the walls. You're allowed to take photos as well.

But instead of taking happy snaps I lose myself in the dancing, free-forming with eyes closed, forgetting everything and anything for an eternity until two girls interrupt.

"Hey I like your shirt. Ooh and your scarf. You aren't Belgian, are you?" says one.

"Belgian? I have to say that's a first. Nobody has ever called me Belgian before. Why do you say that?"

"Oh, you look kind of odd, like quirky. Not a bad thing, I mean. Just, you know, Belgians like to dress weird. I think it's cool."

"Haha. Well thanks. But I'm an Aussie. I guess that's a disappointment?"

The girl slaps me playfully and her friend emits an embarrassed laugh. They continue dancing around me, dragging their other friends across so we form our own enclave.

After more light-hearted banter and an hour or so of dancing, I work up the courage to ask if any of them has a pill. They maintain the rhythm of the beat, subtly shaking their heads in a way that suggests they are neither offended nor encouraged by my question. The music has a stranglehold of them, along with a sense of the night. They've found their level for the evening and are chasing connection and conversation without artificial assistance. We continue to chat away, contorting ourselves in each other's shadows, smiling back and forth.

"Where's the party moving afterwards?" I ask as it heads toward 3am.

"I'm sorry babe, but we're beat. It's home for us soon. Thanks for being great fun," replies the most attentive one.

I wonder if their departure was always in the script. If I'd been more forthright with the romance and less enthusiastic about the ecstasy, would the outcome have been any different? Maybe it's one of those nights where I need to practice contentment. An eight-out-of-ten evening doesn't always have to turn into a ten-out-of-ten.

Warm hugs and kisses on both cheeks follow downstairs at the cab rank. I'm mindful at once of the taxi scene in *Human Traffic*, where my favourite character Moff engages the driver in an obtuse conversation about torture. Taking a lend from De Niro's character in *Taxi Driver*, Moff details how he would love to apply thumb screws to pop singer Peter Andre. Not completely satisfied, he then details a procedure where he would insert a coat hanger in Andre's urethra – the eye of his penis – and crank it circularly to cause maximum pain.

I've not found an E or a girl for the night, so I decide the crowning glory of this once-in-a-lifetime Cardiff bender will be to reconstruct that hilarious exchange. It's only a short walk from Clwb Ifor Bach to my hostel, but I launch into the front seat of a cab with renewed spirits and an indulgent agenda.

"I bet you've watched *Taxi Driver* a million times," I say excitedly, still halfway in the door.

A young Indian man looks back at me from the driver's seat with a fiercely serious gaze.

"I'm sorry, please tell me which taxi driver you are referring to? There are many taxi drivers in Cardiff sir. Which address are we going to?"

His thick accent tells me he has not lived in Wales long. He doesn't exactly fit the mould of the white-haired, weather-beaten cabbie in *Human Traffic,* but I press ahead with the charade all the same.

"Haha. Just having a laugh mate. It's an old movie. Tell you what though, I bet you can't stomach Peter Andre right? Proper prick."

"Sir I do not know what you are talking about. How much have you been drinking tonight?"

"Don't worry about that buddy. It's all above board. Well, I tell you if I ever saw that geezer, I'd have to apply thumb screws, right? I'd gradually wind them up over time...you know, extend the pain like. Then I'd get myself a coat hanger, right, and shove the rusted end down his Jap's eye, ripping it round and round. Proper fuck him up. Then maybe a 12-gauge and it's time to say hello to the almighty. Bye-bye Pete, nobody's gonna' miss you. Boom! What do you say to that?"

The cab driver stares expressionless at the road ahead and accelerates until we are two blocks away from the club. He reluctantly breaks his silence to plead for directions.

"Please sir, the address? And no more talk like this thank you."

"Don't worry I'll hop out here," I say, handing over a fistful of shrapnel, stumbling to the sidewalk and leaving the cabbie mystified.

ENGLISH literature had been Loxton's weakest subject for several years at high school, even though I'd always encouraged my children to write creatively from a young age. Lox was forever butting heads with his old-fashioned teacher Mrs Ramsay, who frequently remarked that his stories and essays were too gruesome or abstract. He, in turn, argued they were factors that shouldn't impact on the work's merit.

Loxton sought and was granted a controversial exemption which saw him transferred to a younger male teacher for the last of his senior schooling. Mr Santini was a stocky, irreverent man in his early 20s who enjoyed sports. The two of them hit it off and Loxton's internal conflicts were transferred into a flourish of imaginative, yet haunting tales.

One of his first assignments in Year 12 was a 500-word story that had to be completed under supervision and without prior planning. Loxton and his classmates had less than two hours to polish it from start to finish. When gradings were handed out, my son had the highest mark of all.

Unbeknown to Lox however, Mr Santini had contacted me on the side. He told me the content of Loxton's story, of a boy who found it impossible to escape his abusive stepfather and was terrified of a mundane future. It ended with him torturing his stepfather and then committing suicide, bashing his own face in with a rock and then diving onto an upright stake on the banks of a creek.

Mr Santini knew as well as I did that Loxton had been spending extended time at the brook behind the school. He was undertaking a complex assignment for geography class which involved him mapping sections of the brook, but he would also stay down there to finish his homework or as a general excuse to avoid being home. Although the theme of Loxton's story didn't shock me, I was at once tearful. Firstly, I was surprised that he would share his feelings so openly and, secondly, I knew how it reflected on my parenting. It felt odd to cry on the *phone to a virtual stranger, but it set in me a resolve to finally seek out help.*

Not a month later Loxton delivered an oral recital in the same class. He wore a wig and read out Kurt Cobain's actual suicide note word-for-word, adopting Cobain's north-western drawl. He stared straight into the eyes of the other students as he echoed the line: "Since the age of seven I've become hateful towards all humans in general."

Mr Santini this time gave him a mediocre mark and warned him about being repetitious in his subject matter. The teacher also phoned me again, telling me how Loxton was at risk of ostracising himself from classmates and becoming an even bigger target than present. Apparently, some kids had started complaining to other teachers that they were getting increasingly 'freaked out' by my son.

By this stage I had already consulted Doug the chaplain about some further counselling or intervention. Mr Santini agreed that he would excuse Loxton from English class for the next few weeks so he could attend sessions with Doug. Although Lox was still not religious in the slightest, he did have an enduring admiration for Doug based on his sense of integrity and appetite for adventure.

The dialogue of these sessions was closely guarded by Loxton. When I pried for information, he said "We just talk about consciousness and perception and stuff. Not everything is about you guys." But I knew he must have discussed the internal workings of our family as he invited – then banished – his sister for counselling. Kim told me Loxton had asked her to corroborate stories about Steve, but Kim refused out of embarrassment. My son considered this treachery and the air between the two of them at home became incredibly tense.

Then it happened that I had an argument with Steve at home on a Sunday night. He hit me twice across the face on the same cheek. All hell broke loose. It felt like we were one of those ghetto families people made fun of on TV. I asked

Loxton to allow me to come to his next session with Doug, so I could verify the stories of abuse at home. It was my way of forcing myself into a position I couldn't back out of. I didn't want to go straight to the police, but I knew I had been far too lenient on Steve's behaviour in the past. Family counselling had to happen.

Loxton saw my cooperation as ammunition in a final firefight to rid the house of Steve.

"You know what you've done…it will never be forgotten," he chastised Steve at the dinner table in the days following.

My husband stared over at me and barked, "Great, Loxton thinks he can't be punished now. He's free to carry on how he likes. Are you ever going to discipline these kids?"

"There's a difference between proper discipline and just smacking people in the head for the fun of it," Loxton interjected.

"I know your plan," Steve replied. "You're going to make me hit you and then call the cops. That's how selfish you are. You don't care what happens to this family. What will happen to Bobby and the twins when you tear everything apart?"

Loxton exploded with unprecedented rage, throwing his chair out from beneath him and standing over the table.

"When I tear everything apart??! How do I 'make' you hit me in the head??! You are absolutely flogging yourself Steve."

"What did you say?"

"You are flogging yourself. That is dead-set the biggest load of shit I have ever heard. You live in a fucking fantasy world. It's totally amazing…do you even realise when you've done something wrong?"

Steve jumped up at once and clipped Loxton straight across the jaw, then rushed him backwards onto the sharp corner of our deep freezer. As the pain washed over Loxton's face, he twisted and swung his stepfather by the shirt until he slammed head-first into the wall. The manoeuvre allowed him enough room to escape out the door and down the driveway.

"That's it. You're never coming back. Never. Find yourself a new place shit-for-brains," Steve bellowed after him.

From that moment we didn't see Loxton for the next two nights.

COPENHAGEN // MALMO

I'M halfway through writing a letter to home when my stomach takes command, forcing me outside to seek sustenance. It's my fourth day of six in Copenhagen, the Danish capital. Denmark is much like the Isle of Skye to me – it's always had an innate draw which can't easily be explained. In my mind it feels like a place of fantasy, of purity, of social progression and extremely beautiful people. It feels like somewhere I need to see before I can begin knowing myself better.

If I delve into that very corner of my soul which believes in reincarnation, I start thinking this sensation of belonging is embedded in a long Viking bloodline. But when I snap back to reality and admit my own shallowness, I consider the sense of wonder was most likely born from many visits to Lego exhibitions as a child. Those long-gone Lego shows featured an intricate recreation of Copenhagen which entirely captivated me. Would that be enough to motivate me 20 years later to spend a small fortune organising flights and a week's holiday in a rather expensive destination? Quite possibly.

I'm loving the city for a number of reasons, among them the array of culinary delights offered. The Danish have an abundance of fantastic fish dishes, delectable sweets and a plethora of pastry goods that I wouldn't normally indulge in. On this afternoon, however, I choose a humble tuna roll from a deli around the corner and trundle back toward my comfy hostel, the aptly named Sleep Inn Heaven.

As I walk the pavement, unwrapping the roll and pressing it to my lips, I feel a shower of ash dumped on me from above. Immediately I begin to anger. What timing! I look at the chimney stacks above and then at my jacket to see if the cinder has burnt any holes. It's a strange ash, fluffy and easily dispersed. I brush it from my clothes and my lunch as I continue to satisfy this burning hunger. The ash grows heavier and heavier until I begin jogging to escape it.

Mid-stride it dawns upon me. I feel completely stupid. This is not ash. It's snow. Finally, after 27 years on this planet and two months in Europe I've finally experienced my first snowfall. To the average man it may not seem much, but it sweeps across me as some sort of boastful achievement. From the burning summers of infancy in Australia, I've followed my heart to a place where ice falls from the sky. Snow is as foreign to me as it would be to a Saharan.

I cannot wipe the smile from my face as I return to writing my letter. The large windows at the front of the hostel allow me to view the snow building up, cloaking the spire of the nearby church, providing a soft pleat to the gutters, enticing children to scramble for handfuls and take aim at one another.

On reception at the hostel is a bearded Danish introvert who is delighting in not only playing 70s and 80s glam rock over the stereo, but has also ingeniously inserted Magic Dirt's *Plastic Loveless Letter* to his playlist. It makes for a perfect moment of culture clash and sentimentality, thrusting the foreign wonder of the present up against the familiar soundtrack to heartbreak I enjoyed at home.

I give the emo the thumbs up and he calls me over.

"You know Christmas beers?"

"Not really. I've heard of them, but never tried them."

"This is a very big thing for us in Denmark. We brew with many flavours. Sometimes strange. This year we have chocolate and licorice beer for Christmas. You should try."

With that he slides from the reception area to the adjoining bar and pulls a half-pint. I'm now sitting in Copenhagen, watching the snow fall, listening to Magic Dirt and enjoying a free chocolate beer. Life doesn't get much better.

Enter Mia, a blonde Finnish student who checks into my room somewhere around the third chocolate beer and an afternoon nap. She's an architecture student from Helsinki, in town following her favourite rock band – Larsen and Furious Jane. For a Finn she is quite short; an elfin pocket rocket with bobbed hair, soft voice and curves in the appropriate anatomical locations.

Mia apologises for stirring me from my kip and, after exchanging pleasantries, we talk for more than an hour of our various travel and musical interests. All sunlight has disappeared when she glances down at her watch.

"Oh shit. You will excuse me? I must get changed."

"Not a problem," I say, waving her off and reclining again into my pillow.

Yet instead of leaving the room to disrobe, Mia stands not more than a metre away and slips her t-shirt over her head, exposing her spotless cream complexion and a white bra overflowing at the cup. She unclips the bra at the back and lets it fall to the ground, leaving me a complete, unhindered side profile of her breasts. Calmly she rummages through her backpack until she finds a towel to wrap around and conceal the magnificent orbs. As if suddenly discovering a sense of modesty, she smirks bashfully, gathers fresh underpants, a blouse and jeans and climbs onto the bunk above me to complete the change out of eyesight.

Still, she is barely an arm's length away, obscured only by the mattress. My imagination is working overtime, picturing her contorting to allow the pants over her ankles, sliding them along her thighs and then bringing them to rest against a picture-perfect stomach.

In the words of one of Queensland's most revered footballers, Chris 'Choppy' Close: I've got a horn that could scare a small dog out from underneath a parked car.

I'm well aware that Scandinavians are more liberal when it comes to nudity, but allow myself a brief few seconds to entertain the thought that she is giving me a signal. Not long departed from Wales and my anti-climactic night in Cardiff, I'm convinced I have become incapable of reading women. Any true red-blooded male must live in constant hope, yet past rejections and miscalculations always weigh heavily on the mind.

Mia shimmies off the top bunk and I half-close my eyes in the pretense that she has again woken me from my slumber.

"Well I'm going to eat down at Pussy Galore's Flying Circus with some friends," she says, as I bite the inside of my lip even harder. "Have fun tonight, whatever you're doing."

"Ah I think I'll go catch a live band at Stengade 18. It's a club I checked out the other night. Good vibe."

"Really? That's where Larsen and Furious Jane are playing. Well enjoy. I might see you there."

And with that Mia flits off into the night as I take the imagery of her topless body to the shower with me.

I'm not long back from finishing my rigorous exercise and digesting dinner when Mia bursts in through the door.

"Forgot my ID," she proclaims, quickly locating it and then turning for the exit once more.

"Actually, I'm just about to walk down to Stengade myself. Do you mind if I walk with you?" I suggest.

"Umm yeah...okay...that is fine," replies Mia with unexpected hesitancy.

We chat effortlessly on the way to the club and inside I buy her two drinks, though she protests. Throughout the support act (which is much too country'n'western for my liking) Mia frequently disappears down the side of the stage. I feign ambivalence and alternate between surveying the room for other talent and discordantly tapping my feet to the beat.

Convinced I need to take command of the situation, I follow Mia to her spot near the stage as the support act winds up. I ask her what she thought of the first band, trying to do my best impression of a shrewd music connoisseur.

"Fantastic," she says bluntly, only momentarily glancing over her shoulder at me.

She has both hands wrapped around the base of a camera and stares intently at the downlights near the stage entrance.

When the first member of Larsen and Furious Jane walks out, she goes all kinds of mental. As the guitarist follows, Mia near explodes, jumping up and down, thrashing her head about and screaming like a hyena. The band settles on stage. Mia and the guitarist exchange several looks, some of which seem like pleasant recognition and others which appear like wary observation.

As much as Mia madly tries to attract his attention and slams her finger down on the camera shutter, the guitarist begins to peruse the room, initiating eye contact with others and then bringing his brow low to convey immersion in the music. Mia grows frustrated and petulant, huffing and shaking her head as his attention wanders elsewhere. She has lost all the casual cool she held back in the dorm in the hours of the afternoon.

I try once or twice to chat with her during the opening half of the gig, but she is a lost cause. Quite sadly Mia is a desperate, slightly unhinged fangirl, pure and simple.

Leaving her and weaving my way back to the bar, I make a conscious decision. Yes, I can grow further disillusioned with the female species and lament my ability to convert spirited conversation into amorous encounters. Or I can recapture that same vibe I felt hours earlier when the snow began to fall, the tunes were top-notch and the chocolate ale did its magic. Fuck it, I'm here in a city I've always wanted to visit, young, fit and single and surrounded by Danish girls who dig indie pop. Hold your head high brother and march on.

Now standing tall at the back of the room with a pint in one hand and the other hand resting nonchalantly in my pocket, I'm disturbed almost immediately by a tattooed siren. Dragging a shorter friend behind her, the tall and slender banshee brushes past my crotch and then holds up her intricately inked sleeve as if to apologise. I shrug off her apology and say "It's okay", but she doesn't look at me again until she is 10m away, grinding against her friend on the dancefloor. She faces away from the stage amid the swaying throng, fixing her heavily shadowed eyes on mine. It seems likes minutes pass and then she twists her hands mid-dance in a movement to beckon me over.

I take the opportunity to play hard-to-get, simply smiling back, then looking away from her toward the stage. In the 15 minutes that follow, I glance back at her a handful of times, hold the line of vision, give her the best brood I can summon and then look sharply away. It's a tense game.

As the band is finishing up and packing away, the stagehands blast a CD over the speakers. It's New Order. Only a few bars into the track I spy Mia moving quickly towards the exit, flustered and with tears streaming down her face. What a fruitcake. I might have dodged a bullet on that one.

Suddenly my beer-holding arm is yanked at the elbow and I turn, expecting to see the inked goddess of my previous flirtations. Instead it's a much plainer looking lass, still with a cute face, but less striking and intriguing than my earlier target.

"I want to introduce you to my sister. She says you're handsome. I think you should come," the girl says in delightfully nervous English.

I'm led right down to the very front of the dance floor, hemmed between the now-abandoned stage and the stampede of people either heading home or seeking beverages.

In the corner stands a petite girl, her face shrouded in jet black hair and only illuminated by the mobile phone she is texting on. When she looks up, a lump immediately forms in my throat. She is the goddess lovechild of Snow White and Winona Ryder in her prime. Her face is pure symmetry, the features of a doll, highlighted tastefully by bright red lipstick and ladybug earrings, and offset by the feistiest of stares.

"You speak English?" she shoots.

"Yes. Well done...how could you possibly know that?"

"You were standing near us at the start of the show. Was that your friend or girlfriend?"

"Wow. You're really good at this interrogation stuff. What if I say she was neither?"

"My name is Mia," she replies, extending her hand sarcastically and smiling.

"Wait, another Mia?"

"Yeah, like M-I-A."

"I get it. It's just the other girl before was..."

"She doesn't matter now. So where are you from?"

I look around to see if the tall tattooed girl is still dancing. She has moved only a few paces behind us with her friend. She is giving Mia No. 2 the evil eye and I feel a total fraud. These two hot women should not be competing for the attention of one giant goofball.

"I'm from Australia...Brisbane if you know where that is. Anyway, it's a pleasure to meet you but I have to duck to the bathroom."

It's only half a lie. I do go to the bathroom first, but then sneak through the fire exit to the upstairs level to clear my head, assess my options and remove any overt signs of eagerness. New Order is still playing and I recognise the track sequencing. It's *International,* one of the favourite albums in my collection back home.

Switching from beer to whiskey, I stand near the window and look down at the snow-covered street. The same phenomenon is happening as the night before, when I drank at a downtown pub with an American backpacker called Hannibal. Just before 1am the streets become flooded with gorgeous women riding pushbikes, artfully gripping beverages while balancing their long legs and five layers of clothing on two wheels. Apparently, it is standard procedure in Denmark to only leave home and go clubbing after midnight. It strikes me as one of nature's great spectacles – like a school of fluorescent reef fish heading naively as one into the deep blue sea.

In Australia the idea of a girl on a bike drinking a beer in the witching hours conjures up all sorts of rough, negative images. In Denmark, where clothing is less revealing, where bicycles are classically styled, it seems an act of grace.

I snap out of my poetic musings as the New Order CD hits track 07 – *Bizarre Love Triangle*. It's literally time to face the music and make a fist of things downstairs. Descending the staircase, I see the tattooed girl and her friend now dancing provocatively with two boys. Mia No 2 and her sister have also been joined by an eager gent, though he is paying more attention to the sister.

I slide into the narrow strip of dancefloor that separates the two groups and dance with my eyes almost shut, feigning general disinterest, doing my best to appear supple and measured, not drunk and socially retarded. Five minutes in and Mia No 2 slaps her palm forcefully into my chest.

"So, they serve drinks in the toilets now? Where did you go?" she inquires, motioning at the glass still in my hand.

I stare back at her from 20cm away, eyes locked, engaged in mutual contempt and rocketing tension. This Mia is almost a full foot shorter than me and I can smell the floral essence of her hiply-styled hair as she delivers me attitude from below.

In one seamless, gliding movement she latches onto my bottom lip, biting her front teeth slowly across the surface, as if peeling the skin of a plum. Her hands grip my forearms and she stands on tip-toes for another taste. Tugging my collar firmly, she presses her chin deep into mine. Then we both pull away and continue dancing as if we were complete strangers.

Occasionally I drift closer to the tattooed girl, who is happy to play along with the flirtatious charade. But again and again I am compelled to smile in Mia No 2's direction. She has a hold of me now, and I of her.

The deft bass of Peter Hook strums enchantingly as *Crystal* bursts into full gallop. We both advance towards each other, brought together in that delusory affectionate state which confuses itself as destiny.

Later I struggle to remember exactly where it was that we exchanged each morsel of our lives; the bits about her being a basketball point guard, a first-year graduate nurse, still living at home with her parents. I detail to her my movements around her city, from the hippy commune in Christiania, to the art galleries and Little Mermaid statue by the docks, to the beautiful cemetery of Assistens, and a day trip across the bridge to Malmo in Sweden.

But share it all, we do; some words spoken at the club, some spoken on the walk home, some in the secretive enclave of her bedroom. In the morning Mia No.2 offers her number and invites me to come watch her play basketball. I truthfully tell her I don't carry a phone overseas and I leave the country in 24 hours. Perfect. There's no chance for me to screw it up.

Poolhall—Jail—Library

BY the time Loxton returned home after his stint on the run, he was already boasting to schoolmates that he was homeless and roughing it on the streets. No doubt he thought it made him look tough, even though the truth was he had been sleeping on the school hockey fields and in the reeds by the brook, covering himself with a tarpaulin and plastic bags. It was hardly the shady backblocks of the Bronx. He'd even used an outside washing machine at a friend's house to clean his uniform. This, Loxton confessed to me when he came crashing through the door two days after disappearing, using the spare key at a time when he knew Steve would already be working.

I'd not slept much more than a few winks the whole time Lox had been away. During that period, I had plenty of time to decide on a course of action for when my son decided to show his face.

"You know Loxton it breaks my heart to say this, but you're going to have to leave home. We can't keep going this way."

"Right, so I'm leaving, not Steve? That makes sense," my son replied sarcastically.

"I've convinced your Nan and Grandad to let you stay at their place for a few months."

"Convinced...convinced? I'm sorry I'm such a fucking burden on everybody. I can't for the life of me figure out why it's got to this stage. Can you?"

"That's enough Loxton. If you had any idea how much it hurts me to do this, you wouldn't carry on this way."

Loxton tried to shield his face as he began silently weeping.

"Fine Mum. You know I've actually dreamt about this day for close to 10 years now. I'm so glad it's finally happening."

With that, Lox upped and left for his room, packing half-a-dozen boxes with his belongings.

My father soon drove up to the house and Loxton filled the car boot, tears still streaming down his cheek.

"No point whimpering about it now. What's done is done," Dad said to Lox, who then slid into the passenger's side and avoided all eye contact.

As devastating as that day was, it was to be the making of Loxton. Though he phoned me several times a week and occasionally visited, he very much became his own man. Lox not once spoke to – or of – Steve for the remainder of the year. Indeed, he would berate me if I ever raised the prospect of the two of them reconciling.

My parents gave Loxton free reign of the entire downstairs level of their house, where he had his own shower, stove and fridge. He paid them $25 a week for his food and board, straight from a government allowance for studying and living out of home. In all respects he was treated not as their grandson, but as a lodger and an independent adult.

The day Loxton left home was the last day he missed school until he graduated. Lox became forged by a resolve to succeed in the face of his circumstance – and no doubt a desire to leave egg on the faces of both Steve and myself. It was Loxton's decision alone to continue his schooling and, unlike others in the same situation, he became obsessive about his grades rather than ignoring them.

Due to his shift to Gordon Park he now had to catch two buses to school and two home each day. He had little scope for visiting friends from the Stafford Heights neighbourhood. All energies and interests became entirely focused. From a noticeable lull in results before he left home, he aced the last three terms, winning both the geography and mathematics awards for his class.

Queensland schools judge their students on an OP (Overall Position), which compares them with other children of the same year around the State. An OP1 is considered best, while an OP25 is the lowest one can receive. Some children may not receive an OP at all if they elect to follow practical, rather than academic, forms of training. Loxton received an OP4, which in a modest school like Everton Park, made him the second-best student in his grade.

Over the course of the year his choice of future career had switched dramatically from becoming an environmental scientist or cartographer to a newfound aspiration as a journalist. Reasoning that he needed a job which would provide variety every day, Loxton was no doubt influenced by his literary mentoring under Mr Santini. An OP6 was the minimum qualifying mark for journalism at Lox's chosen university, leading to ecstatic celebrations at his final grading. Yet there were some misgivings from the wider family, who had hoped he would be swayed towards an interest in the navy and follow in his grandfather's footsteps.

"Why study journalism? You're never going to be a journalist," his Uncle Howard commented.

Loxton, still idolising his uncle and now living under the same roof as him, took it as a particularly stinging remark. Too young to see it as a statement from someone with a total lack of faith in shaping the world, Loxton considered it a blunt assessment of his own personal value. He'd been hanging around his uncle daily in the absence of friends his age, copying all of Howard's depressing punk rock CDs onto cassette and talking cynically of anything and everything. Underneath it all, Loxton had been sure until then that his closest confidant held some sort of belief in his ability.

That insult – combined with another episode around December – exhumed the fiery, tempestuous Loxton that had lain dormant for eight months, buried beneath his books. Loxton attended the graduation dinner with his long-time crush Macy, and the two were regularly linking up at parties, going to the cinema and exchanging mixed tapes. I could never work out if they were actually a couple or whether the affection came totally from Loxton's direction.

The answer to that conundrum came on school-leavers' week, when Loxton and his schoolmates holidayed at Noosa on the Sunshine Coast to celebrate the end of their enforced education. One of my son's best friends for the last three years was Milton, a floppy-haired, freckled prankster who played in the same rugby league team. Milton's father was coach of the team and his mother became one of my better friends in time. In many respects, Loxton adopted them as a second family and the two boys were close to inseparable.

That came to an abrupt end however on the second night in Noosa when Lox arrived back at their apartment and found Macy and Milton in bed together. Not in just any bed either. They were in Loxton's designated room, the one he had paid extra for, dipping into his slender funds in the hope he might impress his crush enough to bring his virginity to an end.

The following morning Loxton rang me, partly to ask for advice and partly to vent. He said he wanted to "knock Milton's head off", but at the same time felt like vomiting. He'd spent the night attempting to sleep on the cold kitchen floor and sounded not at all stable. As Loxton and Macy were not officially together, he had little avenue to object what had taken place and, instead, he opted to sharply remove Milton from his life. For the remainder of Schoolies Week Lox stayed with other friends at their apartment nearer the beach, feeling no need to explain the shift, leaving Milton to reach his own conclusions.

It was at that point that Loxton began drinking heavily, reasoning that sobriety had earned him nothing else save aside academic results. He had been asked to leave home, lost his best friend and his pseudo girlfriend, and was not attracting the interest of any football scouts. From a disciple of the utmost stringent lifestyle, he wavered erratically to a reckless drunk. Lox rebounded from one extreme to the other.

Before Schoolies ended he was found naked in a stairwell, bleeding unconscious on top of a broken beer bottle, reportedly after running away from security guards. That form continued through to Lox arriving back in Brisbane, when my parents reported him sleeping for 17 hours straight.

Poolhall—Jail—Library

A week after returning, Milton's mother rang me to say that Loxton had punched her son several times at a pool party hosted by one of their football friends. Apparently, he had been abusive towards several others on the same night, including yelling nonsensically at Macy and engaging in a street fight with a stranger he accused of dealing drugs. Although I knew what was behind Loxton's frustration, I pleaded ignorance to Milton's mother. It wasn't my place.

Not one to do things in moderation, Loxton continued on this same path through the summer months that followed school. The rapid upsurge in partying required an immediate boost to funds. So, for the first time in his life, Lox secured a proper paying job. I say 'proper' job because he had previously worked at his Uncle Craig's video game store in his early teens, but spent most of his time either playing games or eating food. There had been an acrimonious end to his days at Craig's store, when Steve ordered Loxton to cease working so he could spend more time with the family, something which never eventuated – or ever seemed likely in the first place.

Loxton's new job was at a McDonald's restaurant near the city centre. My son reasoned that it was one of the few roles that would allow him the flexibility of shifts so he could attend university and continue his football ambitions. There was also a suspicion on his part that his Nan and Grandad wanted him out of their house due to his lively weekend activities. This I knew to be partly justified, as my parents expressed dismay at Loxton's eroding fortitude and willingness to help around the home.

I could see that Lox was frustrated within himself at how fast he had let things slip, yet he seemingly had no means to reel in his behaviour. He became shorter and sharper towards me and multiplied his ill feelings towards Kim. His sister had remarked openly at how things had been better at home since Loxton left and he saw this as betrayal, interpreting it as a desire to have him gone and a total compliance with Steve. Kim and I also grew extremely close at this stage and she acted much as a second mother to the twins. Lox was resentful in many ways of our bond.

What had been boiling for months finally reached a head just before university was due to start. Loxton received a letter telling him he needed to pay a fee of $115 before he could attend classes. At this stage he had not been paid for the few weeks he had worked at McDonald's and had not been forewarned of the expense. Loxton became convinced that nobody would lend him the money because he had fallen from favour. And in his mind, the situation became so contorted that he would be expelled from university. He worked himself to a histrionic frenzy and my parents called me over because of concerns for his state of mind.

It had been a huge ambition of Loxton's to become the first kid on either side of the family to complete university. He'd somehow lost sight of the fact that it was also a major goal of mine for close to 20 years. I would find a way for him to have the money by whatever means possible. But this, amid the hypersensitive state Loxton had reached, became the sticking point. He wouldn't accept money from me on the grounds that Steve was the sole income provider in our house. Loxton reasoned that any funds I contributed would be tainted with the scent of the man he hated most and owed the least to. Pride painted Lox into such a tight corner that he gave no avenue for the situation to be resolved, entirely at his own detriment.

"And that's how this is. There is no fucking solution. Do you see why any of this is unfair yet Mum? I'm the one that gets beat around. I'm the one that has to leave home. I'm the one that doesn't have a family. I'm the one who doesn't see his own brothers and sisters grow up. I'm the one that works my fucking arse off and then gets told my ambitions will not happen."

I tried reasoning again that I would pay the uni fees, but he was not having a bar of it. Shocked by the language echoing around his corridors Loxton's grandfather ordered him to button up. With that Lox grew even more upset, bolted off *and grabbed the spare keys from the kitchen, locking himself underneath the house so that nobody could reach him.*

Feeling a weight of regret at inflaming the situation, Dad trundled downstairs and sat patiently knocking on the door, combating the dirgy music emanating from inside.

"Lox, Lox, I'm sorry ma' boy. Your Nan and I will give you back your rent money for the past month. It's your own money that will put you into university, nobody else's. If you want to pay us back later you can. It will all work out square."

Somehow this ticked all the boxes for Loxton's conscience to relent.

He opened the door, barely able to hold his own weight, hyperventilating, topless and with a rusted paint scraper resting on the window ledge beside him, the razor protruding.

NEUSCHWANSTEIN

BEING stood over and chastised by a German guard is a scenario I've imagined since childhood. It has its roots in the dozens of old war films my Grandad and Uncle Howard watched repeatedly in their darkened lounge room. I'd always dreamt about how I would react if transported back in time. Would I be heroic and defiant, or would I crumble and be compliant? There's irrefutable proof of how Grandad handled the situation. His deeds in the Second World War will carry on for eternity. For the rest of the men in our family, there's always that lingering question mark of whether we can ever reach that great zenith of masculinity.

I'm about to find out though. The German guard, far from pleased, is sternly asking for my documents. Already jittery, I slide my passport from its sleeve and present it for inspection.

"Und ticket?" he barks.

I shake my head slowly from side-to-side. I had to make a hurried dash from the airport at Friedrichshafen to my train bound for Munich. There was not enough time for me to decipher the ticketing instructions on the uncovered platform, my extremities frozen and my brain struggling to remember Grade 9 German language class.

"Sprechen sie Englisch?" the train guard sighs.

I nod.

"You must have ticket or you hop off the train! Do you have money?"

"Yes I always planned to pay...," I say feebly as the guard instantly dismisses my reply and instead holds out his hand.

It's another 40-something Euros to add to more than 300 I have spent in botched flight plans trying to get here. I originally had a flight straight into Munich, but arrived at the airport at 7pm for a 7am check-in. Rookie error. With the rest of my itinerary set in stone and funds low, I had a long night tossing and turning, deciding whether to admit defeat and return to

London in preparation for the last part of my trip. Thinking that I may never have a second opportunity, I elected to book another – very expensive – flight the following morning – this morning. All planes to Munich were booked solid, but I did find a space on the first flight to Friedrichshafen, 200km west of my desired destination, at a premium price of course.

The screensaver for my home computer has displayed the same picture for the past two years. It's an autumn shot of Neuschwanstein Castle, at the very southern end of Bavaria's 'Romantic Road'. This monument to extravagance has come to embody the motives behind my trip. It radiates history, elegance, mystery, scandal, a desire for peace, eccentricity, passion and the power of dreaming big.

If I didn't find a way to Neuschwanstein it would leave a massive hole in my trek; as if it were without reason. It's the single most important destination on the list. To not reach it would be a sign that I was, regardless of every other pretense, still willing to accept failure.

Thankfully the Train Nazi steers clear after he collects my ticket fee and I can kick back for the ride alongside Lake Constance to Lindau and then into the heart of Bavaria. Snow is lush in these parts and there are few signs of life near to the tracks. At a town with a name much too long to remember, we are ordered to disembark and wait an hour for a smaller, slower connecting train to Füssen. I shuffle constantly to try and keep some warmth in my feet, eventually spending what few coins remain in my pocket on a hot pastry and coffee at the adjoining kiosk.

The ride into Füssen, a picturesque town under the jagged shadows of the Alps and Austrian border, becomes increasingly glacial, although simultaneously spectacular. Spired rooftops, dark forests and eerie black lakes assemble before the horizon marches steadfastly into the mountains. The snail's pace of the train builds a sense of anticipation and, as it comes to rest at its destination, I spring onto the narrow streets with haste.

In nearly all destinations I have pre-arranged accommodation in advance or sought it as soon as possible upon arrival. However, there is an excitement at Füssen that leads me to lug both backpacks aimlessly for more than an hour. I weave my way around the hubbub of Reichenstrasse up toward Hohes Schloss Füssen (The High Castle) and then lose myself exploring St Mang's Basilica with its giant frescos. Everything is spick and span. Rubbish and graffiti seemingly don't exist in this picture-perfect community.

Past the basilica at the beginnings of the Lech River, there is a moment that I wish I could bottle, for a photograph does not do it justice. With fresh mountain air zipping past my nostrils, I walk down the springy green banks towards the water's edge. The water has a transparency and turquoise nature needing to be seen with naked eyes to be believed. It radiates in such a way that everything surrounding appears to glow, like a liquid jewel trickling wealth and wonder through Füssen's fingertips. Two logs covered with snow suddenly slide off the banks, a display reminiscent of seals gracefully slicing the Arctic water. There is a slight echo and then silence.

After a lengthy pause to absorb the scene, I meander back into town and find a bed and breakfast not long past nightfall. The owner speaks minimal English, so I make a concerted effort to unearth some of that long-lost German tuition. The agreed price is above normal budget, but worth it for a king bed, a heated room to myself and a view to the Alps. I defrost under the doona and fall asleep to television coverage of the European Handball Championships – the women's showdown between Germany and Denmark to be specific.

***   ***   ***

HOHENSCHWANGAU Castle is an essential precursor to Neuschwanstein. For one price you can buy tickets to both and they are only a short walk or horse-drawn buggy ride apart. Hohenschwangau is the less impressive of the two castles, but

Poolhall—Jail—Library

it is here where the dramatic tale of King Ludwig II begins. In advance of my visit I've been reading up on Ludwig and come to find him decidedly fascinating.

Our tour guide for the day, a short, cute blonde with a knitted beanie and mittens, garnishes my existing bank of knowledge with her own gems. Ludwig was raised in Hohenschwangau, eldest son of King Maximillan II of Bavaria and Queen Marie of Prussia. As a child he was described as imaginative, withdrawn and somewhat obtuse, preferring the company of his grandfather to that of his birth parents. In adulthood he held a friendship and obsession with the great composer Richard Wagner which still attracts much speculation. Often Ludwig is referred to as the 'Mad King'.

Engaged at the age of 21 to his cousin, the eccentric prince postponed his marriage several times before officially calling off all wedding plans. His first love, if not Wagner, was his sense of wonderment and ability to become entirely immersed in art, specifically poetry, opera and architecture. He also identified heavily with nature, particularly the swan.

Ludwig II's grand vision for Neuschwanstein was no doubt influenced by his love of medieval folklore, romanticism and fantasy. The guide contends that Neuschwanstein's exact position, upon a ridge that can be viewed from the main bedroom at Hohenschwangau, was meant as a tribute to his father, who died shortly before its construction began. Ludwig had an image of his father waking up each day to see this splendid creation in his honour – or so the guide's story goes.

I'm more inclined to think the second grand castle was inspired by more self-serving reasons. Ludwig inherited King Maximillan's bedroom after his death, so the vista of Neuschwanstein taking shape was solely his. Indeed, it was the death of his father and grandfather four years apart that made available the funds for Neuschwanstein's construction.

In a letter to Wagner before the first mound was turned, Ludwig told of his desire to live in the very location where the new castle would sit, describing it as "one of the most beautiful (places) to be found, holy and unapproachable".

This I thoroughly appreciate as I complete the journey on foot between the two castles, coming to Neuschwansteins's resting place by the side of the Pollat Gorge. A warning sign and temporary fence to my right block the pathway to the uppermost lookout. DANGER – ICE – DO NOT ENTER says the English translation. Yet I know this to be the only spot where the most spectacular profile of the castle can be viewed.

I deliberate momentarily, judging the distance to the jacketed guards and the depth of grip on my shoes. As my decision is reached, two male Brazilian backpackers behind me also lurch for the fence. All three of us are over the fence and running up the snowed-over track in the blink of an eye. The tallest of the castle guards runs towards us, but he cannot catch up.

"Come back! Come ba-a-a-ck!" he shouts in Schwarzenegger tone as we giggle hysterically and draw sharp breaths from the winter air.

A few hundred metres up the hillside we come to a set of stairs that is metres deep in snow and ice. Together we climb around it by latching on to a series of trees growing from a rocky ledge. Soon it becomes evident that we have cornered ourselves on the very edge of the gorge, staring at a sheer drop to stone and gravel below. But a glance back at the castle gives a blissful view.

With minimal room to move, I reach behind into my bag for the camera and wobble nervously on my feet as I try to capture the perfect shot. Suddenly one of the Brazilian boys grabs my waist.

I react immediately, twisting and glaring at him.

"Relax," he says, first gesturing at my feet sliding toward the edge and then up at the castle. "Get your photo."

Realising he only means to assist, I take a good half-dozen frames before we carefully swap positions and I hold him steady while he produces his camera. When it is done, the two Brazilians let out a wild 'Woooo' into the abyss and we exchange high fives.

Backtracking, we dive into the snowy staircase as if it were a play pit, sinking to the depth of our knees and laughing. We continue on a direction away from the castle and come to a footbridge across where there would normally be a towering waterfall. Briefly we stop for more photos before crossing to the other side.

"You like?" one of the South Americans asks while appearing to point towards the castle.

"Yes, very much. It's an amazing place hey?" I reply.

"No, not the castle," he says, shaking his wrist again to draw attention to his hand. Then I see, pressed between his forefingers, a tightly rolled marijuana joint.

"Oh, I see," I chuckle. "Actually, thanks very much, but I'm okay."

The boys grin and shrug their shoulders, before indicating they will continue along the walkway to a higher position in the trees. I've spied another narrow ledge that juts out into the gorge – barely enough for two feet to stand on – and it gives a photographic angle both of the castle and the previous vantage point. I decide if I can align both in the same picture, it will provide me the perfect story to tell in reflection

King Ludwig II himself did not live long enough to witness this figment of his imagination reach completion. After the cost of his project multiplied twofold and his rule over the kingdom slipped to a tenuous position, he was formally deposed on the grounds of insanity. With scaffolding still erected and many key touches needing to be made, Ludwig spent less than 180 days residing in unfinished Neuschwanstein before a forced departure. A day after fleeing he was found dead in the shallow waters of Lake Starnberg with no apparent signs of physical distress or water in his lungs. Debate still rages as to whether he took his own life or was the victim of assassination.

Though Ludwig's closest allies described the demise as horrific and reflected on an existence misunderstood, in many ways it was what the 'Mad King' had courted all along. His desire to become an eternal enigma was granted, albeit at the highest cost.

Perched on the ledge, I wonder what will become of my legacy.

Poolhall—Jail—Library

INITIALLY Loxton found university to be intimidating. His course was filled with 110 students, all of whom ranked in the top 15 per cent of scholars in the State. There was an entire subject assessed on computer skills alone, something Lox felt aggrieved at, given we had never owned a computer and it was a 40-minute journey each way for him to use the university's computer lab. He viewed this as another injustice, a universal conspiracy, designed to prevent him from fulfilling his dream.

Defiant as ever, he would often catch the last bus into town and stay overnight at the university campus so he could monopolise use of the computers and bring his skills up to scratch. Any obstacle put in his way resulted in anger, then a fierce determination to prove people wrong. In his mind, it was him against the world. It was a mindset that served a useful purpose, but disconnected him from any suggestion of being approachable.

When Loxton walked the streets, he would grit his teeth, stare through people like they were dead and clench his fists as he strode to his next destination or objective. To insulate himself from any further pain, he became a robot, completely apathetic to the emotions of everybody else. He didn't conceive anybody could have problems as deep as his, or that anybody else may need a helping hand.

Shutting himself off was his chosen method of survival. Others described him as intimidating and heartless, but when I raised this with him, he flatly denied the accusation. It was if he had an inability to see his actions from anybody else's perspective. If Loxton had been socially awkward in his youth, his aggression in this period only served to isolate him more from potential friends, work contacts, love interests etcetera. He told me he found it difficult at this point to even relate to other people in his rugby league team, often snapping at them and avoiding team get-togethers and teamwork activities.

Within a few months of starting university and saving money from his job, Loxton decided he would move out of his grandparents' house. He shifted to a share house not far from our family home at Stafford Heights, close to his old school friends, but far enough away to keep us at arm's length.

Despite attempts to close the distance geographically with his old pals, it was apparent that Loxton was heading in a different direction at this time. While he was immersed in study, daydreaming of becoming a world-famous journalist, his high school clique mainly engaged in blue collar professions. One became a locksmith, another enrolled in the army, one became a mechanic and yet another turned to plumbing.

At university, Loxton befriended a group of four other boys who were much more academically-minded, but also infallibly irreverent. He had warmed to them after an introductory assignment which tasked all the students with writing a serious news story based on their first lecture. The four boys – Cameron, Dylan, Tiny and Magnus – stood up and delivered an oration that poked fun at everybody else in the room, directly quoting students they had overheard gossiping and noting one classmate who seemed obsessed with the legs of a girl sitting in the front row. Loxton thought it was side-splitting stuff, although his sense of humour and mine rarely correlated.

Mostly though, Loxton found his other uni classmates to be too dour and pompous, so he gravitated towards his McDonald's co-workers as a kind of middle ground. Most of them were also clever kids, but more defined by their love of live music and adventure.

That's where his latest crush Heidi fitted into the picture.

No longer preoccupied in thought by Macy, who he believed had betrayed him on Schoolies Week, Loxton needed another fixation upon which he could focus his attentions.

From the English county of Lincolnshire, she had a songbird's accent and love of indie rock bands that immediately drew my son's attention. She was nice to Loxton in a manner that he was unfamiliar with. Heidi was the only girl that he spoke about for months on end.

Poolhall—Jail—Library

He told me they'd bonded over discussing summer festival line-ups and some of the emerging bands coming out England. At this point in time, many of the 'alternative' American and Australian rock groups that Loxton had been ostracised for liking at high school were becoming more popularised. While he felt vindicated in some senses, it also sent him on a quest to discover newer, edgier bands.

There was no fanfare to Loxton's 18th birthday. He chose to spend the night with a few close friends, drinking on the roof of a three-storey school building rather than have a family dinner. But as soon as he was of legal age for drinking and nightclubbing, he spent most of his spare income on music, whether that was attending gigs, buying CDs from the Record Market and Rocking Horse stores in the city, or covering his walls in posters.

I rarely visited him at home, because frankly it was a hovel. He also shared his new abode with another student who was studying psychology and an older, single council worker who used poker machines as his main source of entertainment. I found it to be a depressing place to be, especially because Loxton had plastered the walls with not only his old grunge favourites, but also newer groups I had not heard of, boasting stupid names like Regurgitator, Korn, Jebediah and Local H. Surprisingly he appeared to have inherited some of my own taste, and I was quietly impressed to see the likes of Black Sabbath, Led Zeppelin, The Police, T-Rex and even The Kinks in his collection, nestled in between posters of philosophers like Kierkegaard, Sartre and Jung.

Anyhow, Loxton received a fright at one of his earliest gigs, at a popular venue of the time, Mary Street. They hosted a live rock band, playing covers each Thursday night. After finishing work, he went there with colleagues only to be met by a huge line-up for entrance. Waiting in line, on a cold June night, the monotony of creeping forward in the line was broken when security guards tossed out two brawling men.

They continued to trade blows until the larger, thicker man began dominating. After savagely knocking his nemesis around, he then dragged him on to the street, continuing to belt him around the head as he placed his victim's mouth across the rusted bars of a drain grate. Standing back, he then brought down his boot viciously on the back of the unconscious man's skull, splitting his cheek right up to his wisdom teeth. Loxton retold the story laughing with brevity, revealing that police soon arrived and the queue began to thankfully dwindle, but I could sense the trepidation in his voice.

Another gig that formed a lasting mark on his year was one called Easy Cheese at the old, now sadly-departed Festival Hall. It was mostly local bands who, again, I knew next to nothing about. But for this particular event, Loxton had hyped himself into a frenzy, certain it was going to be some landmark moment in his life. We spoke less and less as the year wore on, but I vividly recall him mentioning it more than once.

It later eventuated that he had used the event as a reason to finally ask Heidi out, after close to a year of thinly-veiled attraction. She declined, citing a lack of funds, but he insisted he could pay for her. It was then she revealed she wasn't interested in him that way. Loxton took it as another body blow. The years of admiring all these girls from afar, being scarily devoted to one at a time, had not served him well.

To confuse matters, a month later Loxton crossed paths with Heidi at a party to signify her own school graduation. She was uncharacteristically drunk and welcomed him by kissing him on the lips, they argued about her smoking, she vomited bile on his shoes and he looked after her. Later, Heidi swore she remembered none of it. It simultaneously stirred his false hopes and dashed any ideal that she was some angel formed of otherworldly purity.

Loxton almost disappeared completely in the following period. He told me he was concentrating on work and training, as he had his heart set on making a special Under 19s team the following year and needed to be in tip-top condition. It was a semi-professional rugby league squad that provided an early stepping block to the national first-grade competition.

It was hard not to suspect that Loxton was also retreating out of view from embarrassment and hurt.

Only via Kim did I discover in the intervening months over the summer that Loxton had started seeing a girl several years older than him, Gabrielle. She was the complete opposite of Heidi; dark-haired, tanned, loud, uncouth. Apparently, she'd been a former bikini model, but was now a wild-drinking, fast-living woman who lived near the Valley, Brisbane's melting pot of sin and vice.

They were sleeping together. This much Kim had been able to ascertain. None of us were sure if Loxton had been with anyone else in this manner, but it's a hard subject for a mother to broach. We were never introduced to her. Almost as soon as I discovered they had been dating, news came through that they had split.

I harboured fears Loxton had gone completely off the rails at this time, but he had stuck true to his vow to put himself in prime physical shape for the next football season. The next time I saw him, he said he hadn't touched a drink for six months, had become far more muscular, and was carrying as little body fat as I thought was humanly possible.

He'd put on at least 10 kilos in weight and now looked like a fully-grown man, not growing much more in height, but certainly widening across his shoulders, arms and hips. To top it off, he'd shaved his head and grown a goatee. He certainly was starting to look like a rugby league player – or a criminal. I couldn't decide.

Loxton invited me to watch him debut for his new club. I didn't usually attend his games in his late teens. The sport wasn't to my taste and it involved making excuses to Steve about my whereabouts. But I knew how much my son had prepared for this moment and he bugged me extraordinarily to be there.

That day he played okay. He seemed a little overawed, didn't touch the ball much and missed a few tackles, but it was a new surrounding and the kids were much more talented than he had faced in the past. Loxton was disappointed afterwards, but rationalised that he could only improve, relieved to at least get the first game out of the way.

I left the sportsground, but Loxton stayed behind to watch the senior men's games. He later told me he climbed into the grandstand alongside a teammate and started to devour a burger. Then, a tubby middle-aged man with long, frizzy hair, unkempt beard and droopy eyes sidled up to the adjacent bench.

"I thought you played fairly well out there," said the stranger.

"Oh thanks, I appreciate it," replied Loxton, suspecting the interloper may be a talent scout, even though he looked more like a homeless person.

"I reckon if you stayed on your feet a little longer and closed the gap to the attackers, you would have made some more of those tackles," the older man continued.

Loxton became uncomfortable with the critique and stared at the man, then looked away with a sharp realisation.

"You don't know who I am, do you?" the stranger prodded.

Loxton continued to gaze straight ahead at the match on the field, chewing his food.

"Yeah I do. You're my real Dad."

BRITISH CHANNEL // PARIS

PREDOMINANTLY a solo explorer until now, I've opted to spend the last of my three months in Europe on board an organised tour. It pits me on a coach with 50 other young adventurers, all aged between 18 and 35. Most are positioned in the middle of that bracket from around 22 to 29.

There is social stratum to the new environment that has been completely lacking in the preceding weeks. I was able to be anyone I wanted when I traveled alone. I didn't listen to anybody and tried my hardest not to bow to external impressions. The longest period I gave anybody to make a personal judgment about my character was a few nights at most. But suddenly, group dynamics become very important again.

It feels like the first day at school when the bus departs Russell Square in north London and heads towards the Cliffs of Dover. I'm eyeing everybody up-and-down. I take note of their mannerisms, their facial expressions, their tone of voice and clothing, deciding who are the people who will be approachable, who is intriguing, who should be avoided. Others are making polite conversation with those around them, but for the first 30 minutes I offer only a polite "Hi" to the person beside me and spend the rest of it feigning to read the tour notes while observing others casually.

This is my modus operandi these days. I play the long-game when it comes to socialising in groups. I'd much prefer to be the quiet, stand-offish guy that people find difficult to get to know, but then warm to over a period of time. Much better than the extrovert who ignites the party, then burns out and fades away.

Eventually I start a conversation with the bloke beside me. His name is Simon and he's a lean 25-year-old electrician from Western Australia. He's got one son, but has split from his partner and doesn't have custody. Through narrow eyes he tells me that he's been "messed up" in the pot and methamphetamine scene for a few years and this European trip is part of the drying-out process. I enjoy his frank honesty, but make a mental annotation: One to possibly avoid as the trip grows longer.

Before I know it, we are boarding the ferry across the British Channel for Calais. I've always wanted to see Dover. I've got a great uncle who lives not far away in Ramsgate and have heard plenty of family anecdotes about the place. However, the tour bus whizzes into the port, bypasses the town centre, and there is barely time for a few photographs of the famed chalk cliffs before we push off.

Crossing the channel has been another long-held ambition I can tick off the list. I don't know how anybody manages to swim it, but more power to them. Upstairs in the ferry lounge, there is an awkward congregation of the passengers from our bus. It's the first time most of us have stood face-to-face and the air is predominantly stand-offish.

Then a young scallywag with wavy blond hair and a massive grin across his face brushes past me.

"Can I get you an apple juice?" he says.

He turns around and pretends to urinate in a plastic cup, before handing it to me. It's cider and I can smell it.

Without hesitation, I skol the entire contents of the cup in one go, despite it being 10am.

"You madcat!" the boy yells to a few guffaws from the surrounding circle.

I shake his hand and buy him and his girlfriend the next round. I'd spotted the pair of them on the drive down. They were up the front and were giving off a bright, happy-go-lucky vibe.

They're a good-looking couple. He looks like your typical surfer boy. She's a beautiful Spanish-looking girl with a caramel complexion and vibrant, long curls set over one shoulder. Most importantly though, they are both constantly smiling and clearly confident in their own skin.

They introduce themselves as Pete and Juliana. They are from Cronulla on Sydney's southern beaches. It figures.

"So, what do you do for work?" they ask.

"Ah, I work in the media department of a sports organisation. Do you know Queensland Rugby League?"

"Ah get out. Booo! You're a bloody Cane Toad is what you are. Haha. Yeah of course we know Queensland Rugby League. I'm a St George-Illawarra Dragons supporter and Juliana supports Cronulla Sharks."

"Well, what do you guys do for work then?"

"Oh, us?" laughs Juliana. "We've literally just finished high school, but I do work in a café part-time and Pete does some construction work with his Dad."

"Wait on, so you guys are like what age? I could have sworn you were 22 or 23."

"Nup, just turned 18. Fresh out of school," Juliana continues.

Great, I've just made friends with the freshest kids on the bus. That's perhaps indicative of my level of maturity. I wonder if they've even been nightclubbing before?

Ah, what the heck, they seem like great folk. Just roll with it Berg.

"So you guys are 18 too?" pipes up a chubby, rosy-cheeked kid in a thick jacket with spiked hair and frosted tips. "Cooool. Let's get a photo together."

The portly interloper, who later introduces himself as Bevan, then tries to get photos with as many of the other tour comrades as possible.

Once the ferry reaches land on the French side of the channel, our tour guide, Jane, asks everyone to stand up on the bus one-by-one. The task is to tell everyone your name, where you live, three unusual facts about yourself and hold up a colour that corresponds with your relationship status. Green means single and available. Orange means uncertain or confused. Red means in a relationship and content.

I'm one of the last to have to introduce myself and I devote all of the intervening time to unnecessarily contemplating what colour I should hold up. If you asked me to answer instantaneously, I would say I'm single. But gee, I'm 27. What sort of loser is still single at 27? Pete and Juliana have barely graduated and are touring Europe together. Would I say the few emails I've exchanged with Audrey since meeting her in Galway constitute a relationship? She's definitely the kind of girl I could see myself dating seriously, but there are too many loose ends at this point. And I mean, I have been sleeping with a girl back in Australia casually for the past two years, but we both know it for what it is. That's a 'friends with benefits' arrangement. We've discussed it so many times it shouldn't require further analysis.

"So, hey I'm Loxton. I'm a journalist from Brisbane, Australia. Let's see...three unusual facts. My middle name is Panagiotis. I can nail the voice of Dr Claw from Inspector Gadget. And errr, I play the drums."

The last 'fact' is an embellishment. I try to play the drums, but I've actually regressed in my ability. Yet, it sounds like the kind of cool thing that might gain me credo.

Then I reach down, pick up a piece of paper and hold aloft the orange circle.

You coward. You absolute fucking coward. You've just gone and made this a whole lot more complicated and difficult for yourself.

I'm still beating myself up mentally as I walk back to my seat, passing Pete and Juliana, who have switched to the seat behind me. It's their turn to get up.

"Hi I'm Pete. I'm a loser from Cronulla," he begins to loud laughter.

He ends his introduction by staring at Juliana, reaching down and picking up the green circle. "Yeah ladies, that's right, I'm single." More laughter and a few gasps are emitted from the passengers.

Juliana rolls her eyes at Pete, then takes the microphone.

"Hi I'm Juliana. I'm going to uni to study behavioural science and commerce."

She tilts her head, stares back at Pete and drops her shoulders before raising a matching green circle.

All around the bus there is awkward chatter.

The pair return to sitting behind me and giggle uncontrollably.

"Fucking tricked the lot of them," Pete boasts as he claps the back of my seat.

"So, you guys aren't together?" I say, turning around.

"Nah, no way," shoots back Juliana. "We've known each other since we were kids. Our parents are friends. He's dating a girl I used to babysit for god's sake. She's like 15 now. Can you imagine any normal 18-year-old girl dating Pete? We came on this trip together because it's a pact we made at school and our parents didn't want us to go alone."

"Oh shit, really? Boy, do I feel stupid now."

I'm hit with the sudden realisation that I'm in a spot of trouble. I thought Juliana was attractive the moment I saw her. That was well before I knew she was 18. Now I know she's single and we are already comfortable in each other's presence. But, yeah, she's basically a schoolkid.

She's 18 man. Don't even think about it.

*** *** ***

THE final crawl into Paris for our first night of the tour is brutal. French traffic is horrible and the highway is jammed for two hours of the approach to the capital. It's not what I envisaged arriving in Paris would be like, but truth be told I don't have overly high expectations. I definitely think Paris will be proven to be an overhyped cliché and am preparing for it to leave me feeling as flat as a Nicole Kidman film or a pop song by Cher.

After all, I'm the guy who willfully put Hull on his itinerary. I consider myself an intrepid adventurer at this point, not some colour-by-numbers, run-of-the-mill tourist.

As we finally reach our hotel, room allocations are read out aloud. All the couples and friends have been placed together. As a solo traveller, I'm told I'm sharing a room for the remainder of the tour with a tall, dark-haired guy from Melbourne called Liam. He's wearing a grey mohair jumper over a tight black tee-shirt, long black jeans, black boots and a heavy silver necklace. Liam seemed nice enough when we did our introductions on the bus.

No sooner have we hauled our luggage up the stairs to our room, we're told the tour bus is leaving for a night trip around Paris's most famous sights. I sit towards the back of the bus, one row in front of Pete and Juliana, and next to a guy from Brisbane called Mick. I'd discovered a few hours before that he was a bar manager at one of the city hotels I used to drink at towards the end of my university years.

The funny thing with this tour is that around 30 of the 52 people on the bus are from Australia. There's a smattering of Canadians, Brits, New Zealanders and South Africans, but by-and-large the Aussies dominate. In fact, there's at least seven other Queenslanders on board that I've figured out so far. There's a few Australians from migrant families – Vietnamese, Chinese, Chilean – but otherwise it's a Caucasian affair.

It's not exactly what I had in mind when I booked to travel overland around the other side of the planet, but I guess it makes sense that we all fit a particular English-speaking, disposable income type of market.

To the repeated amplification of Rossini's *William Tell Overture* our bus lunges into the Paris night traffic. Successfully surviving the utter madness of navigating the Arc de Triomphe draws a round of applause for our bus driver, a hulking Kiwi with shoulder-length curly hair. From there, we proceed on a mad dash that incorporates whistle stops at the Champs-Élysées, the Eiffel Tower, the Louvre, and Notre Dame Cathedral.

"Don't fret," we are told by the tour guide, "Tomorrow you will have a full day to explore the city at your leisure and revisit any place you wish."

IT HAD been roughly 12 years since Loxton had seen his father, stretching back to when I remarried Steve. How Marty had tracked him down was a mystery. It gave me the creeps to be perfectly honest, particularly as I had been at the same place just moments before. As soon as he arrived home, Loxton rang me and told me about the approach in the grandstand that day. Although we were no longer as close as we once were, my son feared being seen as a traitor and wanted to be upfront.

There can't have been too many more confusing periods in Loxton's life. His father re-emerged just as Lox was following his football ambitions, only months before he started his most significant romance and not much longer before he landed a trial in his dream job.

Loxton treated his Dad just as he did everyone at that point – stand-offishly and with polite but reserved emotion. They kept in touch on a semi-regular basis, although Loxton was forever suspicious about the motives for their reunion. I had a hunch that Lox only went along with it because he was struggling to grow into his own skin as a young man. He'd already made some mistakes with women that gave him elements of forgiveness towards his father's past deeds.

The next part I'll have to retell from the anecdotal evidence of Kim, because I wasn't present when it all took place. The setting was a restaurant bar on the edge of Fortitude Valley, known as Garuva.

Kim had a boyfriend by then, Derrick, who was an apprentice mechanic with a dealership close to the city centre. It was his 18th birthday and he'd chosen to host a small party to signify his coming-of-age. Loxton at first indicated he had other commitments and wouldn't attend, but at the last minute he showed up. It was significant for the fact Loxton and Kim had drifted apart in the past two years over their varying reactions to Steve's behavior.

When Loxton arrived, Kim tried to engage him in an extended update on her life, but Lox stood stone-faced, arms crossed and nodding nonplussed. Once again, he had succeeded in making the atmosphere awfully uncomfortable. Kim could see Loxton looking around to find a place to sit. Garuva was a strange mix; neither a traditional bar nor restaurant. The catchphrase on the front door was 'Hidden Tranquility'. It sounded like the sort of hippy thing Marty would have been into, to be honest. Apparently, you could sit down on the floor behind dark curtains for an intimate dinner, or you could relax in a bamboo and fern setting and socialise.

Loxton spotted a boy who had been in his grade at high school, Brad. They had worked out in the same gym during lunchtime recess at school, so my son broached the topic of fitness. Kim then joined Loxton, attempting polite conversation with Brad's girlfriend. The girlfriend was so quietly spoken that the group had to dip their heads sideways to catch each syllable she uttered.

It was while tilting their heads in her direction that the group sensed a tall figure, gliding towards them. Trying not to be distracted, they continued the discussion until a towering blonde jumped right in between them with a double-clop of her high heels.

"Hey beautifuls." The girl broke the conversation as she hopped in and wrapped her arms simultaneously around Kim and Brad's girlfriend, almost lifting them from the ground.

Struggling for breath, the smaller girls comically attempted to recreate the bearhug. "Hey princess."

Wrapped in one-another's arms, the three girls stood in front of Loxton, continuing to laugh and exchange stories. Almost five minutes later it was if they simultaneously remembered his presence and turned around. Loxton had been unable to immediately make out the face of the new girl, who had his back turned to him until then.

"Hey...," she offered, dragging out a singular word into a warm and detailed greeting.

It was Jen, neighbour and friend to Loxton's high school crush Macy, and Kim's attention-seeking friend from her youth.

Loxton and Jen had barely spoken a word in all their years at school, but Kim observed them click almost instantaneously in the dark light of Garuva. From the beginning, Loxton was periodically ignoring Jen to cut her down a peg or two, making her work for his attention. From her position a metre away, Kim could feel the tension – and initially feared it spelled trouble.

Jen had only recently been the star of a fashion parade, turning up with short, spiraled locks, looking somewhat like Drew Barrymore on stilts. There were plenty of boys currently fighting for her affections, including some of Kim's male friends who were already in attendance.

Suddenly the music stopped and Kim called everyone over to the side of the restaurant, where there was a little breakout area and a sequence of upturned wine barrels with stools positioned around them. It was time to toast Derrick's milestone. The attendees all raised their glasses thrice and handed over their presents.

Loxton was seated at the rear left barrel, along with Brad and his girlfriend, Jen and two other boys who appeared eager to get acquainted with Jen. When Derrick arrived at Jen's present, he struggled with the superfluous, weirdly-bound wrapping paper until two plastic toys dropped out on the ground. At first, he seemed embarrassed, then bewildered, as he bent over and picked up a glow-in-the-dark dinosaur and a cheap, fluoro sword. He held them up for everyone to laugh at and Jen dipped her head in mock shame.

Kim caught Loxton and Jen grinning at each other, their eyes flicking back-and-forth. By the time all the presents were open, the two were engaged in prolonged stares and nervous laughter.

The stand-off was broken when one of Derrick's male friends interrupted and asked Jen what she did for work. She began to reply that she was a housemaid at a popular Brisbane hotel. Loxton eased away from the table, jagging a glance at Jen once more before he left. He sidled up to Derrick and congratulated him on his birthday, buying him the next two rounds of drinks.

The alcohol must have been hitting Lox more than usual, because he invited Derrick and Kim over to the small dancefloor when some retro disco music began to play. Loxton had never been one to dance, but proved to be surprisingly enthusiastic on this occasion. This was a side Kim had rarely seen of her brother. They were flailing around together for less than 10 minutes when Jen left her seat and joined them on the dancefloor.

Kim took a gamble and nudged Jen towards Loxton. It was her way of signaling she knew what was happening and didn't expressly object, even if she still held some reservations.

"Hey do you remember Jen from school?" Kim asked, pretending not to have noticed their flirtations.

"Oh hey, yeah kinda. I'm Loxton if you don't remember me," Loxton deadpanned, sticking his arm out for a rigid handshake.

Jen chortled and limply shook his offered hand. "Pleased to make your acquaintance sir."

Dee-Lite's *Groove Is In The Heart* started blaring over the speakers and, after a lift of the eyebrows, both Jen and Loxton began bouncing around, hamming it up without a care for anybody else.

As the night flew by, the pair dodged back and forth, spending time with other guests, but always meeting back up at some point again, but never touching. At one point, Kim, Derrick, Loxton and Jen left the remaining party guests to find food down the street. Ending up at a 24-hour store at the bottom of the Valley Mall, Jen shunned the traditional fare of burgers and kebabs, instead opting for toothpaste.

"Really? Of everything we can eat, you want toothpaste?" Loxton quizzed playfully.

"Don't knock it until you've tried it," she shot back. "With your breath, I wouldn't think you'd understand. Nah, seriously it's because I have to start work at 6am. What time is it now? Like 2am? My parents don't know I'm out drinking. I don't turn 18 until Christmas Eve. Mum and Dad will kill me."

The age factor injected a little awkwardness into the conversation, but both laughed it off and walked back up the street, several metres ahead of Kim and Derrick.

The four of them caught a cab back to Stafford Heights, Loxton and Jen collapsing in the back seat next to each other, her legs crossed over his.

PARIS // LYON // BARCELONA

OK, I admit it — Paris is actually pretty cool after all. Following our night tour, I go back to most of the same spots in daylight the next day, plus a few additional sites like the Musee D'Orsay, Napoleon's burial chamber and Rodin's statue *The Thinker*. Paris is one of the few places where every block brings something new and spectacular. It's a city of the grandiose and inspired.

I would hazard to guess I've walked at least 20km in the day, allowing me to guilt-free consumption of some baked delicacies on the Champs-Élysées before I catch the train home. I've spent the entirety of the day striding around solo. I'm intent on keeping this individuality throughout the tour, experiencing everything on my own terms. Some of the others on the bus have already formed packs, but I've grown accustomed in the previous weeks to seeing everything that I want to see, when I want to see it. Your first — possibly only — three-month trip abroad is no time for compromise.

No, I have to remember the bus is just a vehicle to get me from one place to the other. The tour makes seeing all the coming countries much more economical than if I had done it alone. Don't get sucked into group politics and allow any of these co-passengers to become a weight around your ankles.

Tonight there is a dinner at the Moulin Rouge. It's not entirely my kind of thing, but I'll do it just to say I've been there. I could use a drink too.

Back at the hotel, I'm fresh out of the shower and putting my jeans and socks on when my roommate Liam walks in. He's styled his hair high like Lyle Lovett and is on the phone to his mother in Australia. He's assuring her everything is okay. She is taking some convincing. Boy am I glad I didn't bring my phone on this trip.

Still, Mum has written to me in the past 24 hours to tell me that several of the places I visited in Hull were the wrong places.

She's looked at the photos and I've gone to the wrong church for my grandparent's wedding and the wrong house for her birthplace. I'm deeply deflated, but simultaneously determined to return one day and complete the pilgrimage properly.

Unsurprisingly, Jen still hasn't responded in any way to the letter I sent her from Ireland. I highly doubt she ever will.

The Moulin Rouge turns out to be an excuse for everyone on tour to get drunk around each other for the first time. Any pretense of it being about fine cuisine and haute couture should be dismissed immediately.

The highlight of the dinner show is not necessarily the scantily-clad dancers, but rather the large, live snake used as a prop in one scene. Unfortunately for the dancers, it is while being held aloft that the snake chooses to take a giant, slimy shit that smears all over a preventative plastic film that has been wrapped around its cloaca. The snake's excrement is so enormous that it begins to drip out the side and form a puddle.

It's a moment of chaos that sets the tone perfectly for what is transpiring in the audience. Think of the dancers as our unfortunate tour guide, the snake as the animal embodiment of the tour passengers, and the slimy great turd as a euphemism for what happens when you inject alcohol into the equation. Before the show has finished, there are three younger travellers who have already vomited and required attention in the bathrooms, Pete has tried to touch a dancer inappropriately, and everyone is laughing drunkenly as much as they are applauding for the performers.

Afterwards the group is encouraged to retreat sheepishly to a bar only a few doors down the street. The licensee has surely seen this kind of debauchery on a nightly basis, but even as a patron, I'm embarrassed in advance of what is about to happen. There's more vomit, a few tears, and a few drunken snogs to set tongues wagging for the next morning.

On a scale of 1-10, I'm only about a 6 in terms of how drunk I personally get, but I do end the evening performing a raunchy version of Britney Spears' *Toxic* on the dancefloor in the centre of an assembled crowd if that is any indication. I'm thankful just about everyone else has pushed it out to a 10 for the night and my impromptu shimmying will barely raise a mention in post-match analysis.

One thing that becomes apparent in many frank conversations had over the course of the night is how many fellow passengers are school teachers. Being that window at the end of the Australian school year, there's at least 10 who have taken the opportunity to let loose abroad. Lord help our nation's future.

Another thing that I take note of is the clear disparity in budgeting. I'm being fairly conservative on my backpackers' budget, but others are clearly here to splurge. At the other end of the scale are the South Africans, who have a 6:1 exchange rate against us, and are thankful whenever a free drink or extra morsel is thrust in their direction.

A South African couple, Wayne and Shelly, are two of the next people to join the little friendship pact formed by Pete, Juliana and I. They are a super positive pair with no ego. Shelly is one of the aforementioned teachers and Wayne works in IT, but is a keen sportsman who enjoys rugby and volleyball. Shelly is the more outgoing of the two, but they both enjoy a good time without making complete jerks of themselves.

I get to know them better the next morning on the long drive south to Lyon, during which our bus driver gets lost twice, much to the dismay of a severely hungover tour group. Shelly and Wayne tell how volatile the situation in South Africa currently is. They recount a past Christmas Eve where bandits disabled their electric fence, climbed over the top of it and stormed a barbecue dinner they were hosting. The bandits ordered everybody into the bathroom at gunpoint and locked the door before ransacking the rest of the house. To make matters worse, Shelly's sister had a newborn baby which was left sleeping in a room downstairs as the invasion continued, prompting a manic reaction.

Thankfully everybody lived, but I can tell from the detailed recreation how traumatising the episode must have been. "You know, some people are only earning $1.50 a day in the poorest suburbs of Johannesburg right now. It stands to reason these robberies are happening," says Wayne philosophically.

As engaged as I am with tales of their homeland, I leave Wayne and Shelly when we reach Lyon and stick to my vow of exploring each city alone. While the remainder of the busload dilly-dallies about determining their walking route, I storm ahead, crossing the Rhône and Saône rivers before climbing up to La Basilique Notre Dame de Fourvière, a hilltop church and art museum that looks down on the Old Town.

It's right on sunset and makes for spectacular photos. I then enjoy a beer in solitary at a nearby café, looking down on the 2000-year-old city. After I soak up the ambience, I head back downhill to the restaurant region and reserve a table near the window for the clichéd consumption of frog's legs and snails. The prices indicate this spot is a definite tourist trap, but experience is priceless right?

I'm still waiting for my meal to arrive when Pete and Juliana stroll past outside with another Brisbane-based adventurer, Harry. Harry is a good-looking, confident chap who has been going out of his way to win Juliana's attention the past two days. I don't handle guys like him well, not just because a small part of me might also fancy Juliana. Men who are showy and naturally good-looking probably evoke a fair bit of jealousy on my behalf. That's my own insecurity shining through again. He comes across as a kind of used car dealer to me; a lot of smooth-talk and not much substance.

The three of them wave through the window and Harry pops his head around the restaurant door.

"Mind if we join you?" he yells over the other diners.

"Not at all," I lie.

*** *** ***

BARCELONA is one of the remaining gems on my itinerary. I love the vibrancy it projects. Of course, reading up on the life of Salvador Dali has only served to increase the attraction, but I'm drawn to Spanish-speaking cultures across the world in general. Barcelona is established in my mind as some magnificent epicentre of sport, music, dance, food, culture, architecture and fiesta.

Not long ago, I watched a documentary about the video production behind Kylie Minogue's *Slow* film clip, captured at the Olympic Pool atop Montjuic Hill. Not that I particularly like Kylie, but that film clip has a certain majesty to it. I love how the positioning of the pool overlooking the city makes it look as if high divers are disappearing into the barrios below.

The pool is one of the first places I choose to visit. It has steel bars obscuring the capture of any half-decent photographs from the outside, so I elect to break into the complex. I'm not missing taking the shot I have dreamt about. Tracking down the hillside, I spot a point where the barbed-wire fence is non-congruent, stop and climb over with my backpack and camera. I'm all alone inside the Olympic venue and leaves are blowing around as I walk to the weathered pool deck to frame a shot of the diving board against the cityscape. The pool has become run-down and neglected in the years since Kieran Perkins secured gold to international acclaim.

There is a loud CLANG and heavy footsteps on the tiles. I take a handful of rushed photos, scarper back to the fence and out of the complex, walking up the pathway to the old Olympic Stadium where the track and field events in 1992 were held. Now it is more commonly used for football matches and concerts like The Rolling Stones and Bruce Springsteen.

Next on the list is the wonderfully eccentric Sagrada Familia, the world-famous basilica which looks like it is melting under the Mediterranean sun. From there, I cut through the back streets, grab a ham sandwich and a glass of Estrella Dam from a restaurant, then walk through to La Rambla and the Gothic Quarter. I give myself two hours to explore the precinct before the organised rendezvous time with the tour bus. It proves more than enough time, as my ever-thinning budget doesn't allow for elaborate spends at any of the shops or markets.

At the tour meeting point, four girls tell how they had their purses stolen off a table at a nearby café. The robbers bolted away and could not be caught. More girls arrive back and tell of pickpockets rifling through their bags as they shopped. By the time everybody is assembled, close to 40 of the 52 passengers have been the victim of some sort of theft. Ferris had warned me in advance of Barcelona that he'd had his laptop stolen there, but I'd pushed that all to one side.

Part of me is relieved I was oblivious to the crime spree occurring around me as I enjoyed my day walking alone. A more vainglorious element of my personality is taking the fact I wasn't robbed as a sign that I'm a bona fide alpha male. They wouldn't dare fuck with me.

"Hey." Juliana interrupts the delusion with a gliding touch of my shoulder. "Can we catch up by the port after dinner? I'll walk down with you."

I've done as many push-ups as possible and drank almost two litres of sangria in my hotel room by the time I'm ready to meet Juliana in the foyer. She's gone for a simple, tight white shirt and black jeans, with her hair tied back. She struts like a woman 10 years older.

"What a day hey? I can't believe that many people got duped by thieves," she starts casually. "Anyway, I've got a few things on my mind. You seem like a really switched-on guy and I wonder if I can pick your brain?"

"Sure, fire away."

It's a longer walk than anticipated to Porto Olympic – not that I mind. Juliana is mostly discussing her employment options after university. She's not sure she's even concentrating in the right fields. Her options bounce wildly between becoming a vet or a photographer or an architect. She might even take a gap year and disappear to Vietnam. Right now, she's arrived at the edge of that enchanting whirlpool where she knows everything is a possibility, but simultaneously doubts she will become anything.

We move on to talking about her older brother. It's clear he means a lot to Juliana. She worries about him like a mother would. It seems he has some girlfriend issues, some mental health issues, some work and aspirational difficulties. We are deep in conversation for close to an hour about him alone, leaving us seated at a traditional Mediterranean café down at the port before we switch to the next conversion.

The sun is setting rapidly to the south, something my Southern Hemisphere mind still finds hard to reconcile. Juliana is facing out to the rolling Mediterranean waves behind me and her face is bathed in flickering tangerine tones. Her perfume smells delicious too.

"And then there's my situation," she says. "I was kind of seeing this guy in Sydney. Well, not really seeing him. He was pursuing me pretty keenly. I'm not that into him. We caught up a few times, but that's it. I don't want to be with him, but I fear what his reaction will be like. You know, this is supposed to be my holiday and I'm stressing about a guy I don't really like that I'm not really with."

I kick back in my chair. We're speaking earnestly for two people who have known each other a grand sum of four days.

"Look I understand what you are saying. I get caught up thinking like this all the time. But it seems pretty clear what the answer is…what your heart is telling you. Break it off. Fuck him."

I'm narcissistically getting off on the fact anybody has sought me out for relationship advice. Also, that and the fact that there is a gorgeous, intelligent young woman sitting a metre away from me who has divulged some of her deepest fears and appears perfectly comfortable around me.

An electric smile suddenly flashes over Juliana's face.

"Oh wow, thank you for listening. I think you're right," she says, leaning in excitedly. Initially, I am startled she is about to kiss me, but she rests on her forearms inches in front of my face, widens her chocolate eyes and begins to whisper. "I think...tonight...I am going to make a play at Harry."

The fucking used car salesman on our bus. The fucking cunt.

There's a lump in my throat that feels like it may take a month to clear. Somehow, I manage to blurt out a few words to break the silence.

"Makes sense. You're both good-looking creatures. He's a lucky guy. Yeah, go for it."

Go for it? You fucking coward. You ultra-polite piece of shit.

I guess, in the back of my mind, I was partially prepared for this. Perhaps I've even been willing it. Things could have gotten tricky if they'd escalated much further. She is almost a decade younger. Think of all the complications that would have brought. Think of introducing her to my mates back in Australia. I'm not the kind of guy that could have held her attention for an extended period of time anyway.

Why do you think so far ahead you dickhead? Always denying yourself the possibility of living in the present. Always holding back, emitting the negative vibe.

Before Juliana's final confession about Harry, I'd noticed others from our tour group filtering into the large bar next door. It has a long beer garden filled with ferns, leading into a white palatial building with tinted windows.

"Hey, we should probably join the others," I say, standing up and turning.

Juliana puts her hand on my shoulder again. "Thanks again for listening."

I head straight to the bar as Juliana mingles with the crowd. One pitcher of sangria purchased for solitary consumption.

I'm ploughing through the sangria as Pete spots me and makes his way over. "Hey buddy," he chirps, "I'd love to fuck our tour guide. Maybe tonight."

The guy is hilarious for a teenager. Entirely brazen. He is the Tyler Durden to my pencil-necked control freak.

Pete also orders a pitcher of sangria and we commence an unspoken race to the bottom of the jug. Sitting on stools, we're up to our third pitcher each before we know it. Things are rapidly becoming hazy and unsteady. We're drinking, well, like teenagers would drink. Which is fine in the case of Pete, but rather unrefined on my behalf.

I've long held an ability to sober up quickly. It's one of the few benefits of being born with a stick in your arse. If I concentrate hard through each drink and consciously deflect any irrational, emotive responses or impulses, I can last until the end of a night without really feeling anything other than tired. It basically defeats the purposes of drinking for escapism, yet I've also found it very useful when things turn to shit or avoiding situations reaching tipping point.

I'm electing to turn on that function when Pete wobbles up from his pew and points towards the dancefloor with the smile of a Cheshire cat. He is soon alternating between grinding up against the much-older tour guide and a posh girl of around 21 from Sydney's northern beaches. Pete can somehow come across as a total lecher and simultaneously the funniest guy at the party.

I'm now drinking with three local Spanish guys at the bar and watching football on television. All throughout the trip I have been learning Spanish from my iPod, narrated by a character with a terrible American accent called 'Johnny Spanish'. It's a chance to test out the basics. But once I have asked their names, enquired what they do for work and commented that the match on television is a great contest, I am lost for further vocab. Instead the three gents communicate with me in a weird, almost primate-like, form of chanting.

"Barca, Barca, Barca," they yell, or "Messi, Messi, Messi."

I feel a hand grip me strongly below my elbow, sharp fingers gripping into the muscles of my forearm. It's Juliana and she's yanking me to get up and join the dancefloor. Save aside from a few killjoys who have left early, everybody else from the tour group is now dancing in a large globular assembly of drunken English-speakers.

Juliana and Harry are already sharing the same cocktail glass, drinking via two straws and having no qualms about each other's personal space. The posh girl being pursued by Pete has relaxed somewhat and seems to be entertaining him having his arms draped over her shoulders while they dance.

Gesturing indiscreetly with her thumb, Juliana identifies a girl with blonde, bobbed hair, dressed elegantly and dancing a few metres away.

"She's a bit of a fox hey?" Juliana laughs, before taking things a step further and physically pushing me in the direction of the other female. "Hey Lox" she continues loudly, "Have you met Lucy? I reckon you'd get along really well. Lucy's an English teacher. Lox's a nerd that loves words as well. Oh, and you're both hotties. Fit as fuck."

There's an appropriately awkward stand-off. We've been introduced for the first time as people who should possibly sleep together, but can manage only a handshake as we both stifle laughter. I've never been described as a 'hottie' before.

Lucy is slightly familiar. I can remember there are two single English teachers on the trip who share a house together. That much I recall from our exercise on Day One when we held the coloured lights up on the bus. I think they were also dancing near us after the first night at the Moulin Rouge and, from memory, seemed amiable, relaxed people.

Poolhall—Jail—Library

This is the first time I've seen Lucy dressed like this though. She's usually rugged up in a pashmina, a dowdy beanie and at least three layers of clothes. No doubt, she's got stunning, piercing blue eyes, but typically she dresses like someone twice her age. In fact, I previously thought her and her housemate might not necessarily prefer the company of men, if you catch my drift.

"Someone is having fun tonight," Lucy drawls as she motions her head in the direction of Juliana, now writhing back-to-back with Harry and letting out 'whoop, whoop' noises.

"So, an English teacher hey? What ages do you teach and whereabouts?" I ask, simply to keep the conversation flowing.

"Do you know the Gold Coast? I teach just near Robina, off the highway. And I mostly deal with senior school; the older kids around 16 and 17."

"I live an hour from the Gold Coast. Small world eh? I bet you feel like you're still supervising kids though with this bunch," I say, referring to Pete and Juliana. "I don't suppose I can get you a drink?"

"Oh, that'd be nice actually. Uno mas vino. Malbec please," Lucy says softly, but confidently.

As I descend back from the platform to the main bar, I kick myself. Asking if I could buy her a drink definitely sounded like I was coming on to her. I didn't even mean in that way. I only asked to escape the situation and by way of apology for Juliana's forthright behaviour. Usually I don't offer to buy drinks at all. It's a rejection-of-power thing. There I go, thinking too much again. I reckon I'm just going to buy this one drink and then go home. Remember to play the long game. There's another three weeks of being on this bus with the same people.

I grab Lucy's wine and order a double-strength mojito for myself to obliterate my nagging conscience. As I return to the dancefloor, Pete is passionately kissing the posh girl, who is standing on tip-toes. I glance across and also kissing, but much, much slower and more intensely are Juliana and Harry.

Their crotches are resting on the respective thighs of the other and they are mauling each other as though they haven't eaten for days.

"Hoo boy," I say as I hand Lucy her glass of wine.

"Yes, I don't think I've drunk anywhere near enough to be like that just yet," she replies. Wait a second. Is she saying this to completely clarify that us hooking up tonight is not a possibility? Or is she saying she would indeed like to drink enough until she loosens up enough to let her inhibitions drop? So confusing.

"Oh, look out," Lucy yells, nudging me to the side just as Juliana charges over, off-balance and full of bonhomie.

"Did you see that?" Juliana quizzes us over-enthusiastically. "I just got with Harry. We were snogging like 13-year-olds. Can you believe that?"

"Didn't see a thing," Lucy deadpans.

"Yeah it was kind of difficult to see. I'm sure nobody will recall it in the morning," I continue, playing along.

Juliana places her hands on her hips theatrically. She hasn't got many remaining braincells tonight. "Phew," she exhales.

Then Juliana lunges forward and grabs Lucy by both breasts in the middle of the dancefloor, latching on through the thin cream-coloured top as if she is about to milk her.

"Lucy, you have amazing boozies. Lox, aren't they great?" Juliana proclaims.

"Well, um, yes, I guess. Anyway, I might grab another drink," I reply as I slurp the remainder of my double mojito in express fashion. Lucy hasn't even touched her wine yet.

The next drink is a gateway for my escape. I have no intention of going back to the dancefloor. There's been a lot to absorb from today and the whole Juliana-pashing-Harry affair has pulled the rug out from under me in an unexpected manner.

I re-join the Spanish men I was drinking with earlier in the night. There is another football game now playing on the screen above the bar. A second double-strength mojito is ordered and I begin to say my farewells to my new amigos.

As the game goes into stoppage time, one of the teams scores and all the local men erupt. They high-five me and start jumping around in a circle. I join in the little celebratory ritual, finishing the last of my drink rather rapidly as I bound up and down.

After a handshake, I make for the exit and just as I am at the front door one of the men quizzes me in broken English.

"Now you go to another club?"

I inform them I am exhausted and make a gesture with both hands to signify I am ready to sleep. I'm definitely going home.

"Ok," he says dismayed, before giving me a hug and lifting me off my feet with surprising strength.

The other two men crowd around and start yelling 'Gol, Gol, Gol' as they pat my head and slap my back. The joy of life is strong in this trio. In fact, the man holding me around the waist is squeezing so tight I can barely feel my legs.

Finally, he drops me down on the planks of the boardwalk and shakes my hand again. Something doesn't feel right. I look around and only one of the other men is still standing with us. The third has disappeared.

Instinctively, I give a subtle pat to the front pocket where I keep my wallet.

It is missing.

I grab the man who lifted me off the ground and pull him in close until our heads are butting.

The sense of deception and betrayal is all-consuming. I'm as angry as I've ever been in my life, accelerated by those last four shots of Cuban rum and an absolutely shit night.

"I'm going to fucking destroy the lot of you," comes a growl that I can barely control.

The level of testosterone and adrenalin is escalating to something I have never felt before.

LOXTON reportedly rang Jen just a little over 24 hours after they had shared a taxi home from the Valley.

The memory of his previous rejections fresh in his mind, Lox tried to temper his enthusiasm, balanced with striking while the iron was hot. He invited Jen out to the movies to watch Something About Mary. Despite his nervousness, later he would discover that, immediately after their conversation, Jen dropped the phone and victoriously danced around her parents' home in her boxer shorts, shimmying up and down the carpeted steps to her family's amusement. *Until then, I don't think my son believed he would ever have that effect on a female.*

The pair hit it off tremendously. Despite some outward incongruencies – Loxton being a noted introvert and Jen being a loud, vivacious force of nature – they had an X-factor as a couple that bound them. They developed little phrases and rituals that were peculiar to everybody else, but particular to them. At first, they only saw each other two or three times per week, but within a month they were together every single day, retreating slightly from their normal social circles.

It was an exciting time for Loxton, who had pestered the editor of his favourite magazine, *Rugby League Week*, to give him a start as a sports journalist. After two years of submitting unsolicited articles each week, the harassment met with some success when the editor and other Brisbane-based reporters had to travel interstate, leaving an important local fixture without coverage.

Loxton was recruited to report on the match and diligently snagged interviews with players from both teams afterwards. He was happy to do the job for free, but was elated to earn ongoing, paid employment when he managed to uncover that two players had signed for a rival professional club.

It was his breakthrough moment. Until then he had volunteered as a newsreader for 4ZZZ, a punk-ish radio station which took pride in fostering anarchy. He'd also volunteered as host of a community sports TV show, wearing some godawful shirts I knew he would regret in later life. Those roles had given him increased confidence in his ability, but securing a job with Rugby League Week was a dream come true.

Without hesitation, he resigned at McDonald's in a move that was meant to represent a triumphant, chapter-closing advance in his life. Yet, when he discovered he would only be paid $200 a week as a part-time reporter, he also took up supplementary roles as a pizza delivery driver and a telephone salesman.

Jen despised her job as a housekeeper, often having much older men invite her to clean their hotel rooms while they were naked. Other times she would find vomit and excrement soiling guests' bright white bedsheets. Therefore, Loxton supported her in quitting and, for a long time, had the sole income in their relationship.

That alone was the only minor source of friction in an otherwise blissful first year for the pair. They loved the same music, the same films, had a similarly absurd sense of humour and were always ready to take on adventure. Within less than six months, they had moved into the same house together, waiting until Jen turned 18 to receive her parents' blessings.

I had previously heard from Kim how protective Jen's parents could be. They had a very different family dynamic to our own. Her parents both held well-paying jobs, they lived in a large, two-storey home in a prime hilltop location, and held regular family holidays and golf days. Loxton had no idea what to do the first time he was invited for a round of golf with Jen's father, uncles and grandfather. He wore a yellow Puma t-shirt and lurid baggy shorts. When it came to swinging a club, he was completely lost.

One night before dinner was served at their house, Jen's father cornered Loxton and asked him pointedly what his "intentions" were for their relationship.

Taken back by the quaint, antiquated questioning and the blunt manner in which it was delivered, Loxton stumbled on his words before making a vow:

"I want to keep improving as a journalist and build a life for us. I adore your daughter and, if everything continues as planned, one day I'd like her to be my wife."

All of it was true, but Loxton felt he had been forced into an uncomfortable position, rather than letting matters develop naturally. He didn't take well to the inference that he might not be trusted.

One thing that Jen tried to play down, but couldn't, was her severe juvenile diabetes. A history of hospital admissions and a constant dependency on insulin lay testament to the gravity of her case. At the worst points Jen would transform, for only brief moments, into a thoroughly hostile creature, ransacking the house desperately for sugar or medication. Most times she wouldn't even remember what she had said or done in those moments. Amazingly this wasn't a major destabilising factor early in the relationship. On the contrary, it brought Loxton and her closer, as he would need to hold her still, monitor her temperature and inject the insulin when she became afraid and disorientated.

I'm guessing Loxton must have divulged practically everything about our home life, because Jen hated Steve almost as fervently as my son. They would rarely visit us at home, and almost exclusively arrived when they knew Steve was out of the house. Jen had been to our place numerous times in the past as a guest of Kim's, so she had possibly formed a strong opinion by the time Lox and her were together anyhow.

Worryingly, I knew that when Jen was 15 she had been stalked by a man 10 years older, who she first befriended at a party. Jen tried to put distance between them, at which point the older man began putting dead animals around her house, phoning late at night and breaking the windows to her bedroom. Unable to tell her parents she was involved with a 25-year-old man, Jen thought killing herself would be the best solution. The climax had been a purposeful overdose on insulin, pushing 120 units through her system, enough to induce a hypoglycemic coma. When she was taken to hospital, she lied and said it had been an irrational mistake, caused by surging sugar levels.

I had no doubt Loxton and her bonded over suicidal ideation.

On Easter weekend 1999 they traveled down to the Gold Coast to spend the holiday period with Jen's family, enjoying a reportedly glorious couple of days at Burleigh Heads. For all their controlling ways, Jen's parents gave my son a fuller appreciation of what family meant, though Loxton did struggle with reconciling the concept on several fronts. It made him jealous, skeptical and confused all at once.

After numerous days of lazing together, tackling each other on the beach, exploring tucked-away restaurants and artisan stores, Loxton and Jen took one evening to chance their arm at the Gold Coast casino. Loxton was by no means a regular gambler or big roller. Within 10 minutes of being at the casino, they hit the jackpot on a poker machine, took the cash and walked away immediately. While they did splurge at the nearby Pacific Fair shopping mall, Loxton purposely put aside half of the winnings.

The following night, before they returned to Brisbane, Jen left Loxton alone in their bedroom, instead preferring to talk with her family, before resting on the couch and eventually closing her weary eyes. Loxton saw this as an affront, bemused that she did not want to fall asleep beside him after what he considered a perfect week.

A crippling paranoia consumed him. This girl had become his everything. If she did not want him as much as he wanted her, what he envisaged for the future was a complete fallacy. Ravaged by intense hopelessness, Loxton exited the apartment, taking a blanket to shield from the chilly surf air. He sat beneath a towering pine tree, on a flat, dark rock overlooking the Pacific Ocean, with his bare feet tucked underneath.

After 15 minutes, a concerned Jen pierced the night air from the apartment balcony: "Loxton! Where are you?"

Lox didn't intend to hide, but did not yell back because he felt embarrassed; embarrassed of his love, of who he really was; embarrassed for Jen for having him as a partner, for having to know him so personally. Jen caught the elevator down, then jogged through the park, looking for him. She stopped at a safe distance when she spied him, cocooned away like a child.

"What...what are doing?" she asked, tears in the corners of her eyes.

Loxton had frozen. Communication was impossible. All he could think was that he was shamefully weak and thoroughly undeserving of what he possessed at that point in time. Instead of being angry, Jen walked over and lifted him by the arm, wrapping him in the biggest of hugs.

"It's okay. I feel exactly like you do some days," *she said sorrowfully.*

Together, they took the stairs back to the apartment, rather than the elevator. Jen asked Loxton to think back to the first weeks they were dating and an incident where she had cried for hours on end.

"That was because I thought you'd eventually discover the real me," she said. "Once you spent time with me, I thought, you would run as far away as you could. I don't ever want to be alive without you."

As they reached the top step, Loxton dropped to one knee, delicately holding her fingers.

"I'm not sure whether I can do this without a ring, but I never want you to leave my life either."

They fell asleep side-by-side on the balcony, nestled together under sprinkling rain. The next day they used the remainder of their casino spoils to purchase the correct jewelry to signify their engagement.

BARCELONA

ONE thing I hadn't previously shared with anybody on this tour bus is my past as a trained kickboxer. Not that I'm professional or anything, but for the past six years I've been learning the art at a run-down gymnasium above a strip club in the seedier part of Brisbane's Fortitude Valley. At first, I started it as a way to keep fit in the offseason for rugby league, then it progressed to something I'd do every night I wasn't playing or training for football, even during the regular season.

A few months before I left Australia, I'd trained for my first proper fight, which was supposed to be held in the piazza at South Bank. It was only intended to be a minor undercard, where both fighters wore shin pads, but I'd prepared for it with a degree of seriousness. I didn't drink alcohol for six months leading up to the scheduled fight, and was training six times per week.

Then, 24 hours before the fight my opponent withdrew without reason and they couldn't find a replacement fighter. The sense of disappointment and wasted effort was immense.

All of this is important to explain my immediate actions when I discover I have been pickpocketed by three men I think are my drinking buddies on the Barcelona boardwalk.

After declaring I will "destroy" them, I headbutt the one who held me around the waist and then throw him violently by the neck into the ground. Taking one rapid step forward, I then punch his friend as hard as I can straight in the nose. I've trained for this particular punch thousands of times against static equipment and sparring partners, but never thrown it with conviction in this type of situation. Blood explodes everywhere and people start shrieking.

Despite the sports that I enjoy, I don't necessarily consider myself a violent man. I don't covet confrontation. Yet, at this precise moment I am completely present in the sensation of fury. There's a palpable anger which has lit my neurons alight and I feel unquestionably confident, powerful and justified in wreaking havoc.

Turning, I sprint after the third thief, who has taken flight with my wallet towards the southern end of the boardwalk and Somorrostro Beach. It takes me a good 300m to catch him, screaming profanities the whole way. I've now started to attract the attention of people along the full length of the entertainment precinct.

Drawing almost alongside my target, I rugby tackle him around his ribcage from behind, slamming his head as hard as I can into the ground. I dig my knees into his calf muscles and pin him below me, banging his head repeatedly into the ground.

"Where is my fucking wallet? Tell me where the fuck it is."

I cannot quell my temper at all. It has skyrocketed to another level.

From out of nowhere, a powerful, muscular body of flesh completely blindsides me, sending me rolling back from the pick-pocketer.

I dust myself off and look up and there is a huge negro bodybuilder lifting the pick-pocketer by the shirt and talking to him loudly in Spanish.

He stares closely at the pick-pocketer and then releases his grip, leaving the skinny robber to scurry away through an alley adjoining the boardwalk.

"He says he dropped your wallet back that way," the man grunts, pointing back towards the nightclub. I glance over my shoulder and the remainder of the tour group has filed out of the nightclub and is now fighting the two other thieves. Pete and a handful of other Aussie boys are taking running kicks at the bandits, who are retreating slowly in ripped shirts, still exchanging insults.

"I don't see a wallet back there. Don't fuck with me," I yell at the black man. "You're one of them. Now tell me where the fuck my wallet is."

My opponent is standing his ground, an unimpressed scowl across his face.

"I'm fucking not one of them. I came here to help you man. Fuck you," he says.

I walk straight up to him, my head barely reaching his chin, then yell as I stare directly up into his eyes.

"You motherfucking cunt. Don't bullshit me. I know how this works. Do you think I'm afraid of you? Yeah, you're a big cunt, but I will take you down. Let's do this. I'm going to kill you. You think you can get out of it this easy? Then you go back and share the money with those pieces of shit?"

"Oi listen!" he yells, inching closer to me before jolting me with a shoulder. "I'm gonna walk you back down this fucking beach and find your fucking wallet you drunk fucking pig. I'm not going anywhere."

Even as he frog-marches me along the beach, I am still hurling insults at him, incapable of calming my emotions. By the time he has moved me 50m, Pete and the others have chased off the remaining pick-pocketers and have run down the boardwalk towards me.

"Loxton, settle the fuck right down," Pete yells, forcefully, but still smiling in amusement.

I turn back to the bodybuilder: "Fuck you cunt."

"You think I won't smash you if you keep this up?" the man says, his eyes growing wilder.

"Try it – you big piece of shit," I spit back.

"Whoa, whoa, whoa," say Pete and the other Aussies as the lunge in to separate us. "He's trying to help you, you idiot."

"No, he's not," I yell defiantly. "It's one of those scams. He covers for them, then goes back and they split the money."

Pete reaches into his rear pocket, then thrusts my wallet into my stomach.

"You dickhead. This was like 10 metres from where they stole it. You must have sprinted straight past it. I've checked and the bank cards and your driver's license are there, and there's still a few Euros in it."

I flip open the wallet and the bank notes are all intact, but the coins have been taken.

"How much do you reckon they got?" Pete asks.

I search thoroughly and do my calculations. "I reckon about 25 cents."

Everybody bursts into laughter except me. I'm still furious they took anything.

"Now you should go home to bed," says the muscle-bound intervener.

"And you should fuck off," I respond thanklessly.

Pete and the others turn me around and put distance between us and the stranger, who death-stares me into the distance, before he pops in his headphones, shakes his head and continues to walk north along the beach. He was probably just a worker from another nightclub on his way home who thought he should stop me from killing the Spaniard.

"I can't believe you bashed three guys because they stole 25 cents," Pete cackles.

"Euro cents," I slur with some cheek. "They're worth more than Aussie cents."

We make it over to the remainder of the tour group, gathered around a water fountain near the taxi rank of a cul-de-sac. Juliana has been vomiting into the fountain.

"That was awesome," she proclaims. "You kicked arse."

Lucy is helping to look after Juliana and gives me a bewildered, unimpressed smirk.

"You were kinda a fuckhead at the end though," chimes in Harry over the top.

"Shut the fuck up pussy." I give him an icy look that lets him – and everybody else – at once know my true feelings towards him.

Pete pipes up again. "You do know you're covered in blood, right? Fancy a swim in the Mediterranean?"

Without saying a word, I take my shoes and socks off and run down to the beach, sensing Pete is just a few footsteps behind me.

When I wake up the next morning, I'm laying in a wet t-shirt and jeans in the bath tub, sand spread all over my body, battling a pounding headache.

If there was anybody that didn't know me on this tour before last night, they certainly know me now.

So much for playing the long game.

LOXTON's natural father had pleaded him for forgiveness many times in the past, but had more success once our son was finally in a stable relationship. I gather Loxton wanted to bury the demons of his past and he became more amicable towards everyone – surprisingly enough, including Steve.

I think he and Jen thought both sides of the family were all one giant crazy soap opera, but outwardly they tolerated us at the very least. It made it all the easier that Loxton and Jen were now sharing a house with Kim and Derrick, meaning we could see everyone when we popped in to visit.

Loxton had bleached blonde hair at this stage and, in the past few years had coloured his locks everything from purple to black to electric blue. Jen had pink streaks through her naturally blonde hair, for reasons I found similarly hard to fathom.

Later my son was to adorn himself with a barbell piercing through the cartilage at the top of his ear, as well as through his tongue. In his first year at his new football club he was nicknamed 'The Animal' on account of his wild, thrashing style in tackles. Always a fan of the Muppets drummer, he chose to get the character Animal tattooed on his right deltoid in bright red and orange ink.

He was definitely coming out of his shell and expressing himself in ways he had not felt comfortable before. It meant we would sometimes catch Loxton singing or even dancing – if that's what you'd call it – when we called around and they were listening to rock music.

But this increasingly exhibitionist behaviour didn't always sit well with his sister, who confided she thought Loxton had changed for the worse. She'd been accustomed to him being of a particular demeanour through his youth, and perhaps as he became more open and less withdrawn, Kim feared the brother who shared the same travails of childhood had now disappeared. They began to butt heads more and more when they were back living under the same roof.

Poolhall—Jail—Library

Although Loxton and Jen had tried keeping their engagement a secret, Jen had started wearing the ring and several people suspected a looming wedding may be the case. Kim was one who spotted the new jewellery and was most forthright in asking them both if they had some news to share. It was her brother, one of her best friends and they all shared a house together. She figured she had a right to now.

When it was confirmed that the pair were engaged, they swore Kim to secrecy until they could properly announce it. This threw Kim into an immediate huff. She told Loxton and Jen she felt disappointed and deceived that they hadn't confided in her freely. In reality, Kim had two motives affecting her at this point in time. The first was that she had been together with Derrick for a lengthier time, and begrudged the fact he had not yet proposed to her. Secondly, she suspected her own imploding relationship may not yet reach that stage at all, for Kim and Derrick were consistently arguing, and the confrontations were increasing in ferocity and spite.

The straw that broke the camel's back came when Loxton permitted Marty to collect him from the home he shared with Kim, and drive him to a football match. While Loxton was in the process of reconciling his father-son relationship, Kim had no interest in getting to know Marty better. Being two-and-a-half years younger, she had only flitting recollections of her natural father, knowing him predominantly for providing a nagging sense of abandonment.

When Loxton arrived home later that evening, Kim flew off the handle at him. She reminded Lox it had been a condition of him being in the house that he did not reveal to his father where he lived. Loxton thought she was over-reacting and could only recollect her saying she wanted to have "no contact" with Marty. In actual fact, he had reprimanded his dad for parking directly outside and coming inside the gated front fence.

A bitter slanging match erupted along the length of the house until Kim stormed out crying, drove straight to my house with Derrick and shared details of the conflict. Several incendiary text messages were then exchanged between Loxton and Kim. It became clear, via the severity of the messages' content, that living under the same roof would no longer be an option for them.

I asked Derrick to call Loxton and invite him over, so that I could mediate the situation.

Loxton's old Toyota Celica screeched into the driveway within 30 minutes, and he marched to the front door with Jen in tow. Thankfully Steve had opted to take the other children and disappear from the ensuing skirmish, sensing the level of hostility about to unfold.

"Remember how Kim used to punch herself in the stomach to make herself cry and then tell you I'd hit her?" Loxton began loudly. "This is exactly like that. You have always – ALWAYS – taken her side. What a surprise she's coming running to you now. Unable to handle her own shit like the big, fat crybaby she is."

I stood my ground. "Loxton that's enough. Are you going to let me talk?"

"So you can stick up for her?" he responded in an instant.

"No Loxton. There are very, very good reasons why Kim is upset and, frankly, I am too. I...I said it was your own decision if you wanted to see your father again, but I can't lie if it upsets me. It hurts me deeply. After everything he did to us. You knew all that."

"He did all that stuff years ago," Lox contended. "Yeah he was unfaithful. He probably lied a lot. I'm sure you thought about being with different men as well. Everybody makes stupid mistakes. I know that better than most people. And, you know, I don't really like him anyway. I'm just trying to forgive him and have some semblance of a normal family again."

"I know Loxton, I know," I said. "It...it's just very hard whe..."

Kim interjected in a tearful rage. "How could you fucking talk to him? He used to fucking touch me for god's sake. Are you okay with that?"

Loxton paused, visibly hit by the revelation. He searched for the appropriate words.

"Kim, I swear I didn't know that. I vaguely remember something about him abusing someone being discussed when we were young, but I thought it was a story so we didn't have to see him again. I thought it was just something we were supposed to tell the children's court. I thought maybe Mum alluded to that so we would never leave her. After what happened with you and the fuckhead over the road, and those times Steve touched you...I take these things deadly seriously."

Tears were unexpectedly starting to well in Loxton's eyes. Beside him, Jen held his hand and tried to dry her own eyes. I then remembered her own prior experiences with the older admirer that stalked her.

"You don't remember at all?" I replied incredulous. "You were older than Kim and she remembers. You really don't remember the things he did. Or at least you don't remember the way things happened in reality."

I was too hurt to be diplomatic and sensitive to Loxton's feelings at this point.

"Are you saying he touched me too?" my son asked sharply.

I squared my jaw in pain. "He did it to you before we broke up. Then he kept doing it to Kim afterwards when he still had access. You were actually the one that told me when you were a boy...that you walked in on him touching Kim."

Loxton was now putting his hands to the side of his face and crying more freely.

"What do you mean he used to touch me? You've never told me that. I don't remember any of this and I remember everything." He was bright red and eyes dilated in pain.

"I did tell you," I replied. "You must have blocked a lot of things out."

"Surely I'd remember that." Loxton was pleading for it to be untrue. "Why do I remember everything else so clearly?"

I passed a box of tissues to Loxton and shrugged sympathetically and apologetically.

Then I felt it well up inside me. Involuntarily I turned my head sharply to both sides to try and subdue the pain that was returning from more than a decade earlier. It all felt so real again. So tiring, so nightmarish.

"He used to touch you in the bath. Not in a normal fatherly way. He was a very strange person. Sick. Sick is what he was. That's one of the reasons I tried to stop him being alone with you. There were so many things that he did."

I could no longer restrain myself from that point. I became a blubbering mess, overcome with the torment of my memories. Crying turned to a deep, pained moan that I had no control over. Later Loxton told me that it sounded as though I had just witnessed the death of a child or a fatal car accident.

He and Kim moved to comfort me, but I had to relinquish every last bit of truth; expel it from my chest.

"I tried to stop him from doing things so many times," I screamed. "I couldn't stop him from anything...even from doing things to me. Fuck him. Fuck him. You know what he did? He used to kidnap you and take you away from me and make me do things to get you back."

I began gesturing wildly.

"He was so...so screwed in the head – crazy – that he used to think all the time about me fucking Andreas, his best friend. He would accuse me of looking at him. I didn't like Andreas at all, the big, fat, hairy grub. Then, one time, he took you away for a few days and he rang me. Your father said the only way he could get over his jealousy was to watch me have sex with Andreas. I told him he was sick. He also wanted to have sex with his younger sister – your aunt. He said he wanted to be her first so that she knew a real man. He should have been in a jail. I told him that. I didn't want to fuck Andreas. Ever since I knew *your father, he was the only man I had been with. Then he got me to lie there and have his sweaty fucking fat friend fuck me while he watched with a drink. You were in the next room. Just the thought. It makes me so sick. You've got to understand I had to do it. Please understand. It's not what I wanted."*

BARCELONA // ARLES // NICE // PISA // FLORENCE

THUNDEROUS, yet mocking, applause greets me as I drag myself to the downstairs buffet. I try to slink into a tucked-away corner to escape the attention of the tour group. But after last night's performance on the boardwalk at Porto Olympic, I'm the talk of the bus.

The tour leader edges behind me as I dip a spoon into my hangover-relieving concoction of yoghurt and granola. She places a gentle hand on my shoulder.

"Just checking you're okay after last night? I heard you got into some trouble down at the port?"

"Yeah, it's all good," I say, shrugging off her concern.

"I mean, it sounds like you handled yourself well, but I thought I'd double-check," she continues. "It didn't really seem like something you'd get caught up in. I was a bit shocked to hear."

Well, now you know woman. You poke the ginger bear hard enough and this is eventually what happens.

Lucy is standing outside as we load our baggage on to the bus for an eight-hour drive to Nice, via the World Heritage ruins in the Roman settlement of Arles.

She is smirking the same bewildered smirk I can recall from the final moments of last night. Or at least, what I thought were the final moments.

"Do you remember you knocked on the door of our room when you got back from swimming? It must have been bloody freezing," she quizzes.

"Errm, no."

"You were checking to see if anyone was still partying. Safe to say, I had my sleep mask on by that time. Suzie and I had been looking after Juliana, making sure she wasn't sick on herself. Then I just crashed. Anyway, you did get me out of bed and we talked at the door. You don't remember any of it?"

Poolhall—Jail—Library

"No, not a thing," I apologise. "Look I'm really sorry how I behaved last night. Sorry if I ruined the sleep for you guys."

"Good, don't do it again," Lucy jokes. "No, it was entertaining. You've livened this trip up a bit. But yeah, maybe hang low and get some rest on the bus today."

And that's exactly what I endeavor to do, curling myself in a ball next to Pete and trying to compensate for what feels like at least six hours of missed sleep. Mind you, it's hard to doze off when the bloke next to you is singing renditions of The Darkness at the top of his vocal range.

Mercifully the bus pulls into a service station near the Spanish-French border and, while everyone grabs warm food, I order two bottles of San Miguel beer to aid my prospects of sleep. Mick, the bar manager on tour, factually points out that San Miguel is in fact a Filipino refreshment, not a traditional Spanish one.

Either way, it assists me in catching some zeds until we journey right up to the heart of Arles, stopping not far from a vintage children's carousel. There's only 90 minutes allowed for exploration. I've heard Arles is home to an amphitheatre that looks like a miniature version of Rome's Colosseum, so this is the first place I venture to. The venue still hosts bullfighting and concerts in modern times.

I'd read up on Arles a little before the tour, partly because there is a rugby league foothold in this part of the world. It was also a place of inspiration for Van Gogh. Despite what others on the tour may think of me today, there are some grey cells occupying my cranium.

In Arles, then later in Nice, I follow my patterned behavior of wandering solo and removing myself from the main group. I just find it so much more rewarding than being in a cluster, milling about aimlessly.

The two-day layover in the French Riviera is a chance for me to get back some semblance of fitness again and I walk as much as I can on both days. In Monaco that includes doing a lap of the Formula 1 track in darkness while the remainder of the group venture to the plush casino to fritter away their money – or more likely, their parents' money.

My reasons for wanting to see Monaco are more from the perspective of geographic and demographic curiosity. It's one of the smallest sovereign states in the world in land size and also one of the most densely populated. I've been fascinated by population density from as young as I can remember. There was a point in primary school where I read encyclopedias feverishly for anything to do with Bangladesh, because it had such a dense population. Indeed, I still support Bangladesh in cricket because of the affinity I developed back then.

Growing up in Australia, density fascinated me. Our nation was so sparsely populated and the notion of overcrowding seemed so foreign. It intrigued me to consider the pressures high population density would place on the environment, on government infrastructure, on transport systems, and the way it would change human relationships and interactions. Then, when I progressed to high school, I became probably the only kid in my class who hung off every word when we discussed Malthusian Theory. I still carry many of those teachings with me as gospel in everyday present life.

When people discuss things which I consider elemental – like climate change, population distribution, or birth rates – without full thought for eventual consequences, I grow frustrated and despondent very quickly. I'd go as far as to say my beliefs on sustainable demographics affect most aspects of my adult life. I don't pursue a top-flight career in Sydney because of it. I support greater, more relaxed migration to regional Australia because of it. I'm not inclined to ever have children, for a large part, because of those early learnings.

With all of this in mind, it's probably for the best I'm walking around Monaco by myself, taking it all in, through my own prism of interpretation. I doubt anybody else on this tour is contemplating such grave matters. They all spent hours and countless dollars dressing up for tonight's casino visit, and here I am, walking the streets in a cheap, striped long-sleeve top, cargo shorts and my joggers, without any sense of regret or fear that I'm missing out.

When I meet up with the others at the scheduled pick-up point, yes I'm as equally fascinated by the Ferraris, Lamborghinis and other opulent surrounds, but for vastly different reasons.

***   ***   ***

THERE have been many, hushed discussions on the bus the past few days about how we are going to source ecstasy tablets before a scheduled visit to Space Electronic Disco in Florence. I've been among them, but certainly am not the instigator. There's less than a month before I return to a new contract with the Queensland Rugby League and that's the last thing I need appearing in the newspaper. It's bad enough I got caught for drink driving this year, a day after my kickboxing fight was cancelled.

For those with a predilection for party drugs, listing the words 'Space Electronic Disco' on the official itinerary is like waving a flag to a red bull. The Asian kids on the trip are particularly hyped for it and are joyously recalling tales of past benders. They aren't big drinkers, so I guess they consider this to be their moment in the sun.

Even when we stop to snap photos of the Leaning Tower of Pisa, there's chat about whether the African men who are selling watches and statues – hurriedly packing all their belongings into cardboard boxes whenever a police officer approaches – might be able to source us a quantity of disco biscuits. I'm not sure that's what Galileo Galilei envisaged when he imagined dropping two round objects from the city's famed landmark.

Although I don't let slip, my enthusiasm for ecstasy is truthfully waning the closer we get to the much-vaunted night. For one, I'm mindful of the mushrooms in Amsterdam and the period of torture I suffered on the comedown. Secondly, my performance at Barcelona hardly requires an encore. Thirdly, I've started to pick up the earliest signs of a chest infection and feel increasingly rundown. As soon as we arrived in Florence, I set out for a fast-paced 5km jog, followed by bodyweight exercises. I felt the rapidly cooling air burning my lungs with each inhalation and suspected I may get sick. Now, I'm paying the price for ignoring that intuition.

There just might be a fourth factor playing with my mind too. Once back from the ill-fated jog, we head as a group to a hidden trattoria, where we are ushered into a candlelit back room. The space is so cramped, it is impossible to move your chair without maiming at least two people. If you want food or more drinks, there is no option but to remain stationary and hope the waiter will attend to you. Trying to wriggle out and walk to the counter would be like trying to push to the front of a mosh pit.

Mick starts a particularly erudite conversation around our table of eight, mostly male, travellers: "Which three girls on the bus would you most like to shag?"

Mick has nothing to lose at this point. He's already hooked up with two of the oldest desperados on the tour by this time, and has no qualms about his reputation. One of said women has turned into a Stage Three Clinger and has been following his every move like a hawk, but Mick really couldn't care less. He already has his eyes cast to the future.

Running through his top three, Mick reveals number three is Shelly, the bubbly South African girl, whose partner Wayne is sitting within earshot. Even more brazen, he nominates No. 2 as the wife of a Melbournian man who is seated right beside him.

"Yeah, I can't argue with that. Fair play. She is pretty hot," the husband chuckles.

"And then...drumroll please...," pronounces Mick. "Number one is that minx of a school teacher from the Gold Coast. Have you seen her dressed up? What an absolute dark horse. She could give me detention anytime. What's her name? Lisa?"

Taking a pause from their beer and wine, the assembled committee of perverts gives a collective reply: "Lucy?" They agree she is a worthy nomination.

A strange knot has already formed in my stomach and I join the conversation seconds too late. "Yeah I think it is Lucy."

With that, Lucy looks up from her entrée on an adjacent table and gives yet another one of those smirks. She has a damn different smirk for every occasion.

"What are you guys talking about?" she quizzes in a strangely playful, yet authoritative, voice.

"We were just seeing how that bruschetta tastes? We haven't received any food yet," I lie.

"Really?" she replies disbelievingly. "Hmm...it's actually a bit dry and bland. Disappointing. Not what I was expecting after the great food of the last few days. Let's hope the main courses are better."

Our table nods back together in agreeance before returning to a more hushed conversation. "Damn, I almost feel bad for saying I'd fuck her," whispers Mick. "She's a bit sweet. I bet she's a church girl."

As our nominations for top three shags continue around the circle, Lucy consistently features in discussions. Everyone seems to agree she is some kind of untouchable symbol of wholesomeness. Mind you, also featuring heavily in voting is Juliana, who Mick artfully excluded from his initial nominations on account of his friendship with Harry.

When it comes to me, I palm the question tactfully. "Gee. Come back to me. I'm still deciding who my third will be."

Except, mercifully, that opportunity never comes. Our meals are served, we tuck in ravenously and, as the alcohol takes effect, the conversation breaks off into multiple tangents and never returns.

When the night ends, the Tetris-like arrangement of the restaurant means I stay seated until everybody is up and moving towards the door. Last out, I find Lucy waiting behind for me on the cobbled street as everyone else migrates as a group.

"So, what were you guys really talking about? I saw you look over a few times," she pries.

"We were playing a game to see who could remember everyone's name on the bus. You're a bit of a quiet one, so a few of the guys had no idea," I lie again.

"Likely story. You were making fun of my stupid hair, weren't you? I can't get the fringe to sit straight in this weather. I love the European cold, but my hair hates it," Lucy continues, paranoid.

"Look, don't stress about it. I'll level with you. All the boys were nominating the cutest girls on the bus. You were popular." This is only a white lie.

Cue yet another one of those smirks and a bashful glow. "Oh really? I still don't believe you. Those boys must have low standards," Lucy quips.

We laugh and continue behind the others, dragging our feet as conversation turns to all the artistic wonders and landmarks we hope to discover throughout Italy the next week. It's spirited, meaningful conversation.

Just before we reach our hotel, Lucy pauses a second.

"So, who did you nominate? Who are the cuties on the bus?"

I scramble for an answer. Do I say something like 'A gentleman never tells his secrets?' or maybe a dramatic 'You, my beautiful rose. You take my breath away'?

Instead, this comes out:

"Definitely Pete. Have you seen how many local girls he's kissed so far on this trip? You know he went back to a French chick's house in Nice? He reckons she was an absolute wildcat. I'd have to say Pete is the cutest creature on the bus, for sure."

Lucy laughs absurdly and punches me in the arm. "Alright then mister. See you in the morning. Statue of David time. Yay!"

I WAS in such a state of hysteria after the revelations made to Loxton and Kim about their father that both asked if I required a doctor or ambulance. Declining, instead I buried my head into their shirts as they hugged me from both sides, sobbing until they were soaked through to the skin. It was one of the most painful, yet cathartic, days of my life. I had held those secrets for almost two decades.

"Don't think I'm stupid. Please don't tell anyone," I pleaded.

Loxton squeezed me tighter. "I'd never do that Mum. None of us here doubt a word you say. I'm very sorry you had to go through this."

"I've never even told Steve," I revealed.

"Look Mum, you are beyond courageous. I can't believe that someone would do that to you. You're even more courageous for telling us. I promise you this: Marty is as good as gone from my life. He will never see me again."

I don't know a time that has impacted my son's mental health more than that day.

Jen reported that Loxton went home and stayed in bed for the best part of a day-and-a-half. He called in sick on deadline day for his magazine.

The nausea in his stomach stemmed from two root causes. He felt he'd betrayed Kim and me for allowing Marty back in our lives. No matter what angle we tried to approach it from, Lox could not forgive himself. He was distraught that he had remembered things so incorrectly.

Secondly, Loxton had invited his father to his 21st birthday party, which was less than a fortnight away. He'd also accepted some money to go towards the costs. Now the only option was to ring his father, confront him and sever all ties.

Loxton later detailed to me the full phone conversation:

"I'm just calling to tell you this is the last day we talk." It was a rehearsed opening, but the only way Lox could get through the conversation.

"Oh yeah...?" Marty returned, slightly panicked, slightly angry.

"Yeah. It'd be better if we didn't talk or see each other anymore."

Marty laughed. "Where has this all come from?"

"Maybe you should have a think about what Andi and you did. I don't want to see you again you fucking sicko"

"What do you mean? Do you have any reason for this?"

"You know."

"What?"

"You know."

"I don't know Loxton. You'll have to tell me."

"It's not my place. This is all fucked up. Why did you have to do this? Why, fuck you?"

"Don't swear at me. You better have a good reason for talking to me like that. Fuck me, hey?"

"Yep...fuck...you."

"Is this something from your mother?"

"It's not from her. It's from you. It's what you and that other fucking bastard did."

"Oh, tell me." Marty now had his back up. "Tell me, what exactly did we do?"

"You know. You two took me away and then fucked her. You made her fuck Andi. That's fucking rape you fuckheads. I'll fucking kill you both."

"And what proof do you have of this? You mean you want to never see me again because something your Mum said that might be true...that's not true."

"Yep."

"C'mon Loxton. You're smarter than this. I never bloody did any of that. How can you believe that?"

"It's all I have to go on. Mum brought me up and she wouldn't lie about that. I saw her face. I wish I didn't have to do this, but I wish I didn't have a father who was a sick fuck."

"There's two sides to every..."

CLUNK. Loxton hung up in Marty's ear and gripped Jen's hand in silence.

*** *** ***

WITH all this happening in the background, Loxton went ahead with his 21st party, revealing to shocked and whispering guests that he had asked for Jen's hand in marriage.

A week after the party the young couple moved into a new-ish apartment towards Loxton's grandparents' house – my parents' house – at Gordon Park.

"She's my soulmate," Loxton confided of Jen to me in unusually open conversation. "After everything that's gone on these last few weeks; she digs me out of it. She understands. We just get each other."

Their first few months at the new apartment were like a honeymoon prior to the as-yet undecided wedding date. Whenever I would try and catch up with them, they'd be on some adventure or out at some restaurant – back at Garuva where they first met, at Tulio's, a delicious Italian buffet at Aspley, or down at the Scalded Cat Café. They bought antique furniture together and watched every movie that seemingly ever existed.

Gradually, Loxton's Uncle Howard began to have faith in Jen also, a massive step forward in the eyes of my son. Howard had snidely called Jen 'The Stork' for months beforehand, on account of her height, and Loxton didn't take kindly to the ridicule. After all, Jen had been invited to trial for the Australian women's volleyball team ahead of the Sydney Olympics, and Loxton only saw her size as a thing of beauty and athleticism.

Then again, Howard had never really talked to any of Loxton's friends and was quite threatened if anybody else became close to his nephew. That he started to accept and converse with Jen was a weight off Loxton's shoulders and an endorsement that had no parallel.

Work opportunities continued to pile up for Loxton. He became a more regular and trusted correspondent for the sports *magazine, which was just as well, as their lifestyle caused bills to mount.* As relationship and career took precedence, Loxton began to noticeably drop his commitment towards playing rugby league.

Some weeks he would only train once a week, persuaded to stay home to make up for lost time in the office and because Jen grew lonely without him there. One night he returned home and changed clothes, determined this time he would get some exercise and fulfil his commitments to the team.

Yet Jen begged him to stay, saying she felt strangely unwell. Loxton was tempted to shrug it off, but bit his lip and remained at home. Through the night, Jen experienced pain and tiredness that was unusual, even for a diabetic.

"I think we need to get you to the hospital if you don't improve by the morning," he said.

But come the crack of dawn, Jen ran from their bedroom to the toilet. She emerged 10 minutes later, a look of shock and bewilderment painted on her face.

"Something really weird is going on," Jen said. "Come look at this."

As she pointed to the bloodied contents of the toilet, Loxton held her with a sense of urgency.

"That's it. We've got to go now."

Thankfully Jen had a family physician who knew her from childhood, adored her and agreed to meet at his clinic immediately. The doctor had formed a tight relationship with Loxton, having met several times when Jen required new insulin or took a bad turn with her diabetes.

However, on this occasion he requested Loxton remain outside. After what felt like an eternity, the doctor's big wooden door slid open and Jen ran out instantly, straight past Loxton in the waiting room, out through the glass front door to the carpark.

"You'd better get out there," the doctor told Loxton glumly.

My son jogged after Jen and caught her crying against a concrete pillar.

"I've lost a baby. It was only a few weeks old, but it's gone now. Probably a good thing. I couldn't have one safely even if we wanted to." With that, Jen broke down bawling in Loxton's arms, but then just as quickly, turned off the tap and controlled herself. "It really is okay. We don't need a baby hey?"

For a few weeks they kept their news to themselves. Then Loxton divulged the secret to me one day in the kitchen.

"Mum, I've never wanted kids, but this has made me think a lot. Maybe some people are so wonderful that you should have children with them to perpetuate their memory and attributes?"

Loxton definitely appeared more rocked by the loss of the baby than Jen.

However, he suffered after that in a way that was as much his own fault as it was terrible misfortune. Lox became ultra-protective of Jen. He viewed their relationship as 'us against the world' and would barely let her out of his sight. Unfortunately, he reverted back to the same uncertain, jealous, awkward boy he'd been in his teens.

If Jen wanted to spend time with her family or friends, Loxton would question why she preferred their company. The more he tried to cling to her and told her she was his everything, the more he scared her away and prompted her to rebel.

"I think she's going to leave me shortly," Lox offered one day from nowhere. "There's six billion people in this world, so why would she want to spend her life with me? The idea that your true love could come from the same city, the same school, the same friendship circle is just stupid on my behalf. She can do much better."

"I think you're going off the deep end Loxton," I countered. "You'll self-destruct if you keep thinking this way. Just take things at face value. Don't try and cling to her. There's that old saying: 'If you truly love something, set it free'."

Poolhall—Jail—Library

Loxton completely mistook what I was trying to say. He thought I was imploring him to break up with Jen, not simply to give her more freedom and space, and to be less negative.

"You know what I say to Jen whenever she tells me she loves me now?" my son said.

"No, what?"

"I just stare her in the face and say 'Why?'. Why would she choose to love me of all people? I'm a fuck-up."

FLORENCE // ROME // VERONA // VIENNA

"I GUESS red wine might keep me alive," I say, half hanging out of my bedsheets towards the door and sniffling

This morning's planned trip to see Michelangelo's statue of David never did happen. Nor did the walking tour around the rest of Florence. I made it as far as the Ponte Vecchio – a medieval arch bridge at the centre of the city, where lovers place padlocks with their initials on them – before I turned around and came straight home.

I'm really struggling with my health. I haven't been this sick in ages. I'm burning a fever and my lungs feel like they've been hit with an algae infestation. After lying in bed and blowing my nose most of the day, I've now got Pete, Juliana and Lucy standing at the doorway.

"C'mon Loxie," Pete goads. "Space Electronic Disco tonight dude."

"Yeah baby. Woot!" adds Juliana for extra effect.

"Don't forget the wine first though. Wine is where it's at," chimes in Lucy. "We've got that dinner amongst the ruins with those other two tour groups."

"This is my time to shine," declares Pete. "Fresh ladies who don't know what a creep I am. Bang, bang, bang!"

I'm actually flattered the trio would remember my room number and bother to call past. I'd more or less planned to sequester myself in this bed for the rest of the day and avoid all human interaction. But now that they've stopped in, I can feel my arm being twisted.

"OK so definitely no pills for me tonight at the disco," I preface the conversation. "But I guess red wine might keep me alive."

"So that was two ecstasy pills for Mr Loxton," Pete pretends to scribble on an imaginary notepad.

"Good lord," I reply.

"That's all we needed to hear. Now let's get ready to part-ay," freelances Juliana.

Lucy stands at the door and rolls her eyes. She's anti-drugs. This has already been firmly established. "A wine might be the smarter choice Mr Loxton," she advises.

Tonight's intersection of three separate tour groups is like a Jagerbomb at 5am. The sexual proclivities of our group do not require any encouragement. There are so many flirtations and brief hook-ups already happening, I'm sure I'm oblivious to at least a handful. Now we're going to mingle with another 100 young adventurers high on life, where you don't have to see any of them ever again.

Sounds like a perfect recipe, right? Throw in endless bottles of wine, delicious food, an imitation Italian temple converted into a chic playhouse and the promise of amphetamines afterwards.

We've been told to dress up tonight. The guide wants us looking our finest for the dinner and Italians can be quite fussy on who they let into their discotheques, she says. Accordingly, I bring out my shined black shoes, iron my black trousers and button up my white collared shirt for perhaps the only appearance this overtly formal ensemble can expect on tour.

The bus smells of 50 dissonant perfumes and aftershaves. With the odours combined, the air could be bottled and marketed as a new fragrance – 'Urgency and Desperation'.

We sit on the stationary bus for a good 10 minutes without the engine even starting for our departure. There are two spare seats and the guide is watching the digitised clock that sits on the bus dashboard. Out of the front door of the hotel spills Suzie, Lucy's teaching colleague. She is dressed in a jacket and pants that suggest she may have just returned from Alpine hiking. Everyone seems puzzled as to what would hold her back.

"Sorry, bloody Lucy needed me to hold her hair in place," Suzie yells to the entire bus. She's definitely a bit more uncouth than her roommate.

Then Lucy ascends the steps of the bus. The humble chariot is lit up by playful whistles on both sides of the centre aisle. Lucy is wearing an intricate knee-length white lace dress that suggests she might be ducking off to a wedding somewhere. Her hair and make-up are impeccable. There's been noticeable effort on her behalf, but the result still manages to be classical. Her blue eyes squint through tapered lashes as she finds her way to the last remaining seat, a generous cleavage highlighted by the downlights.

"Holyyy sheet," says Mick audibly from several rows away. He doesn't even try to disguise how impressed he is.

"Yo hot momma," teases Juliana from further down the bus.

When we arrive at the temple for dinner, the driver struggles up a steep driveway before parking at a grand entrance. All the way, leading down to the dining area below, are a series of arches with white drapes set over them. The tables and chairs are set out like a banquet hall, also covered in pristine white linen.

The other tour groups have already arrived and, if we thought Lucy had gone the extra mile in presentation, we're blown away by the packs of unknown girls who are flaunting hours' worth of preening.

"Right, now's your chance to pair up and make a grand entrance," enthuses tour leader Jane.

I feel the slightest tickle down the outside of my hand and sense two soft, small fingers looping around to interlock.

Lucy smirks. "Shall we?" She invites me to lead her into the function, mirroring each other's gait as we stride shoulder-to-shoulder.

I'm trying to stay nonchalant, but it must be asked: What on Earth is happening here? She is a bona fide stunner. Easily the hottest girl in the vicinity. Actually, I take that back. The hottest *lady*.

Why would she bother choosing me? I'm like the nerd in one of those American spoof movies who somehow lands the prom queen. She saw me lose my marbles in Barcelona and still wants a piece of this? There must be something wrong with her.

I'm so caught up in the moment, that as I escort Lucy to a free table, pulling out her chair politely, I totally lose track of where our friends have been seated. We're soon surrounded by a few of the older couples on tour, who although perfectly nice, are not our usual crowd.

"Oh, it seems we've become estranged from the group," Lucy pronounces in mock horror.

"I don't think I could go drink-for-drink with Pete tonight anyhow," I reply.

"Oh, that's right. You're dying of man flu, aren't you?" she jibes. "But a drink does sound quite nice doesn't it?"

I let Lucy lead the charge when it comes to drinking. The last thing I need after a course of anti-biotics is to get wasted in front of three tour groups, sitting next to Mother Bloody Teresa.

Lucy is opening up. She is originally from Mackay. One of her brothers is an aspiring musician in Brisbane. Another works in finance in London. The London brother has a flat in a posh part of town and is getting a little too big for his boots, Lucy chides. Her parents are hard-working, honest people from Queensland's north with a rural upbringing. They encouraged all their kids to be well-educated, like to get outdoors and are regulars at the beach.

"Would you like another glass of wine?" the Italian waitress asks in an adorable accent.

"Why not?" Lucy replies with abandon, before turning to me. "So, what about your family?"

"Well, I'm the oldest of five kids," I say matter-of-factly. "And my parents died in a car crash shortly after the youngest was born."

The second part is complete fabrication. The first part is not even 100 per cent factual if you count all my step-sisters and step-brothers.

However, this is definitely not the first time I've lied to someone that my parents are dead. Especially if I'm talking to someone from a stable, nuclear family. It's much simpler and dignified than explaining the true story.

"Oh, that's terrible," says Lucy. "I'm sorry."

"It's okay," I respond. "It's all history now. Life only goes in one direction and that is forward, right?"

What a bare-faced liar. Trying to sound like Mr Positive Mantra is perhaps the biggest misrepresentation of all my fibs.

We continue to chat and Lucy reveals she has few friends, just a small tightknit circle of girls from her hometown. She doesn't spend an awful lot of time with anyone outside of work on the Gold Coast. She's dedicated to becoming as good an English teacher as possible. She likes to read and listen to music a lot and is fascinated by science, especially human biology.

"So...," begins my $24 million question. "Nobody special in your life then?"

She sighs and taps a bracelet against her wine glass. "No. I was with a long-time boyfriend until a little over a year ago and then we broke it off. I've had the odd date here or there, but it's not really my thing...dating that is. I just find it so fake and contrived. It's a snake pit."

As much as I lack self-confidence to seize opportunities, even a fool would be blind to all the green lights popping up. Lucy keeps 'bumping' into me at every city. She came and practically ripped me out of bed this afternoon. She's been single for over a year and just happened to choose me to walk through the grand entrance with her.

But then those familiar ghouls cross my train of thought. Lucy doesn't need a guy like me in her life. I'm the most unfit I've been in a long time. I'll be flat broke in two weeks. I was literally dragged to her and introduced to her by the 18-year-old girl I had fleeting thoughts about romancing just a few days beforehand.

Nah buddy, you can't do this to Lucy. She doesn't deserve a jerk.

And really, I do have to question what my reasons for being attracted to Lucy are. Do I just like her because she seems to like me? Do I just like her because all the other boys on the tour have put her on a pedestal? Is this an ego trip? What if she wasn't this good-looking? What if Juliana had snogged me in Barcelona instead of Harry?

I make a conscious note to skip the next glass of wine. I need to think this shit through.

As if on cue, Juliana and Harry, Pete and Mick, and the South African couple – Wayne and Shelly – saunter behind our chairs.

"Well, look who it is," announces Juliana. "The cute couple." Juliana hangs an arm over Lucy's exposed shoulder and hugs her from the side. "How are things over here? Things are getting a bit cray-zee at our table."

"Yeah," Pete says simply, bulging his eyes wide open, holding up wine glasses in both hands, then letting an unfamiliar girl in a tight-fitting dress squeeze past him.

"Are you excited for Space Disco later?" asks Juliana, without giving time for a reply. "Anyway, we just came over to say hello. We're social butterflies you know baby? Better keep moving."

All six of them insist on chinking glasses as they depart. I detect a sense of begrudging from Harry and Mick.

Shelly is the last to touch glasses and looks at us with eyes of sweetness and sincerity: "You do make a great couple."

As they waltz off into the crowd, I let out a burst of laughter. "I am definitely going to avoid those six for the rest of the night. I don't think I'll do the disco afterwards."

"But, aren't you going to…you know?" Lucy quizzes, making a weird gesture that could suggest somebody having an epileptic fit. She's trying to ask me if I'm taking drugs tonight in the exact way you'd expect a god-faring, English teacher with no experience of narcotics would.

"Oh, hell no," I confirm. "I'm being absolutely truthful when I say this is the sickest I've been in my adult life. I feel like I'm running a temperature of 200 degrees."

"It's not the company?" Lucy asks sarcastically. "You don't reckon you could make it out for one drink? Let's just see what the place is like and then we can go home early if you like. Don't leave me alone with these lunatics. Haha."

Lucy is successful in her pleas and, after another hour or so chatting effortlessly over dinner, we trek out to Space Electronic Disco. I fork over the exorbitant cover charge and, only metres inside the club, I'm met by an overly keen Thao, the Vietnamese drug aficionado on tour.

"Sweet. You're here Lox. Those local guys I was hoping would come through with the pills haven't. You can help me find out if anyone else here is carrying," he enthuses.

"Ah, look Thao," I say. "I actually wish I was home in bed right now. I'm not going to have a big night. Sorry mate, I know I'm being boring. I had grand plans to hit it hard tonight, but I'm not feeling it now."

Thao is downcast and a little angry. "Mate this is Space Electronic Disco. This is Florence. We're on the other side of the world man. When are we ever going to be back?"

"Maaaate…," I begin to reason before signalling that I've arrived with Lucy.

"Oooh," says Thao with a sudden realisation. "I see. Enjoy your night. Hopefully I'll be enjoying mine too soon. Remember, if you suss anything out, let me know first."

Poolhall—Jail—Library

Lucy has followed me into the club so closely that her breasts have been grazing the middle of my back for the past few minutes while I conversed with Thao. We join the throng on the main dancefloor, but spend most of our time mingling and talking with the other tour group members, catching up with anybody we've missed the last few days and maintaining an air of geniality.

There's a good half-dozen who are still sniffing the club for ecstasy, but I can sense it will all fizzle out to nothing. Most are too scared to approach anybody. I'm glad I dismissed the possibility early.

I find myself later dancing opposite Lucy upstairs. She's not one for making a spectacle of herself, but we're having solid fun bouncing along to acceptable club remixes of A-ha and Bowie, skipping the naff songs in between. We chat as we dance, which necessitates moving closer together and talking into each other's ears above the volume of the music.

Lucy smells fantastic. She looks gorgeous. I genuinely enjoy her company. The physical tension between us has definitely raised a few notches in the past half-hour. If I had swallowed a pill, things would either get very hot'n'heavy from here or I would make a gigantic tit of myself. They are the only two eventualities in that circumstance.

But in my relatively sober state, I'm again thinking that I shouldn't lead Lucy on or take advantage of her eagerness. I'm too physically drained to consummate anything in my present form. I'd only give her a terrible performance. Besides, I need to figure out in my head what she means to me. Is this attraction forming just because she is at close proximity on the bus? Have we been drawn together like magnets because we live within driving distance in Australia? What if Audrey from Galway was in this very club right now? Who would I pick between the two of them? Both intelligent, pretty, witty women.

Overthinking this situation has taken the bounce out of my step, and as Juliana and Harry slide over to dance with us,

I welcome them into an expanded circle, creating more space between Lucy and I.

There's an unspoken rivalry with Harry that I'm sure is not entirely imagined on my behalf. I probably am threatened by him if I'm to be honest. He has jet-black hair, could even have a touch of Mediterranean blood in him, has a quickfire answer for any scenario and a killer smile. He's a charismatic opportunist who never misses a beat. Harry is everything I am not.

Although I feel it's becoming old news, he lured in Juliana first and now he and Lucy are smiling at each other and giggling away, at the same time that my own misgivings grow. I'm on the downward slope of enjoying the night. I can feel pessimism rising and am probably correct – don't let Lucy give me false hope and vice-versa. Give the girl space. Don't fuck with her heart. Or your own.

"I think I'm going to go home," I offer abruptly, indicating my throat is killing me. I say goodbye in such quick terms that nobody can stop me or try and convince me otherwise.

***   ***   ***

ROME is home to some of the most desirable destinations on any tourist's itinerary. Yet for me, it is also where my health reaches a nadir.

If it wasn't for my eagerness to see places like the Colosseum, Trevi Fountain, Pantheon, Spanish Steps and Circus Maximus, I would stay in bed the entire 48 hours we are here. Instead I try and wake up prior to anybody else, catching public transport to the tourist hotspots before the sun can provide much heat to the Italian capital. I cross my intended destinations off like they are shopping list items, not places of wonderment.

After a frustrating visit to the pharmacy where I try to translate my need for echinacea, I head back to the camp site just as many of the group are getting up to commence their day. My designated roommate Liam has become an increasing oddity over the course of this tour. We've barely seen each other most days, and when we have crossed paths it's usually after midnight when we're both drunk, or when he is walking around chatting on his phone to his Mum.

One night in Nice he sleep-walked and pissed at the end of his own bed. Another day he walked in on me naked in the shower. A few times our beds have been so close that we've rolled over and touched hands or snored in the other's face. We don't share a single mutual friend on the tour. Our interactions are stilted, awkward moments that can't pass quickly enough.

"Are you still sick?" he says as I re-enter our cabin.

"Yeah, I'm really sorry mate."

"It's okay. But if it's alright by you, I might request to move to another cabin for a few days. I've already had a touch of sickness on this trip and just want to be safe," explains Liam.

I'm secretly relieved. I'd love a few days in isolation. Our cabins are nestled in quiet, leafy hills well outside the centre of Rome and I set about sleeping the rest of the day away. My temperature fluctuates wildly. I'm not entirely sure whether it is the effect of the surrounding winds momentarily calming the unseasonal Roman heatwave, or my body's complete inability to maintain homeostasis.

In the moments I am not dead asleep, I ponder my relationship status far too much. I decide to give Lucy a wide berth. She probably is attracted to guys like Harry as well.

I don't sit with her or, in fact, anywhere near her on the bus the next few days, though I am constantly mindful of where she is located. I can remember every word Lucy says to me when we cross paths briefly at pickup points, but am convinced we'd be no good for each other.

Venice was one destination on the trip where it could have been anticipated that romance would flourish, but for me it is the exact opposite. I end up dragging my sniffling nose and sorry arse around the canals with Simon, the boy I sat next to on Day One, the one who separated from the mother of his child and is weaning himself off meth.

We don't talk a lot and, at the end of the day, I ask him whether he wants to join the rest of the tour group for a traditional dinner, set to feature violin serenades.

"Oh man, I can't," he says. "That collectors' store we stopped in before…I bought 200 Euros worth of Japanese vampire manga porn. I won't have any money until my Mum can transfer some more."

What. The. Actual. Fuck.

I stopped in that store to get my Mum postcards and spoons and he somehow found cartoon vampire smut on DVD?

CONVERSATIONS about Jen started to become more critical.

The more Loxton doubted her love towards him, the more he found fault with her.

She was putting on weight, he said. She was much more concerned with her family than keeping things happy at home. She was wearing shirts to provoke interest from other boys. She should stop smoking.

Criticism was Loxton's antidote to insecurity, He desperately wanted Jen to respond to any of these accusations. Any outward willingness to change on her behalf would have convinced him he still held a special place in her heart. Instead Jen took the opposite tact. She wanted him to show he still loved her by accepting her, warts and all. She wanted him to relax and not be so over-bearing.

Then Loxton made an irreparable mistake.

"She was searching for wedding dresses, but couldn't care less if I was in room," he explained. "So, I said to her: 'You seem more in love with the idea of being married than you are in love with me'. We had a big fight. I went to bed and when she came in, I told her maybe it was just me realising I actually didn't love her. Mum, I've never made a girl cry like that. I broke something inside her."

From there, things became extremely rocky between the pair. From one of the most intense romances I'd witnessed, they became heart-breakingly fractured.

Jen moved back to her parents' house twice, but returned after Loxton begged her. Whenever disagreements came to a major boiling part, he'd tell her he didn't love her again. It was his nuclear option and way to drive a knife through her heart and finish on top.

Except, he never did finish on top in this scenario, as he'd always regret his actions, loathe himself more, and pine for Jen when she walked out on him.

"How many times do I have to hear you don't love me before I go for good?" Jen asked him in one desperate stand.

I could see the mental state of them both deteriorating.

Then, just before Christmas in 1999 a bombshell dropped – Jen's own parents, who lived such a charmed life from an outsider's perspective, announced they were splitting. Jen's father was found to have been engaged in an online affair with a lady in the USA. The lady's username was 'The Walrus' and photos in hidden computer files showed she was an overweight lady with glasses and children of her own.

Jen knew about her parents splitting before anybody else, but was initially unaware of the infidelity aspect. The subsequent cascade of revelations brought her world crumbling down. Most of us observed that Jen's father had appeared the more loving and committed of the two parents, so the whole matter came as a huge shock.

The extent of the impact on Jen became apparent when she was placed in a psychiatric hospital. Loxton had grown up visiting his Uncle Howard in similar wards and witnessed first-hand how his personality shifted for the worse when medication and electro-convulsion therapy were introduced to the mix. Thus, my son rallied against his fiancée being admitted to the hospital, which placed him firmly at loggerheads with Jen's mother in an ongoing, heated confrontation. Eventually her mother bulldozed over the top, unwilling to negotiate in the face of serious health risks to Jen.

Loxton's profound sadness and despair at the situation came in direct contrast to news he had recently been commissioned to author his first sports book by a small publisher. He took time off from his normal job to complete the final chapter, and split his time between working on the manuscript and visiting Jen at lunch and in the evenings. Medical staff warned him numerous times he shouldn't visit too frequently, although Jen encouraged him to stay at her bedside and to fall asleep together. It was only a matter of days before Loxton realised this hospital was unlike the ones Howard had been interred within, putting his mind at ease.

Poolhall—Jail—Library

Once the book was finished, Loxton needed to travel to Sydney to be present at the launch. This marked his first time venturing to Australia's biggest city and he wanted Jen released from hospital so they could fly there together. The request was denied, so instead he rang her twice a day from interstate while away.

On the eve of the launch there were troubles, with the publisher under financial duress. The prospect the publisher would halt or cancel production continued right up until the fateful day, when Loxton was to be present at the Institute of Sport with several leading rugby league coaches. At that stage he didn't care whether he would be paid. He merely wanted his work released to the world. The book ended up being released and Loxton was remunerated in full, however the publishers skimped on materials and distribution. It was a day of wildly mixed emotions for Lox, as I found when I called to congratulate him.

He also revealed to me that Jen had opted to begin a course of anti-depressants while he was away, which bothered him a great deal. Loxton was vehemently against drugs all throughout his youth, and I've seen no evidence that his stance has changed in adulthood, aside from his many insane hairstyles.

Jen was released from hospital before Loxton could return from his week-long commitments in Sydney. It was decided she would stay at her parental home to help her mother through the divorce, begin studying a course in childcare, then move back to the apartment shared with Loxton.

Lox extended the lease on their unit by another six months, but Jen became a rare visitor to their shared home. My son said to me he thought the divorce of Jen's parents might make her value their relationship more, but the opposite was true. She had lost faith on many fronts. She'd grown up in a home where everything was rosy for 20 years only to be told it was all a big lie.

"Maybe I don't believe in us as much. People don't seem to stay in love forever," she confided in Loxton.

Jen began putting up walls and was clearly mentally disengaged the next time I saw her at my home. Some of the ego and callousness I'd seen in her youth – when we only knew her as Kim's friend – began to resurface. I have no doubt though, it was a reaction to the exceptional circumstances of the time.

"I don't want to have to beg her to put more effort into us," Loxton despaired.

At one point, Jen moved back in with Loxton, they had a fight, and she moved back out again just as quickly, with her mother driving over to transport her belongings. Loxton hated when Jen involved her parents in the middle of disagreements, primarily because he thought disagreements should stay between couples, but also because he didn't have the same option.

There were two carloads needed for Jen to move out, and between trips, Loxton urinated over the remainder of her belongings in much the same way he had urinated on his father's bus as a child. It was indeed an infantile response that only further deepened the division.

From that moment, Jen would not answer any of Loxton's phone calls or text messages. He managed to eventually ascertain from Jen's younger sister that she had moved down the Gold Coast to live with a female friend for a while.

Loxton couldn't accept that Jen wouldn't even dignify him enough to respond. He simply couldn't cope with that fact. He visited me and cried openly, growing despondent to a point where he was hyperventilating and stuttering his words. I moved beside him on the couch and stroked his hair as I would when he was a child. It was the only way I could think to calm him.

Unbeknown to all of us at this point, Loxton had stolen some of Jen's possessions – her insulin vials. When he left my house, still upset, he was blaring rock music from his speakers and apparently called his estranged fiancée again on the phone, this time successfully reaching her.

As Jen picked up the phone, Loxton said just one word: "Goodbye".

VIENNA // MUNICH

I'M PRESENTLY drifting through a pirate musical that has engulfed my entire room. After being sick for almost a week, more than a quarter of this entire European leg, I've pulled out all stops to get healthy in the days before Christmas.

Earlier today I went down to the sauna and sat inside it an hour while the Austrian locals pranced in and out, completely nude. I was willing to endure all sorts of shrivelled, old man penises and rotund bellies flapping about near my face, solely in the quest to put my health back on track.

After the sauna I then climbed the stairs back to my hotel room, where Pete thoughtfully gave me a bottle of cough syrup. I took two hearty swigs and went to lie down in bed. Our Viennese hotel is one of the plushest accommodations we are set to enjoy on this tour, designed to look like a giant glass pyramid from the outside.

I've opened the window and am lying on top of my freshly cleaned bedsheets, feeling refreshed from sweating so profusely in the hour preceding. Magically, the room is transforming into a bright yellow cartoonish hue. Through the window squeezes a dark-stained pirate ship, and it sails across in front of my eyes, expanding in size rapidly as it drifts. Finally, it comes to rest on the far wall, as if projected there by some hidden audio-visual equipment.

I hear chanting begin, at first discordant, but then harmonious, building louder into orchestral proportions. I try to use the television remote control to turn down the volume because I fear disturbing the other hotel guests. The sound is at eardrum-breaking point.

As one, all the pirates before my eyes link arms, and starting dancing across the wall, continuing their cheery performance.

I finally click that I am dreaming. I try to force myself to wake up. Instead, nothing changes. All that happens is I make some loud grunting noises that sound like a woozy dog.

The pantomime continues and now the pirates are taking turns to give solo performances, their cheeks blossoming and their song delivery strong and inventive. I try to force myself to wake up again, but cannot.

"Knock, knock," says Pete as he opens the door to my room.

"How did you get inside my dream?" I slur to him.

"Bahahahaha. What the fuck are you talking about? This isn't a dream. You're awake you mental case."

"Wait a second," I say, using one arm to push myself up from the bed.

"You've been making these loud weird pig noises," Pete continues to chuckle.

"Yeah I've been trying to wake up," I say. "Wait a second, if this isn't a dream, can you see the pirates on the wall?"

"No," Pete replies incredulously. "You are tripping big-time."

"What the hell was in that cough syrup? Did you slip something into it?" I question.

"It's just standard cough syrup, I think. I got it from the store, so it can't be too strong. Have you had anything to eat today at all? Maybe you were so dehydrated from the sauna that it's hit you hard. Do you think I should call the tour leader or a doctor," he says with surprising concern.

"No...it's actually quite...enjoyable," I smile. "So, you definitely don't see any pirates? Gee I wish you could see this. It's a reasonably elaborate production."

Pete hands me two glasses of water.

"If you don't mind mate, I might save the water for a little while and ride this show out to the end," I say. "Who would have thought that the cough syrup in Vienna would get me higher than a night at Space Electronic Disco?"

"You're a crazy fucker. I'll leave you to it and bring some food up," promises Pete. "Wait until I tell the others about this."

Later in the night the group is scheduled to attend a Ludwig van Beethoven tribute performance. At the pick-up point, Lucy approaches me for the first time in days.

"I hear you've already been treated to one show today," she laughs, referring to my hallucinogenic episode. "Lucky you."

Nothing is spoken about the intervening period between us having deep and meaningfuls in Florence and this stilted conversation. It's almost like both of us refuse to recognise either the previous moments of intense flirtation or the proceeding dead silence.

At the Beethoven dinner and concert, we sit at the same table, but not together. Lucy is way more into the classical music than I am, and after a few wines, as the evening grows long, she invites me up to dance. I politely decline as I'm still sober, trying to annihilate the final strains of sickness. I'm also remaining steadfast in my opinion that I shouldn't lead her on.

I feel like I'm probably being a jerk for denying the waltz, but otherwise I'm on the up-and-up. The pirate hallucination and afternoon laughs with Pete have injected much-needed mirth back into my mindset. I'm being chatty with everyone around our table, can finally taste food again and don't feel like falling asleep constantly.

*** *** ***

MY RETURN to drinking is saved for the special location of Munich's Hofbräuhaus the following night, Christmas Eve.

We've all been given a 'Secret Santa' recipient – the name of someone else from the tour, drawn out of a hat at random. I get Bevan, the chubby kid who loves taking selfies with everyone. Each 'Secret Santa' gift must be 10 Euros or less in value and wrapped, then handed over to the tour guide.

Invoking memories of when Jen bought Derrick a plastic dinosaur and sword for his 18th birthday at Garuva, I scour Munich's outdoor Christmas markets until I find two bizarre plastic moulds of wrestlers. One is purple and one is green.

There is no hidden context to my present. I just hope it messes with Bevan's head a little.

My mind flits back to that fateful night when Jen transformed from my sister's previously annoying friend to somebody who carried the essence of life wherever she went. God, I fell so completely, naturally for her. I still remember the chance meeting at Garuva so vividly.

Jen was dressed entirely in black, a double-strapped top, pin-striped pants and exaggerated heels. She dwarfed me. Looked absolutely statuesque, but sexy as hell. Her top rode up at the back whenever she extended her arms. Her skin, her smile, her sass; she had it all.

I'd always secretly thought she was the cutest of my sister's friends and, although Kim didn't know, Jen and I had flirted at a volleyball tournament previously. Jen was a gun at the sport, beating everyone and anyone, regardless of if they were older or younger, male or female. She played a school championship final with no shoes, in baggy comical pants and with her hair tied up messily like she'd just risen from bed. Whenever she won a point, she would do a little jig and pull funny faces to herself.

It flicked my switch. I liked her moxie.

Then when she bought Derrick that damn stupid dinosaur for his birthday, I dunno, it just appealed to me. I remember, that same night, she ended up stubbing out her cigarette on the same plastic stegosaur when I told her I didn't kiss girls who smoked.

Our attraction was entirely unforced. I've struggled immensely to feel that with anybody since.

***   ***   ***

ONCE Christmas gifts are bought, we all rendezvous at Germany's premier beerhall. Although the Hofbräuhaus's links to the rise of the Nazi party are discussed, we do not dwell on them, instead diving straight into steins of beer. A portly, elderly waitress in traditional garb floats between tables carrying four steins in each hand. We try to replicate her efforts, but fall woefully short.

Such is the power of peer pressure and group dynamics, several members of the tour start by skolling as much as they can from their first stein. I'm not one of them. I've learned from partaking in that kind of malarkey too many times in the past. Instead I set my sights on finishing three steins for the night, equivalent to three litres, six pints or around eight schooners of beer in an evening. That's a figure I can reach without compromising either my masculinity or my health irreparably.

I'm nestled in the corner of our table. To my left is Pete and to my right are Juliana and Harry. Directly opposite me is Lucy who, as per normal, looks like she just walked out of a salon. I'm not usually into women who spend an awful lot of time on their appearance, but she is hardly your stereotypical high-maintenance chick. By day, she could pass for the little old lady from the Tweetie Pie cartoon. There's no fake tan, more often than not she's in something long-sleeved and classical, and she doesn't go overboard with make-up. Ladies don't need to when they've got eyes like hers.

Our meals of pork-knuckle and sauerkraut are a welcome and delicious interval to our task of imbibing as much beer as we can in just over two hours. After easing off alcohol the last few days, my tolerance to booze is not as impressive as some of the others. A guy from Townsville and Wayne from South Africa lead the charge and are close to the bottom of their second steins before we know it. Lucy is having a go at conquering a single glass, but she is sipping her way through it at snail's pace.

There are plenty of laughs to be had around the table as the night progresses. Everyone is well and truly in the yuletide spirit. Even Harry and I are chinking glasses.

Poolhall—Jail—Library

Because we are seated directly in each other's line of sight, it's impossible for Lucy and I to not cross gazes at regular intervals. There's not a great deal said between us, but I do catch her eyes flickering up at me multiple times. I know I'm subconsciously taking note of her every minute movement. At the times where we stare at each other simultaneously, she smiles and her eyes reveal both warmth and a tinge of sadness.

Most of us pile on the bus before its scheduled departure time, decidedly tipsy. A few stragglers, namely Pete, decide to stay behind at the Hofbräuhaus to continue amorous pursuits with local drinkers. I'm mostly focused on holding my bladder for the 30-minute ride home. I downed two-and-a-half steins, not quite making it to three. Meanwhile, those who made it all the way through three glasses appear very jolly indeed.

With no hesitation, Lucy and I sit together on the trip, a small, but significant thawing of our little stand-off. We discuss what we'd otherwise be doing in Australia on Christmas Eve, surrounded by those we love and the all-consuming heat. I can tell Lucy is a very family-oriented person. She's also a very serious, calculated communicator. That might scare some people off, but I see it as a reflection of my own style.

The fella from Townsville who has smashed down three steins is arguing with his wife in the hallway as we all retreat to our separate rooms. Lucy and I stay behind as mediators and try and convince them for an hour how wonderful their respective partners are, how they are on the trip of a lifetime and should savour this time together. No sooner have we negotiated world peace, than we hear a loud thumping on the locked glass doors of the hotel foyer.

It's Pete and a German girl in her mid-to-late-twenties. They've just stepped out of a taxi. I bet Pete has used the same story that he is aged 25 again.

"Let me in fuckers," he yells.

Snow has begun to fall heavily and Pete is shivering in a thin skivvy. He rubs his hands as I unlock the entrance, and he walks past me, showing the girl around the hotel. They inspect some artwork, then disappear out the back doors where there is a little shielded arbory. I can hear them laughing around the side.

"Well that wasn't too clever, was it?" I say to Lucy. "Now I'll have to wait here to let them back in again."

"I don't think they'll be back in a hurry," Lucy smirks.

"You could be right. Hey, I don't suppose you want to grab a cup of tea back in my room and watch the countdown to midnight on TV?" I blurt. "It'd be a shame to spend the first seconds of Christmas alone in such a beautiful part of the world."

I don't know where this sudden shift in confidence and thinking has come from, but I'm just trying to be genuine. If you enjoyed someone's company and found their conversation interesting, you would invite them in for a cup of tea at midnight on Christmas Eve, wouldn't you? It wouldn't matter if they were male or female, right?

There are two beds in my room. I'm sharing with Pete tonight, having negotiated a switch with Liam. As I put the kettle on, Lucy lays down on the bed nearest the door. I turn around and am faced with a predicament. Do I sit casually beside her on the bed? Do I jump on the other bed and possibly offend her? Or should I just stay standing to avoid making a decision altogether?

I chicken out and go for the last option, remaining in an upright position and chatting away as our drinks boil. Then comes a tap, tap, tap at my ground floor window. I peer through the glass to the darkness and see Pete's ugly head a foot away.

"What's up?" I say as I slide the window up.

Pete's now only wearing boxer shorts and it's close to zero degrees. "Look man, really sorry, but can you let me and the fräulein use the room? It's fucking freezing out here. I promise I'll be quick. You can trust me on that."

I can't contain my laughter and signal to Lucy we should vacate the room. I hold the door open as near-nude Pete and his blushing beauty sneak through.

Snickering, Lucy and I set up camp with our cups of tea down the hallway. We can hear sounds of rough, uninhibited sex echoing along the walls. Someone is being slapped intensely.

We watch the clock hit midnight, several people let off fireworks and cheer in the distance. Then comes the sound of Pete bellowing "Merry Christmas! Ho, ho, ho!", pausing mid-shag to declare his conquest to everyone.

LOXTON was found by Jen passed out bleeding on their apartment balcony next to a knife, a bottle of wine, a syringe and two vials of her insulin. Jen had called one of her friends and two of Loxton's friends to rush over after his worrying phone call, but none were close by. So, instead she raced up from the Gold Coast herself. She woke him and immediately fed him bread to raise his blood sugar.

There were light marks along Loxton's neck where he had run the knife and a small chunk taken out of his forearm from where he landed on the utensil after passing out. His skin was freezing cold.

Thankfully there had not been enough combined insulin left in both vials for Loxton to suicide. Jen informed me of what had happened, returned to the Gold Coast, and I booked my son in to receive emergency counselling.

Disappointingly we found the counsellor to be a bit of a simpleton, full of mindless optimism and unsubstantiated faith. Neither Loxton nor I have ever tended to gravitate towards people who are ultra-positive. Loxton told her that although his relationship breakdown instigated his suicide attempt, he thought of killing himself daily anyhow.

It took the moving of mountains to convince Lox to talk more, and when he did, it wasn't exactly what I wanted to hear. He revealed he'd continued to grapple with the same self-hatred and feelings of uselessness, even when he was achieving things that others thought were inspiring. He traced most of his thoughts back to how he had been treated by Steve, who I remained married to.

Minus any resolution or sense of satisfaction, Loxton and I left the session, not intending to return for scheduled follow-ups. But just before we reached the door, Loxton stood and spoke more freely with the counsellor.

"Are you happy yourself, having to spend every day between these drab walls, listening to people like me talk of despair, probably being paid a pittance, growing overweight

Poolhall—Jail—Library

and becoming more distant and unexcited with your partner?" he fired.

"All I want to know is this: Can anybody be pleased with what life has to offer, particularly as you grow old and everything becomes familiar? Why can you be so sure death is worse than that? The truth is you don't know the answer, but you're willing to try and stop other people who have reached that conclusion of their own accord."

With that, Loxton stormed out to his car, revved the motor and waited for me to catch up.

"That was uncalled for Loxton," I snapped.

"Was it? Or is everyone else being deluded?" he shot back spitefully before dropping me home in silence.

After a few weeks where he seemingly disappeared off the surface of the planet, Loxton informed me he was moving in with Jay, one of his most loyal and stable childhood friends. He was a calming influence on my son, and soon Lox had set up a punching bag underneath the house, bought a drum kit and was back playing football with several other old friends.

The boxing bag came in for particular use after he tried to re-establish contact with Jen around the time of his 22nd birthday.

"No, I don't want to see you for your birthday," she said bluntly. "You didn't love me. You only ever wanted somebody to love you. Who you dreamed me up to be is a person that doesn't exist."

Jay stepped in by taking Loxton to one of their favourite restaurants on his 22nd. It was Tulio's Italian, the same place on the northern suburbs where Loxton often went with Jen for special occasions.

A short, chirpy waitress stopped at their table.

"Hey aren't you the guy with the really tall, blonde girlfriend? We haven't seen you in here for a while," she said.

"Um," my son replied with a revealing pause. "Kind of."

And that's how Loxton met Sasha and things became even more confused.

The two of them hit it off with back-and-forth banter that Loxton usually found difficult to engage in. Jay encouraged Lox to pursue the new girl and that's exactly what he did. The next day he went to a florist and ordered a dozen red roses and a chocolate in the shape of a heart.

"But who was I supposed to address it to?" Loxton later said as he detailed the fledgling romance. "So, I sent the roses the restaurant and just wrote 'To the cute waitress with the short, dyed hair'. I don't know how to describe her Mum. She just seems like a really sweet and nice person. You know, the day after I saw her, I sat on my lunch break at work and started thinking 'Maybe I should change the world rather than moan about it?'. It's the first time I've ever thought that way."

It was fantastic, as much as it was surprising, to hear Loxton talk that way. That was, until he revealed more to the story.

Sasha had responded to an email address left on the card with the roses. She said she had a long-term boyfriend and was in a happy relationship, but left the door open for Loxton and her to catch up for a drink sometime "as friends". She stayed true to her word and they met up for a smoothie one afternoon following work, with nothing untoward taking place.

Figuring Sasha was taken, Loxton was defenceless when, out of the blue, Jen called him a few weeks later and wanted to give their engagement one last go.

The pair plunged into a new relationship of the same breakneck intensity of their first year. Loxton seemed to be happy again and there was an undoubted chemistry between them, so I wasn't entirely upset, even if I prepared myself for what I thought was an inevitable disaster.

Loxton was elevated to state editor of Rugby League Week at 22, a remarkable achievement he was justly proud about. In that regard, he continued to hit all sorts of milestones with his writing and career. However, as he matured, he found not *everything rested on the prestige of being published. He became alert to the politics of his workplace and the ethics behind the overarching parent company. Some of his passion diminished. At the end of the year when there was a restructure, Loxton opted to take a payout of more than $10,000 rather than keep his job. It was the most amount of money he'd ever had coming into his bank account at once.*

What Loxton didn't tell Jen was that the money wouldn't be deposited for a month. He gave her his bank card the night before a gala ball for the Brisbane Broncos NRL team and told her to buy herself a dress. Thinking Loxton was flush with money, she spent $270 on the dress. When Lox found out he went crazy. He'd only had a balance of $282 and there wasn't enough money for a taxi to the event.

"Mum I was so furious. I thought it was so selfish of her. We had to catch the bus for 40 minutes in the heat in our formal wear," he later told me.

"But when we finally reached the ball, I had to admit she was completely stunning. Even alongside all these professional athletes, I thought we made the most perfect couple. Then...I guess I mustn't have forgiven her completely, because I started drinking wine at a stupid pace. Usually I don't drink wine. The next thing I knew, I was waking up at my place the following morning and Jen was nowhere to be seen. My throat was killing me.

"I called her parent's house and she just answered and said 'Why would you bother ringing me?'. I had absolutely no idea what she was talking about I swear. 'Don't you remember last night?' she said. Apparently, I'd stood up and abused her in front of everyone. We were at the table between the television journalists and the Broncos players, and everyone was looking at us. I told her to fuck off at the top of my voice and made a scene when she stormed out. I can't even forgive myself after that, let alone ask her to forgive me. There's no point even trying to salvage the relationship."

I think what killed Loxton's spirit more than anything was that his whole life trajectory pivoted on a moment in time that he couldn't even remember. He really struggled with that concept. One day he was still planning to marry this girl, then the next day that possibility no longer existed.

MUNICH // LUCERNE // MOUNT PILATUS

AS PETE screams "Merry Christmas" down the hallway to us in the throes of passion, I look over at Lucy and we both break out in laughter again. It's been a good night.

"Hey, Merry Christmas. It's been awesome getting to know you," I say, opening my arms for a big hug.

We stay locked for longer than normal friends, cuddling each other carefully without crossing any boundaries.

Disengaging from the hug, I pause for a split second as my lips pass Lucy's cheeks, but then successfully avoid temptation altogether.

We're both red in the face and let out matching sighs before sitting down shoulder-to-shoulder and chatting until the sun is almost up. When Pete opens the bedroom door and bids farewell to his lady friend, I can finally get some sleep.

*** *** ***

LUCERNE is perhaps my favourite city so far in mainland Europe. I knew prior to arriving that it had a picturesque lake and was a regular haunt of Carl Jung's, but strolling the streets of the central Swiss city introduces me to so many more intriguing aspects.

Perhaps it's been through reading Jung on this journey, but I have an instant feeling of familiarity and calmness when our quartet begins exploring by foot. Today it's just me, Pete, Juliana and Lucy wandering around for large portions of the day. There's been some minor falling-out between Juliana and Harry and she's not sure he is the right guy for her anymore.

This is what I've been preaching all along with the 'play the long game' mantra. It's all well and good hooking up in the first few days, but if you grow to dislike someone on a tour, it's pretty hard to get rid of them – or to not be the one discarded yourself. As it stands, there is more than a week to go on our trip and we still haven't properly celebrated Christmas or New

Years' Eve yet. It'd be a shit time to go through a relationship meltdown, particularly when we've all paid thousands of dollars in advance for this fleeting, memorable period of our young lives.

I'm at a point where I'm confident there is no more residual feeling from me towards Juliana. I like the kid for sure, but she's just that – a kid. We've definitely evolved into something like an older brother / younger sister dynamic. I've got her back and she's got mine, but the physical and mental attraction has dimmed. With a degree of certainty, I know we will stay great friends long after this trip is over.

To me, if there is one female I end up with on this trip, it's going to be Lucy. The conversations and moments I share with her are on another level. But it's a matter of knowing whether to gamble on crossing that bridge.

Maybe Lucy and I are just meant to be really great friends too? Maybe that's all she wants? She's a bit more reserved than I am, and if we return home to Australia together and I start partying with my mates again, will she be a dead weight or will I have to confront and address my own immaturity? I don't want to envisage that scenario just yet.

Here I am, over-thinking the situation again, but what gets me this time is that I'm certain Lucy is cut from the same cloth. I don't feel bad for over-thinking a situation that involves another over-thinker. I don't want to walk into this gunfight only to have been out-thought by my counterpart.

I just can't envisage a scenario where, if Lucy and I kiss, this is going to end in any other scenario than another engagement down the track – and probable, immense heartbreak. She is too much of a nice girl, too much of what I want in my future, for this to be treated like a potential holiday fling.

We either have to keep things strictly platonic between us or keep our distance.

More than any other day on tour however, I find myself waiting for her to catch up to me in Lucerne. I'm not charging off into the distance today, not doing everything solo. When Lucy, Juliana and Pete head into a shop full of trinkets, I dutifully stand around until Lucy, in particular, is finished shopping. When we walk the 14th Century Kapellbrücke, the wooden chapel bridge through the centre of town, it's her I'm discussing the intricate murals with. When we reach the Löwendenkmal, a carved stone Lion monument, I volunteer to take her photo against the impressive backdrop.

Even at lunch, where we re-join the rest of the group, I'm trying to guard a seat next to me at our table for cheese and chocolate fondue. Without thinking, when Lucy arrives I nudge the seat slightly out, opening the way for her to join me. I've well and truly let my guard slip. Rational thought is no longer prevailing.

Post-lunch, we are tasked with making our way to the cable cars for the awe-inspiring ascent to Mount Pilatus, which rises through the clouds and shadows adjacent Lucerne. Mindful I've perhaps been smothering Lucy, I volunteer to go ahead when the attendant asks if one more person could join the group of strangers in front to complete a full gondola.

The ride up is breathtaking, unlike anything else I've ever done. The first section of the climb keeps a relatively quick pace, gliding past towering trees and above skiers and tobogganists. I don't think I've seen this much snow in any of the previous cities combined. Our outlook over the smaller mountains and surrounding towns is astonishing. Each element of my personality is being appealed to – the geography geek, the adventurer, the sportsman, the spiritual thinker.

My camera, the trustiest sidekick on this whole epic journey, comes out of my backpack and gets a workout until we are at stage two of the climb. There is a station where one cable, serving the bottom half of the mountain, stops. Then there is a part where a second cable shoots skyward, disappearing into the unknown. If I thought the first part was steep, I had no idea.

The second leg is clunkier and slower, and the gondola swings wildly in the wind. There is no whooping and hollering from snow bunnies below us on this section. In fact, the deathly silence beneath us is matched by a drop in chatter on the gondola itself, as we hold our collective breaths. On some parts, I have no idea how someone managed to erect the pylons for the cable cars to follow. It is barren, unforgiving land below us now. The whole thing is an engineering marvel.

We power up towards one part which feels like it may be the summit, only for our trajectory to suddenly drop. My stomach plummets and I grip on to the edge of the vessel. Around me, people are adjusting their footing and trying not to look down out of the windows. There is an immense abyss over which we are now tightrope walking. If the cable above us fails, we will plunge hundreds of metres to a rocky, freezing death. Rarely, possibly never, have I ever experienced such a peak of adrenaline. We creep tentatively towards our goal.

Docking at the final station, I exit and walk up a ramp that brings me to an unbelievable viewing platform. There is stark Alpine scenery all around. I can't resist darting off down a series of trails I find, taking me along cliff edges, past secreted Swiss military installations and through a series of caves. This place is an absolute highlight – and I get to see it all on Christmas Day!

That's right, it's Christmas. I'd almost forgotten. The next two nights we get to stay at a 115-year-old hotel perched right on top of this very mountain. Again, I don't know how anybody managed to build anything at this altitude, traversing the terrain we've just passed. This says untold manner of things about the capacity of human ambition and resourcefulness. I'm on a physical high which feels like I'm floating on clouds in more ways than one.

I've previously read about the capacity of the Swiss to defend their nation in the most ingenious ways, carving aircraft runways into the side of mountains, setting up high-tech missile defence systems and tunnels. They are a 'brains over brawn' nation and you have to admire that. Their willingness to test and exceed everyday limits projects them as a highly intelligent and innovative populous.

Before I can return from exploring the fringes of the mountain, the remainder of the tour group has arrived, collected their keys and dragged their luggage 100m through snow from reception to the main hotel building. When I enter reception, I spot a solitary internet station. This will surely become flooded once everybody returns from unloading their baggage.

With urgency, I slide over and log in. I haven't wished anybody a Merry Christmas back home. I'm hoping a couple of them might care enough to have dropped me a message too. Sifting through a short list, I spot an unexpected email from Audrey. I say unexpected, because in the almost two months since we slept together in Ireland, communication has been hit-and-miss. I've kept her updated reasonably regularly of where I'm at on my travels and the adventures I've encountered. Most of these messages have been met with two- or three-sentence replies, so I naturally assumed her eagerness was minimal.

It should figure that she now contacts me when I've let correspondence drop off on my behalf. That's how girls work isn't it? Or at least that seems to be the case from my experiences.

Audrey writes that she recently endeavoured to reconcile with her ex-boyfriend, but he was jaded from their previous split and didn't entertain the idea. She's now finished all her exams at Salzburg and has more time for keeping in touch. If we happen to be in the same vicinity in the future, we should catch up, the email says. Otherwise, Audrey writes, we should stay in contact and pick each other's brains on matters of life and love, seeing as we have such similar senses of humour and world outlooks.

It's definitely a case of sliding doors. If Audrey had bothered to contact me even two days earlier, I would have been a short train ride from her home in Austria. Instead she was trying to stitch things up with an ex-partner while I was coughing up phlegm and enduring out-of-body experiences with imaginary pirates.

Destiny just so conspired that the past two days have also been the two days where I've finally become comfortable letting Lucy get close to me. I don't hold misgivings or bitterness towards Audrey. She's one hell of a catch. Truth be known, if she'd bothered to touch base earlier, I would have thought of few things better than a rematch on her home turf.

But she's missed that opportunity.

I open a reply message and begin typing.

"Hey Audrey, Fantastic to hear from you, although I'm sorry to learn of your recent travails. Funny that you should mention life and love…I've met a girl who lives not far from me in Australia.

"I think it could get serious."

I ONLY asked Loxton if he was gay as an off-the-cuff remark.

It had been six months since he and Jen split for good and he showed little signs of being interested in other women. Of course, I'd earlier heard this new girl Sasha was on the scene, but that never seemed to go anywhere. Loxton enforced several times that they were simply good friends and often caught up to talk over things like sociology and philanthropy.

In that same period, Loxton changed a lot of the male friends he was hanging around. While he still maintained a close core of trusted childhood friends – Jay, Jabba, Rocky – he was hanging out an awful lot in the Valley. That district I knew from my youth as a place where only vagrants, drug-takers and homosexuals frequented. I was convinced Loxton was neither of the first two, so I had a growing suspicion it may be the latter.

His new friends were not sports-minded like most of his previous pals. They were all skinny, pale guys who liked repetitive electronic music. I found it hard to keep track of which new friend Lox was hanging out with on any given week. Loxton also changed his car, swapping his old street vehicle for a more upmarket executive's car. He began collecting tattoos. His hair changed through all the colours of the rainbow, although this was not necessarily anything new.

Loxton was also paying a lot more attention to his physique around this stage. Although he'd always enjoyed competing in sports, now he was taking more of an interest in the muscle sculpting and nutrition side of things. He'd go to the gym most mornings and do some form of fitness at nights.

There were enough red flags popping up to warrant some suspicion of his activities. Unlike most single boys his age, Loxton would barely talk about girls when we visited. He was always blabbing on about welfare systems, or the environment, or new business ideas. To that end, he reminded me a lot of his natural father...a dreamer. He rarely did normal boy things.

He was in my kitchen one day and we'd been conversing easily enough beforehand, so I thought it was a prime opportunity to bring things to a head.

"You know son, it wouldn't matter to me if you decided you didn't really like girls," I probed.

"What the heck are you talking about Mum?" he yelled back. "Not you as well. You're like the fourth or fifth person that's said that."

"Well, there's no shame in it," I reinforced.

"My friends are saying this, Uncle Howard said it to me. Jesus, am I that interesting that people have to analyse my life? I'm not gay Mum. I just don't see the point blabbing on about girls. They're not the most important thing in life. Love is a bit of a hoax if you ask me and that's whether I'm straight, gay or a polar bear," he said before storming toward the door, offended.

Then he paused, choking on his words. "Mum I just feel numb to everything. Nothing makes me feel passionate about anything. I'm trying. I'm trying to take new interests, but it's not working. I feel like a piece of shit cast adrift in the sea. The last few years the only thing that mattered to me was being someone that Jen wanted. I've lost touch with what appeals to me or what I aspire to do. I'm totally lost. What makes it worse is that, if Jen rang me today, I'd still go back to her. It doesn't make any sense, but if there is ever a chance she's coming back, I don't want to be the one who has shut the door completely. I'm not in any state to be someone else's boyfriend...not now, maybe not ever."

One familiar person who did re-emerge more prominent in this period was my brother Howard. It was like he became Loxton's source of grounding, even though Howard continued to be haunted by psychological problems. He still believed that people were chasing him for matters which had happened a decade earlier. Loxton liked to think he had become his uncle's protector, reversing their roles from his youth.

Despite finding Howard's negativity a struggle on top of his own concerns, I believe Lox saw someone who was worse off than him emotionally, yet had immense potential. Recognising that in someone else gave Loxton the smallest notion that life was not something you could just give up on. He always maintained that Howard was the smartest person he knew and deserved to find love and a purpose.

Each Friday Loxton would drive over to his grandparents' house, where Howard still lived, and take his uncle for lunch, to pay any bills, and check out music stores and a military memorabilia shop. Loxton figured it was a form of relief for both Howard and my parents, who often struggled to see eye-to-eye despite their obvious concern for each other. Howard believed our parents were too controlling and pessimistic, while my mother and father struggled to comprehend how Howard could never free himself of his debilitating thoughts.

In hindsight, it wasn't a great situation: a downcast and depressed Loxton trying to guide a paranoid schizophrenic who thought his own parents were more negative than him. That's our family tree laid out with embarrassing accuracy for everyone to observe.

Many times, after they caught up on a Friday, Howard would ask to stay at the house Loxton shared with Jay. They'd watch comedy movies and then Howard would fall asleep on the couch. But, over time, Howard migrated to the foot of Loxton's bed. He'd rest on the floor at the end of Loxton's bed like a canine, completely fearful people would break in and kill him otherwise. It was extremely odd, but Loxton swore his friends to silence and vowed he would take care of Howard no matter what curious behavior he exhibited.

This went on for a good six months, until there was an unexpected intervention.

After pleading that they were just friends and confidants, Loxton began sleeping with Sasha. She had broken up with her long-time boyfriend, and had dated several other boys briefly before confessing she did, in fact, have a crush on Loxton. He reciprocated. This seemed to put an extra kick in his step for a while and they were soon officially a couple.

However, unlike Loxton and Jen's extended honeymoon period where they barely fought in the first 18 months, Loxton and Sasha were constantly arguing from the start. A redhead paired with a Sicilian girl was never going to be a placid love match. It would have been only two weeks after they declared they were in a proper relationship that Loxton, his eyes full of hatred, visited me and said Sasha had gone missing at a party and later confessed she had spent the night fooling around with another friend – a female friend.

Loxton was gutted and tried to end all contact, but Sasha kept chipping away at him until he would discuss the matter. She was confused she said. It had all been a mistake. She was committed to Loxton and wanted to prove so by moving in with him.

The only problem with that equation was that Jay became quickly fed up with their volatility as a couple. He wouldn't allow Sasha to move in and, in order to preserve his friendship with Loxton, suggested they both move out together.

That's exactly what happened and, less than a month after being together, Loxton and Sasha pitched in together and relocated to a house on Stafford Road, only a kilometre away. Loxton no longer had as much time for Howard, or indeed anybody, and always appeared sullen and pre-occupied on the rare occasions we caught up.

"Mum, I've been offered a job in Townsville, working in media alongside the North Queensland Cowboys," *he revealed on the phone one day.* "I'm in two minds about whether to go. It's a good career step, but I've already got good work down here with the Broncos and my freelance contacts. It's a big move away from everyone. I think what's going to swing it is...I need to get away from Sasha. I can't take much more of her

Poolhall—Jail—Library

moods. If I relocate to Townsville, I think she knows we won't survive and she'll walk away."

Except that's not how the situation worked at all.

Loxton packed his belongings and left, but didn't have the heart to tell Sasha he wanted to break up with her. He'd never been the one to end a relationship on his own terms in the past and he couldn't picture himself in that role. In his mind, people who ended relationships were always the bad people.

So, naturally Sasha ended up following shortly behind. She thought she was welcome. And because of my son's reticence to make a tough decision early, he stretched out their feuding for the foreseeable future.

With that tumult in the background, Loxton began to settle into a new job where the expectations were decidedly different to Brisbane. On his first day he was admonished by his editor for having blue hair and sent across the road to the barber to have it shaved immediately. He argued that he had sported blue hair for most of the past two seasons when working with the Brisbane Broncos.

"You simply won't fit in up here. Townsville is not a city for blue hair. We don't suffer fools in this neck of the woods," he was told in no-nonsense fashion.

After contemplating quitting inside his first few hours at work, Loxton bit down on his pride and stayed. It was a confronting period in many aspects. The heat was only a few degrees more than in Brisbane, but it sapped Loxton of energy in the initial months to the point where he was sleeping an uncharacteristic amount of time. He picked up two tropical bacterial infections that further lowered his immunity and fondness for his new surrounds.

Sasha found employment at a restaurant on a café strip near the centre of town, but was stalked on several consecutive nights by a homeless man who took a shine to her. He would follow her home in darkness. With only part-time work available, Sasha also volunteered at a centre for the needy, where many of the attendees had substance abuse and mental health issues. She would dispense them medication, toiletries and food, but often be castigated at in return.

"Thanks bitch," was a common phrase Loxton told me about.

My son reported feeling there was a lot more violence in the new city, witnessing street fights, fights in family restaurants and, of course, fights outside the many bars which serviced a population with a high military and mining concentration.

The sole shining light in his life at this point was a chance to train alongside the Cowboys' professional NRL squad. Loxton had requested permission to spend a week with the top squad, preparing exactly as they did. The exercise served several purposes, winning the trust of players and allowing him to write first-hand articles about the club environment, while also fulfilling a childhood dream.

He battled through the week, reporting increasing soreness on every day, and having ice baths frequently to minimise the effects. He felt the coaching staff dished out special punishment to him because he was a journalist – a snitch and an outsider – and he was left with a bloodied nose after one boxing session. Another time he reported losing all strength in his legs on weighted lunges and staggering noticeably at the gym in front of chuckling players. Vomiting happened as a daily occurrence.

Yet for whatever absurd reason, Loxton was incredibly proud of undertaking and surviving the experience. He could admit he was never going to be athletically talented enough to make it to that level competitively, but he got to briefly taste it by using other abilities to scale that mountain.

Loxton's driving force was becoming the best sports writer he could be and everything else took a back seat. He travelled away most weekends with the team, and was rarely at his own home in Townsville, let alone having time to come and visit us in Brisbane.

Indeed, one of the very few times we saw him in those next two years was at Howard's funeral.

MOUNT PILATUS // ST GOAR

THEY say the first step is admitting you have a problem.
Committing in email to Audrey that I thought Lucy and I might "get serious" is the point where I've finally admitted to myself it's what I want deep down. I can continue keeping her at arm's length as a means of caution, or I can grasp the rare opportunity of a woman who I consider genuine relationship material.

"You do know that you're allowed to let yourself be happy," is a phrase my friend Rocky has said to me often these past few years.

Anyhow, the time has come to open our 'Secret Santa' presents as part of the tour group's Christmas festivities. We've assembled in the more modern Bellevue building to the southeast of the mountain, surrounded by chocolate and cakes and glühwein.

"Have you tried the glühwein? It's scrumptious," Lucy says sweetly as she stands alongside me, cradling a warm glass in both hands.

I heed her recommendation and walk over to the accommodating hotel staff, who ladle out a glass to sip. It is extremely delicious and very morish. The temperature and spiced cinnamon flavour make it easy to guzzle down.

Bevan opens my present of the two plastic wrestlers and yells out "Err, thanks" to nobody in particular. It's not as comical or show-stopping as I thought it would be. When it comes Lucy's turn, she opens her present and receives a masquerade mask, along with a small, postcard-sized piece of artwork depicting the Alps. Someone has been much more thoughtful and kind in selecting what she receives.

My present is rather tiny, only around half the height of my hand. It's been messily, but tightly wrapped. I rip it open with brute force and out comes flying a black figurine with an erect penis. The rest of the tour group erupts in laughter. It's a fertility statue. I'd seen them for sale at various markets along our route.

Juliana, slapping her thigh in hysterics, yells out above the crowd: "You like that Loxton?" She's got me good.

Lucy is smiling and mockingly shaking her head, again playing the schoolteacher who disapproves. We watch as everyone else takes turns to open presents, then we eat a small meal which is served on high circular tables scattered throughout the venue. You have to stand to consume your dinner.

A dilemma has been created by the placement of the tables. Those with the best view through the windows are also situated nearest to the door, which lets in freezing night air each time someone passes in or out. I ask Lucy if she wants to grab the table with a premium outlook over the Matthorn and the valleys to the south.

"OK," she agrees. "But I better top up our glühwein to keep us cosy."

Lucy returns with a smile, takes a healthy swig of the toasty alcoholic beverage and then stands so close that our arms are brushing. After daintily chewing and swallowing a small morsel of roast lamb, Lucy leans in.

"Can I ask you something?" she says. "Is everything okay between us?"

It's not what I was expecting at all. I thought we were going to tip-toe around this confusing dynamic until both of us were drunk enough to do something that would either consummate or completely destroy any mutual affection. I hadn't bargained on having a mature, mostly-sober conversation to tackle this head-on.

"What do you mean?" I feign. "Of course, everything is okay between us."

"Great, I thought I'd just check," she replies, before we return to conversation about our favourite parts of the tour thus far, plans for the few remaining days, and juicy tidbits of gossip about fellow tourists.

Then, without warning, Lucy takes control of the wheel, turns the chatter around and heads back to the same coordinates. "You're not an easy guy to get to know Loxton. You are aware of that aren't you? I feel like we've become really good friends – great friends in fact – but sometimes you act like you don't want to be around me. I've seen you like that with other people too, so I'm just not sure if this is something particular to me, or you just have times where you want to be left alone?"

"Wow, you've really over-analysed the situation," I chuckle, before noticing a look of hurt descend over Lucy's face. She's trying to have a heart-to-heart and I'm belittling her for having the courage to speak up.

"Alright, fine then. Everything is hunky-dory. Forget I said anything," she snaps, but with enough guile and politeness to make it non-confrontational.

"How about we finish this meal, get another drink and go and mingle with the rest?" I suggest. "It's Christmas. And whatever you think, I'm really glad I'm spending it with you. You are a special friend and I hope it stays that way long after this trip is over."

Wow. How's that for taking it up a few notches? I'll raise your "great friend" and give you a "special friend" category. I've also dared to mention the forbidden topic that nobody on tour seems keen to broach: What happens to all our friendships when it's time to fly home?

From the moment I say I want to remain close to her after this trip ends, you can feel a tingling in the air. We both sport grins that are hard to subdue. As we join in frivolities with everyone else, the alcohol flows freely and rapidly. Everything becomes a blur.

At one stage we all walk outside. There's a snowball fight. There's a point where I hold Lucy by the hips as she pretends to drop forward to the adjoining ravine. I invite her, Pete and Juliana back to my room, which has one of the best vantage points in the hotel. We find and drink more wine. I almost kiss Lucy as we squeeze together to peer out the window to admire the view. Pete challenges me to a nude streak across the top of the mountain. I accept the challenge. There's wild cheering by dozens of people. I'm walking around freezing, wearing just sports shoes. I drink more wine.

I wake up on the floor of the communal showers to the hotel holding a bottle of red that has spilled everywhere. It looks like I'm bleeding to death.

I can't remember much clearly. All I know is that I definitely didn't do anything with Lucy.

I need help. I need to stop doing this shit.

***   ***   ***

ST GOAR is almost invisible on the map. It's a tiny speck that you wouldn't otherwise notice unless you went looking for it.

Tucked away in the Rhine Valley, this preserve of cultural hallmarks is defined by its cuckoo clock shops, it's hand-crafted ceramic steins, wine cellars, stuffed toys and the ruins of the Burg Rheinfels, a castle from the 13th Century.

It's also cloaked in thick snow as we approach on the tour bus, descending through a winding mountain pass.

Things have thankfully not been as awkward as expected with Lucy in the two days that have passed since Christmas Night. We have hardly seen each other, but from what I understand, she spent Boxing Day nursing a hangover of similar proportions to mine. She's not sitting next to me on the bus today, but directly in front instead. A few times she's turned around for brief conversations.

There are never any great stretches of time between consumption of alcohol on a trip like this. One of our first appointments in St Goar is to trek down to a magnificently preserved, darkened cellar, where there is an assortment

Poolhall—Jail—Library

of dessert wines lined up. I'm tempted not to drink, but the setting is perfect. Juliana elbows me in the ribs as I lag behind.

"You better not pussy out again," she says. "I'm reserving you a spot right next to Lucy."

With that, she throws a scarf from a distance at the seat next to where Lucy is setting up.

"Please keep a spot for the beautiful couple," Juliana pronounces indiscreetly. "You guys are so cute."

"We are not a couple," both Lucy and I protest in unison, which sounds like an indictment on its own.

I mockingly throw my hat on the seat next to Juliana. "Better reserve this one for Harry too." It brings a scowl from Juliana. They are still amid a rocky on-and-off period of their romance.

Lucy and I slide into position side-by-side on a long bench, almost directly at the centre of the tour group. The German sommelier regales us with details about the building's history and of the peculiarities of each wine we are about to consume.

From the outset, there's a sense of brazenness and a new level of familiarity from Lucy. She taps my hand and exclaims "Mmm, this one is really nice" as the first drink is served. She squeezes my thigh gently to catch my attention when she remembers a funny story to whisper. When she excuses herself to go to the bathroom, she wraps one hand behind my back and uses my bodyweight to lever herself up from a seated position.

Whatever I did when drunk on Mount Pilatus has clearly not deterred her in any significant way.

"Are you sure that you two are not a couple?" asks one nosy tour group member who I've barely spoken to before.

"Oh, come on," chides another. "I think they've been getting it on for weeks."

"Don't worry," interrupts a third. "You two are really well-suited. I say good on you. What a lovely place to find happiness."

In the less-than-10-minutes Lucy is away from the table, our relationship status becomes the focal point of all discussion. When she re-emerges and tries to surreptitiously slide into her previous spot, she is met with a round of applause and heckling that catches her off-guard.

"What...are...you...all...clapping...for?" she smirks, before turning her interrogation to me. "What did you say while I was gone?"

"I didn't tell them anything. They're good enough at making up stories on their own," I deadpan.

Lucy shrugs it off and polishes the second and third servings of wine. Both are exquisitely sweet. We nibble on cheese and dried fruits provided in the centre of the table. Everyone is getting a touch jubilant and it's only the afternoon.

*** *** ***

OUR hotel in St Goar has a downstairs bar where we all agree to meet for a quick feed later at dinner time. Most people return to their rooms in the intermediate to get changed and spruce themselves up after the long bus ride and a few hours of wine tasting. I sweat out a decent 30 minutes of exercise, put on a tight blue shirt and my good jeans, and spend an unnatural amount of time styling my hair, before making a way down to rendezvous.

It's soon clear that consuming food is a secondary priority of most people, keen to kick-on with a few more drinks after opening their throats earlier. It's barely 8pm before the first round of Jägermeister is passed around. Hotel staff clear the dining tables and rearrange the room to encourage dancing. A DJ sets up next to the bar and begins spinning tracks.

This secluded hamlet becomes the place where everybody realises the trip is quickly coming towards an end, and we bond as a collective, shaking and shimmying the night away. With snow still falling heavily outside and nowhere else to go at this hour, each man and woman is savouring the moment and losing themselves in the night.

Everything remains perfect until a puzzling disagreement between Juliana and Harry erupts. I'm too busy enjoying myself to even notice what starts it. There are rumours Juliana has kissed a girl and this has sparked the confrontation. I'm not so sure, but I assume it is quite likely due to jealousy on one of their behalf. There are accusations shouted across the room, then both storm off in different directions.

"Come on, we better go sort this out," Lucy says, grabbing my arm and leading me upstairs where we encounter Juliana angrily muttering to herself on a landing, tears in her eyes.

We calm her, remind her to enjoy the trip. I tell Juliana that Harry clearly likes her and it will all be sorted out, even though deep down I think he's an A-grade jerk.

Gradually, over the best part of an hour, Juliana starts to mellow in her emotions, but she refuses to re-join the party, heading off to bed instead.

As Lucy and I descend the staircase back to the hotel bar, we notice a side door on ground floor. It leads out to a pathway which runs alongside the Rhine.

"Come on, I want to show you something," Lucy says enthusiastically.

We detour outside, jogging through snowfall to the banks of the river. Lucy is crossing her arms for warmth, and rolls the neckline of her top up so that it protects her nape from the night air.

"See those two castles on the opposite side," Lucy says. "One is called the Katz castle and the other is the Maus. I was reading about them this afternoon. Apparently, the occupants of one of the castles said they would devour the other."

"I did notice one of the castles on the way in, but not the other. That's interesting," I reply, my teeth chattering.

"I think it's cute," Lucy states.

"What? That the occupants of one castle would want to eat the other?"

"No silly. Just the names. Katz and Maus. I think it's cute."

Lucy playfully punches me in the chest and I respond by rubbing her arm and back to try and help her keep warm.

We are standing directly in front of each other, alone in near-silence – interrupted only by the rush of the river's waters and the distant thump-thump of our tour group party, now several hundred metres behind us.

"So...everyone truly thinks we're a couple hey?" Lucy says as we turn and begin to walk further away from the hotel, towards a swing set and playground.

"That does seem to be the consensus," I reply with tongue-in-cheek formality.

"Well...what do you think?" Lucy prods.

"I think...," I begin to say, my throat gasping for air. "I think we should give them something to talk about."

And with that, I turn to face Lucy again, staring from centimetres above directly into those beautiful blue eyes of hers. I grab both her hands and she responds by curling her fingers to interlock with mine. Steam is rising from our mouths as we tilt heads at opposite angles and close the distance. Our lips explode on impact with an immense release of endorphins.

It's a first kiss that lasts at least five minutes.

It is an electric, delicate, heart-racing smooch that rivals anything I've ever felt before.

LOXTON admitted himself for regular anger counselling after less than six months in Townsville. I later learnt that the malaise of his relationship with Sasha and his despondency with everyday life had brought about at least three incidents of serious self-harm in this period.

"I've never met a girl who knows how to enrage me quite like her," he confessed. "I'm afraid of what I might do if this continues. I told her I wanted to kill her after one fight in her car. I pulled her seatbelt tight until it was almost choking her. Mum, you know me; there's nothing I hate more than violence against women...particularly after everything our family has been through. I need to make myself a better person."

I genuinely lost count of the number of times Loxton and Sasha broke up when in Townsville, and could not keep track of when they had resumed the relationship. She moved out of their home at least twice, and they ended up living under separate rooves even when they were together towards the end.

On one of the extended stretches when they had split, Loxton flew to Brisbane to attend a musical festival with a few friends. He also caught up with Kim, with whom he'd now mended all bridges. She'd become his confidant through the rollercoaster ride of his love life.

While Lox was in town, I beseeched him to come with me and visit Howard, who had been admitted to psychiatric hospital again. Loxton was initially hesitant, fearing how upset the visit could make both of them. However, he eventually put aside his reservations.

"Mate, how are you doing?" Loxton offered, trying to sound upbeat when Howard was finally permitted to enter the hospital's communal area.

"I'm not so good," replied Howard flatly, shaking uncontrollably as he tried to light a cigarette.

As much as we tried to connect with Howard and lift his spirits, he was downcast, staring at the floor through our unsuccessful attempts at conversation. The medication had turned him into a zombie and he had discoloured skin on his pale face from electro-shock treatment. In the end, it was me who left distraught, begging Loxton to take me home. For the brief few days Loxton was in town, he forced himself to return and see if he could prize a smile out of his uncle, all to no avail.

A matter of weeks later each member of the family received the phone call we had all feared, yet knew would probably arrive one day. Nothing could prepare me for the torment of the situation however. I passed the news on to Loxton, who by then was back in North Queensland.

"Lox, Howard has gone and done something stupid and this time I don't think he's going to come good. Several days ago, he was released from the psych ward. He went home to Nan and Grandad's house and slashed his throat with a razor. It was deep. Deeper than last time. They took him into hospital and operated on him, but somehow he managed to hide soldering fluid in his belongings. Once he woke up from the operation to fix his throat, he drank the soldering fluid. He has completely burnt out his insides. His oesophagus basically doesn't exist. They've had to replace it with tubing. Now the soldering fluid has leaked to his major organs and it's slowly dissolving them as well. He's on life support, but his body is slowly shutting down."

"I'm going to ring work and see if I can fly down tomorrow," Loxton said, exasperated. "I've got no money left after the last trip. I don't suppose you could help me? Or maybe Nan and Grandad could?"

"Unfortunately, I can't assist with money Loxton," I replied. "We're broke too. In any case – and I know this is hard to face – but I don't think he is going to be alive by the morning. From what I'm hearing, he probably won't wake up and I don't know if you want to see him in his current state. I know you're not religious son, but maybe say a prayer or light a candle or just play a CD that reminds you of him. I think that's all any of us can do. I know he meant so much to you."

"Mum, please don't refer to him in the past tense," Loxton begged before excusing himself to end the conversation.

The devastation felt by all of us was acute, but Loxton, Kim, Howard and I shared a special bond that stretched back to some of the most difficult moments in our lives. We'd survived that together, but now one of us had chosen to leave this Earth as a result of their own hand. I held massive concerns that one suicide attempt was about to become two.

When Loxton finally got a flight to Brisbane, it was as we'd feared. Howard had already passed, surrounded at his death bed by my father, his brothers and Steve.

"You let Steve go there? To be with Howard in his final moments of life? He had such contempt for the man. I can't believe you'd do that," Loxton said despondently.

"Now is not the time Loxton. Steve went there to represent me. He's my connection to those last few moments. Let's not argue today," I pleaded.

Loxton made the mistake of bringing flowers for his Nan, who was catatonic at the happenings of the past week. We'd all been specifically instructed not to bring flowers, but the message did not reach Loxton. My father scolded Loxton for disobeying the request, which led to an unusual exchange of terse words between the two, then Loxton broke down crying and locked himself in the toilet.

Once they had mended their bridges, Sasha showed up out of nowhere at the wake, without explanation. Loxton had obviously told her what had happened and asked her to attend, but as far as we all knew, they were no longer together.

It was a day of utter confusion and devastation, with Christmas just a matter of days away.

BERLIN // HAMBURG // AMSTERDAM

OUR game of cat-and-mouse with the other members of the tour group is continuing, despite last night's dalliance exposing the true feelings between Lucy and I.

While Lucy makes no hesitation in riding the A4 and A9 to Berlin beside me on the bus, we don't kiss or even hold hands in front of the voyeuristic pack. If anything, we're probably more reserved than we have been in St Goar, Mount Pilatus and Lucerne. Lucy lets her guard slip momentarily and falls asleep on my shoulder, but soon adjusts herself when she realises the error of her ways.

Berlin is such a prized destination for me that I'm honest with her from the outset.

"I've got a lot I want to see today. I'm probably going to be moving at a frantic pace. Do you mind if we do our own thing and meet up tonight?"

The German capital is in the midst of a blizzard when we arrive. That's not an exaggeration. We gather around an electronics store at the drop-off point to watch a news bulletin about surrounding countries which have already been hit hard. In France, 10,000 people have abandoned their cars. Power has been cut-off in Austria. Slovakia is issuing avalanche warnings. There are widespread reports of vehicle accidents across the continent.

A sense of urgency and real danger hangs over the group. In the face of fast-falling snow, I head to Checkpoint Charlie, to the Holocaust Museum, Brandenburg Gate, the Reichstag, and follow the Berlin Wall as it snakes through the city, chipping off a piece to take home. I normally despise people who deface historic sites, but convince myself the wall is so large that my 10cm portion won't be missed. Later I regret it, convinced I've earnt bad karma.

As night falls, I grab a lucky photo of the ruins of the Kaiser Wilhelm Memorial Church. Left as a reminder of the bombing

Poolhall—Jail—Library

raids of World War II, the church is being inundated with snowfall, building up next to its footings. As I take a picture, a large snowflake drops right into the centre of view, reflecting red Christmas lights which have not been taken down. The trickery of rose-coloured luminance fills the frame, appearing as though a magical orb has plummeted from the sky.

I've spent most of the day covering the city by foot through thick slush, so when I discover the planned night time adventure is a walking tour of East Berlin's trendiest bars, my feet groan for relief. Wanting to catch up with Lucy, I ignore the significant temptation to have a quiet night in.

I'm immediately glad for my dedication. Lucy has pulled out all stops to look her most stunning tonight. She's wearing a new pashmina and shirt, pinned together with an eye-catching brooch. Balancing on high heels, she is the epitome of grace and elegance.

As we traverse from bar to bar, Lucy and I pull away sneakily at intervals to exchange covert kisses, hiding ourselves behind corners and in the darkness of laneways. We're still confident nobody knows for sure whether we're an item or not.

The evening is going swimmingly, conversation is effortless and invigorating. I'm exploring one of the most important world cities with a clever, warm-hearted woman who makes me feel intensely alive. It provides reason for pause and thanks.

Then, as we take a steep wooden staircase to an uber-cool underground nightclub, Lucy loses her footing, reaches behind to grab my hands, but slips from my fingers. Her high-heels skid over the wet timber and she slides down at least 10 steps, bringing her with a thud to the floor.

I rush down, but in the second or two that it takes me to reach her, she has already started crying in pain. Tears are flowing over her face as I try to help her back on her feet.

"No, no, ouch," she yells, ordering me to leave her alone.

I've not seen her lose her composure like this.

"I'm sorry...sorry I couldn't stop you falling," I say meekly.

Juliana arrives and places her arm around Lucy to calm her. There's every fear that she has done something which will require first aid to her back, hip or legs. Finally, after sustained coaxing and clearing a circle in the nightclub, we manage to prop Lucy on her feet, and she stumbles to the female toilets with Juliana.

Half-an-hour later, her eyes raw from crying, Lucy re-emerges and taps me on the arm.

"I think I want to go home. I don't think I've injured myself seriously, but I can't believe I've made a fool of myself in front of everyone," she says.

I attempt to convince her to stay, to chill out and have a drink to calm her emotions. "Nobody thinks you've been silly. We were all just concerned." But Lucy is having none of it and signals that she is leaving the club with immediacy.

Following behind like a puppy dog to street level, I hail a cab and check once again that Lucy is okay and doesn't require a trip to hospital.

"I think I'll be okay, but if you can stand the shame of being seen with me, I wouldn't mind you joining me in the taxi," Lucy says. "I highly doubt we're tricking anybody that we're not together anymore."

Once back at the hotel, I assist her to the foyer and the lifts, then into her room.

It's a weird situation. She's clearly in excruciating pain, but she's inviting me inside when everyone else is out partying. The intensity of the last 24 hours has me questioning what the correct thing is to do. How far should I be reading into this?

"I want you to have a look at my leg," Lucy instructs. "You've probably seen most injuries playing rugby. Maybe you can tell me how severe it is?"

Lucy lays on her bed, fully-clothed and face-down. I test the ligaments around her knee. From my amateur clinician's perspective, nothing seems out of order. I bend her knee up and she has full range-of-movement. There's no tear in her hamstrings and quads, we ascertain. Then I prod softly around the soft tissue of her upper leg.

It soon becomes apparent the only point of pain is in her right buttock.

"Look, I think it's just deep bruising. It probably hurts like hell regardless, but that's my diagnosis. Do you want me to get you some ice?" I enquire.

"I guess you could just scoop some ice off the street, the way it is bucketing down. No, I'll be okay," Lucy laughs. "Don't take this the wrong way, but would you mind actually looking at it?"

"You mean...look at your bum?" I chuckle. "I'm hardly going to say 'no' am I?"

Without saying another word, Lucy reaches with her right hand and softly pushes down the waistline of her pants, exposing just the upper half of her derriere. My eyes are immediately drawn to her brand-new black G-string. I swear teachers were never this hot back in my day.

Secondly, I observe a very inflamed, dark purple bruise that extends further south beyond the visible limits.

"You've inflicted yourself a beauty there," I say.

"What is it?" she replies with concern.

"It's a fairly nasty haematoma."

With that, Lucy sits up at surprising speed, no longer grimacing with every slight movement. She kneels on the bed and looks past me into a mirror over my shoulder. With more haste, she rips down her pants until her whole right cheek is exposed.

"Oh my god. That is horrid!" she exclaims.

"That's not exactly what I was thinking," I say with lifted eyebrow.

"You can go now," Lucy informs me.

"But Lucy..."

"No. I'm actually very embarrassed. That is super ugly. I can't believe it's grown discoloured like that so quickly," she continues.

"Do you really, genuinely want me to leave this room?"

"Genuinely Loxton. It's time for bed. We only kissed for the first time last night. I'm not that type of girl. Besides, I don't want you going home and telling all your mates how you hooked up with a girl with a bright purple bum," she snickers.

"Yeah, sure. No dramas. Okay then, I'm sorry if I offended you," I say with contrition.

"No offence at all. Now kiss me good night and leave," Lucy says with a smile.

I wrap my fingers tenderly along her jawline and we press our lips together passionately as one bum cheek remains hanging in plain sight.

"Ok, now shoo," Lucy laughs, shamefully pulling the blanket over her exposed bruise.

I backtrack towards the door slowly, giving her every chance to change her mind.

She doesn't.

*** *** ***

HAMBURG is a city my grandfather visited during the war. He played a part in its liberation days before the final German surrender.

To this day Grandad and I remain incredibly close. He's my idol in several ways, mostly for the strength he has provided our family in the most trying of times. He is the one family member who I believe never quit on me. At his heart, he is a very decent, loyal, loving man. There haven't been a great deal of male role models in my life who have been able to show me what masculinity looks like in combination with compassion.

In tribute to Grandad, I spend most of my brief time in Hamburg walking along the docks, taking a heap of photographs of landmarks he will hopefully recognise on my return. Lucy doesn't venture out all day or make contact with me in any way once we are off the bus.

I run into her roommate Suzie on the streets and ask nonchalantly how the patient is faring.

"Still feeling sorry for herself," she replies sharply. Suzie strikes me as a tough character who struggles with Lucy's softer edges. "No, in all seriousness, she is hobbling quite a bit. I don't think she could comfortably walk far today."

"Oh ok. Well tell her I hope she's feeling better soon," I venture.

"You do know Lox, you are allowed up to our room?" Suzie says. "We're all adults here. I know what's going on between you two. You don't need to pussyfoot around."

"Of course, you're a smart woman Suzie," I fire back.

"I was actually going to suggest that we switch rooms in Amsterdam," says Suzie. "It's New Year's…it's the last two days on tour…it's goddamn bloody Amsterdam. Who knows what could happen? I think I'll let you kids enjoy your time there."

"Um, thanks," I say hesitantly. "That sounds nice, but I don't know if that's what Lucy necessarily wants."

"You really like her, hey?" Suzie says with suddenly-unearthed emotion.

I leave her question unanswered and head back to the hotel to take care of overdue emails.

Stepping inside the elevator to ride up to level 10 of our hotel, I'm taken aback when Lucy appears, preparing to hop off at ground floor.

"Oh hey," she says, startled. "Shall we do a brief catch up in the lift? How was your day?"

I press the button to close the door and Lucy joins me for the brief ascent through 10 floors.

"It was pretty cool, I mainly…," is all I get out of my mouth before Lucy mauls me.

She slams me into the side of the elevator and pulls my collar tight as she locks lips. It's entirely unexpected aggression.

"Sorry, I just had to get that out of my system," Lucy apologises. "I've been cooped up in the room all day."

When we reach my floor, I whisk Lucy out of the lift before she can return to ground level. In one movement I scoop her into my arms and press her up against a giant window that looks down from the hallway to the snow-covered streetscape below.

We are making out ferociously, bodies pressed firmly together, although fully clothed.

"Mind my tender buttocks," Lucy giggles.

I'm gripping her with all my strength, lifting her against the window until she can almost lock her legs above my waist.

I give her one final peck on the lips, then drop her to her feet as quickly as this all commenced.

"I'm not that type of guy Lucy," I say wryly, before waving her away. "Now shoo."

*** *** ***

OUR time in Amsterdam begins with a live sex show at a theatre and everyone trying to score as many drugs as they can. Those who were too timid to procure ecstasy in Florence are now exchanging cash for illicit substances like there is a global shortage. Because smoking weed and eating space cakes are legal here, it also loosens up a few of the goody-two-shoes who otherwise wouldn't imbibe.

I've already approached Liam to see if it's okay if Suzie switches into our room, so I can stay with Lucy the final two nights. He's nonplussed, but I really couldn't give two hoots at this stage. I wish I'd had a roommate I'd hit it off with to share this remarkable adventure alongside, but it hasn't happened that way. I'll just have to make do with sleeping alongside the most gorgeous girl on the trip.

Unsurprisingly, despite multiple warnings from tour veterans, many of the younger, virgin pot smokers are completely torched within the first few hours of reaching the city heart. There's a handful who are vomiting, another few who are wigging out, and several who don't make it as far as a scheduled canal cruise on the first night. The tour guide is having conniptions trying to round them all up like stray cats.

I'm being a clean-skin this time around in Amsterdam. I had all the lunacy I needed the first time I was here with Jerome. It would seem wasteful, with 48 hours to get to know each other better, if I chose to spend half the available hours left with Lucy off my nonce. She's not even remotely interested in that sort of thing.

In fact, I'm becoming paranoid as the hours tick down that I haven't figured out what Lucy wants very much at all.

Maybe she just wants a companion to round this trip off with? Maybe she simply wants someone she can cuddle up to and include later as an item of gossip for friends? Maybe she won't want to know me at all when we land on the other side of the globe?

She overwhelmingly comes across as a 'good girl', but how many 'good girls' ram themselves up against men in elevators like she did yesterday? How many 'good girls' buy new G-strings and expose their bum for boys they don't know very well? Am I going to kid myself that a woman this pretty doesn't attract interest on a regular basis back at home?

I'm doing an exceedingly good job of talking myself out of a romance that has been served up on a platter.

"I'll tell you something, Loxton," Lucy confides when we break away from the group to take a walk, prior to the cruise. "I really did not think you would go for me on this trip. I thought you were too cool for me."

"Me? Too cool?" I respond, bewildered.

"Yeah I've always been a bit of a nerd, a bit quiet," she says.

"That's just how I like them," I joke back.

"No, honestly, I saw you early on the trip and thought...the clothes, the hair, the music, the sport...you were very much into a different scene than me," Lucy continues.

"I don't think I'm too cool for anyone, especially not you," I try to reassure her.

"I was convinced you had a girlfriend back in Australia that you were covering up. You do know you are a good-looking guy? You're a handsome fella. You're incredibly intelligent, quick-witted and know so much about the world...," she says, before I cut her off.

"That's enough of that. This head has never been called good-looking. I just whittle away gems like you with persistence," I confess. Many a true word is said in jest.

"And another thing – you don't take compliments well, do you?" Lucy says.

"Nor do you," I plead with a smile. "Let's just enjoy this in the moment and let it see where it takes us."

Somehow, in the space of five minutes, I've safely navigated around my own neurosis as well as Lucy's.

The canal cruise turns out to be an unmitigated success. For the first time, Lucy and I openly display affection in front of others. She holds my hand when we talk with fellow travellers. We kiss politely, but passionately, at regular intervals. When we're dead-tired at the end of the night, we find a booth seat and enjoy the final moments of the journey draped in one another's arms. Nobody bats an eyelid, and most are congratulatory.

Our only hiccup comes upon return to the hotel. Liam has not only reneged on the deal of sharing a room with Suzie, he has brought home one of the older ladies on tour, one that slept with Mick early on. In their stoned and amorous state, they've locked themselves in their quarters, meaning Suzie, Lucy and I must share one room. It's not exactly what we envisioned. Lucy and I spoon together on one bed, keeping everything strictly above board while Suzie snores a metre or so away from us.

*** *** ***

Poolhall—Jail—Library

DAM Square, the epicenter of Amsterdam, is absolute madness on New Year's Eve, as one might expect.

We're in a group of a dozen tourists who've elected to share the final night of 2005 together, the crowning glory of almost a month living in each other's pockets. Pete is leading around the posh girl from Sydney's northern beaches – the same one he kissed all the way back in Barcelona. Juliana and Harry have patched things up and are dancing away. The South Africans are having a ball. Then there's a handful of single hangers-on who are milling about, thinking this might be the chance for them to snag a companion for the opening hours of 2006.

There are people stretched as far as you can see. It feels like a dance music festival that has taken over an entire city. A stage has been set up in front of the Royal Palace and the sky is filled with lasers, energising beats and elaborate pyrotechnics. People stream into the square from the multitude of bars and koffieshops under the full spectrum of drugs and drink.

Down backstreets, large crowds gather around men who have taken it upon themselves to stockpile enough fireworks for their own personal lighting show extravaganza. Loud booms emit from the side of canals as they ignite lengthy trails of red firework chains, crackling along the pavement and ending with pronounced explosions. Car alarms are going off all across the surrounding suburbs. Some of the amateur blasts are strong enough that I fear they may flip a small vehicle.

The collective hearts of all assembled are pulsating. It's especially the case for our group, which has the added vulnerability of heading into the unknown. Having followed tightly regimented, mirroring schedules on tour, tomorrow we become free radicals headed on wildly varying paths. For instance, I'm flying out to Australia less than 48 hours after arriving in London. Conversely, Lucy and Suzie will be grabbing a bus and spending two weeks exploring the north of England and Scotland before returning to the Gold Coast.

The temptation is there to try and lock everything down, to try and discuss or determine exactly what the relationship status is between Lucy and I. Are we going to meet up back in Oz? If so, when? Am I free to see other people until whenever we catch up again? Is she? Are we boyfriend and girlfriend or a holiday romance that served its purpose and time?

I figure the best course of action is to avoid that discussion altogether and treat Lucy like a princess for the few remaining hours that we have guaranteed in each other's presence. Whenever we move through the crowd, I can sense myself being over-protective, shielding her like she's a newborn duckling, nudging people out of the way and ensuring not a hair on her head is touched. When we visit a bar to drink cocktails and beer from massive novelty glasses in the shape of boots and trophies, I offer to order and pay for everything.

Lucy's not very talkative tonight. She seems preoccupied in thought. Her default manner of communicating is stopping dead in her tracks and kissing me, or taking photographs of just the two of us. Lucy does this with such frequency that I'm sure it frustrates our companions. We're the embodiment of two pathetic lovesick puppies.

At midnight the atmosphere around Amsterdam is palpable. It's a sensory overload as lights, sounds and vibrations along the ground combine in a confronting climax.

After celebrating and wishing everyone within earshot a happy New Year, Lucy and I slink off together to the side of the Royal Palace. We kiss up against the exterior walls for what feels like an hour, not talking, just sighing, exhaling, panting, gazing at each other with a longing for some certainty out of this crazy situation.

I hold Lucy like she's a china doll. This stranger has somehow become one of the most precious things in my life. I'm dedicated to showing her how a gentleman treats a lady.

She bats her eyelashes at me, looks deep into my soul and purses her dainty lips together, delicately pushing out the words:

"Can we...just go home...and fuck?"

LOXTON didn't confide in me of Sasha's infidelity – or should I say infidelities – until their relationship had well and truly run its course.

That she had been cheating on him, with multiple people, around the same time that Lox had gone through Howard's suicide, was something that beggared belief. Just as alarming was the fact my son didn't feel like he could tell anyone about his issues for more than two years.

Lox first spilled the beans to Kim, who subsequently asked why he bothered to stay with Sasha when he was so blatantly unhappy. He maintained that the shame of her affairs would reflect more negatively on him than anybody. If his colleagues from work, teammates from football or sparring partners from kickboxing knew that Sasha had saw fit to cheat on him...what sort of man would he be?

He didn't want people speaking about him as the journalist who couldn't satisfy his partner. It opened him to ridicule and subjugation on many fronts. Or, at least, that was the complex Loxton carried around with him.

Shortly after revealing to Kim what had been occurring, Loxton also drove to visit me and lay out the facts. He was deeply embarrassed, but felt that he needed to explain it to me as a mother and woman. Loxton's greatest concern was that I might think he was becoming like either his father or his stepfather. He wasn't walking away and jumping from one girl to the next. He wasn't an abusive, violent man who intended on leaving a trail of heartbreak behind him.

"I just don't understand why you would think you deserved to be treated like that yourself," I told him.

"I struggle to think I'm worth more than that Mum. I really do," came his reply. "Not many people have loved me in this lifetime. I'm afraid the next person to love me might not even exist, or might be the last."

In the preceding months, Loxton had relocated back to Brisbane from Townsville. He'd made that decision in the wake of Howard's death, deciding his grandparents needed him around more than ever – and vice-versa.

In the final stages with Sasha he'd also taken a step down to work for a suburban community paper so he could concentrate on getting his personal life in order.

When it all fell apart, Loxton was floating aimlessly, nothing keeping him on an even keel or making him feel inspired aside from his continued devotion to Wests Mitchelton Rugby League club. He began partying an increasing amount, spending most of what he earnt on drinking over weekends.

The same friends that were trying to dig him out of the rut – old friends Jay, Rocky, Jabba and Eddie – were involved in similar behavior. They meant well, but across the spectrum they were going through problems identical or closely related to the ones Loxton had experienced. Some of them had been cheated on, some were lacking self-confidence, all were arguably struggling with discovering a sense of purpose. I thought the lot of them drank far too much.

While Loxton had professed his innocence and desire to become a good man, I could see his values slipping thereafter. Following Sasha, there were a string of girls that came and went in quickfire fashion. I can't say I got to personally meet any of them. My son would oscillate between being boastful of his conquests and the brief rush of self-esteem they delivered, then at other times, pining for Jen and the purity and direction that his first real relationship had provided.

I had to remind him several times that Jen was almost five years in the past. She wasn't coming back. That ship had sailed.

Loxton liked to believe he was capable of anything if he put his mind to it. This was one of the positive mantras he rested on to give him reason to live during fits of depression. Yet, that same stubbornness and determination was at the root of his inability to surrender when it came to Jen. She remained a black mark on his CV he wanted to amend. I don't think he even wanted to win her heart back in the end. He just longed for her to tell him she forgave him and he was a decent person.

It seemed that was the only validation that mattered to him through a bleak period until he found two focal points.

First of all, Loxton was invited to become the first full-time media manager for the Queensland Rugby League (QRL). Then secondly, his friends set a distant target date for them to travel overseas on a joint adventure.

Of the very few things Loxton had a deep faith in, one was rugby league and the other was the state of Queensland. That he could combine both passions and work for an organisation as well-known as the QRL convinced him that he still had something to offer. He dreamt of doing something he believed was of a communal good, and this was definitely his niche. He threw himself completely and utterly into the role.

Because he worked so heavily in this period – and has indeed until now – Loxton was able to begin to save money in a way he hadn't for several years. When his friends mentioned an international trip, it gave him something to build towards and look forward to. He wasn't interested in owning a home or a sports car. Envious of those who jetted abroad, he saw it as a chance to finally spread his wings.

When it came to the crunch, all of Loxton's friends postponed their travel plans due to a shortage of funds or conflicting commitments. At that point Lox made what I thought was a significant decision – he decided to go ahead alone.

I won't lie that his trip has caused me all sorts of stresses, especially knowing he is out there travelling by himself. His moods plummet and rise with alarming frequency. Perhaps I haven't expressed that my reservations are just that, reservations. I didn't want to stop him from heading overseas. But that seems to be how he has interpreted some of my cautionary tales. It's why he cut me out in the final weeks before departing.

I feel deep down like he was always meant to travel. He's been fascinated by flags and countries, encyclopedias and *atlases since he could walk and talk. One of Loxton's favourite things to do in childhood was sit on my lap and look at tourism slides through the eyeholes of my View-Master. How nations came to be formed – both through geography and history – is a shared interest that always captivated his attention more than most.*

Loxton's loathe to admit it, but we've got quite a lot in common. And of those things we don't hold in common, we compensate for each other and balance the other out. I've never made good on my promise of returning to England since I flew to Australia in 1967, but it's something I've been able to do vicariously these past few months.

I'd say it's unlikely my son and I will ever see eye-to-eye over some things. I just hope all my children continue to be my eyes to the world.

AMSTERDAM // BELGIUM // LONDON // BRISBANE

LUCY'S body is wedged between my legs. We're on the final bus ride back to London, due to arrive at 6pm.

Both of us are facing out of the window as we speed through Belgium. We're effectively spooning in a sitting position, Lucy reclining into a void I've created by hitching my left leg onto the seat. The back of her hair is pressed into my chin and my arms are wrapped around her torso. I'm experiencing a pervading sense of contentment. We're watching the closing scenes of this holiday play out on a blurred landscape that whizzes past the window.

The tour guide is walking up and down the aisle, checking everybody has made arrangements to get home safely from Russell Square upon our return. The poor lady is only in her mid-to-late twenties, but has been made to play Mother Hen to a pack of social incompetents for large parts of this trip.

She smiles when she sees Lucy and I locked together. "I'm glad you two are finally comfortable letting it all hang out."

We return her a smile of warmth, then go back to being nuzzled together in silence.

After our one-and-only stop in Belgium, at a petrol station no less, Lucy fetches me a package from within her backpack. It's a small rectangle, covered in gift wrapping, with a bulge on one side.

"I've been meaning to give this to you."

Hoping dearly it's not another fertility statue, or at least one that doesn't make me feel so grossly inadequate, I unwrap it with care.

Spilling into my hand is a white badge with the words 'Out, damned spot' written across it in faux blood. It's a quote from Macbeth. We discussed it at dinner way back in Florence, what seems an eternity ago now.

"I noticed your jacket has badges of rock bands and revolutionaries, but none to do with literature. You're supposed to be a writer, aren't you?" she quips, raising her eyebrows with one of those million individually identifiable smirks.

I don't have the heart to tell her that, as an English teacher, she's read far more Shakespeare than I likely will in my entire life. If it were something like Chuck Palahniuk, Irvine Welsh, or even Hunter S Thompson, that'd fit the bill.

Her present is thoughtful and meaningful, nonetheless.

I then unsheathe the main body of the present, which I've already determined is a paperback book, but have not yet ascertained the title. It's *The White Cities: Reports from France 1925-39* by Joseph Roth, the famed European newspaper correspondent of the early 20th Century.

"I remembered how curiously excited you were by Arles and I think you mentioned Avignon in another conversation," she says, blushing.

"But that was way back...like the day after things went mental in Barcelona. Those are things you've picked up on from very early in the tour and stored away," I probe, surprised she'd recall the detail.

"What can I say? I thought you were alright. Quite possibly, I noticed you before you noticed me," she reveals.

"And me being a deranged man on the boardwalk at Porto Olympic didn't manage to convince you otherwise?" I say.

"Let's say I chose to overlook certain things. Moving on to the next topic...do you like the gifts?" Lucy enquires.

I pull her close and plant a kiss on her cheek and then her lips, twisting so we can face the diminishing 3pm sun. It bakes the surrounding fields in orange, shines through the window and covers us in an otherworldly haze that adds to the serenity and surrealism of the moment.

We barely say another word for the remaining hours to London. Instead we hold each other tight, and I alternate between compensating for the sleep I missed the night before, and racking my brains for how to say goodbye.

*** *** ***

AFTER convincing myself the best thing to do is subdue my eagerness, I opt to decline when Lucy invites me for one last farewell drink with Pete and Juliana at the terminus in London.

I make up an excuse about needing to catch up with Ferris and Jerome that night, which is partly true, but I omit the fact I'm not meeting with them for another two hours.

Until then, I go and shield in another pub a suburb away, drinking alone and trying to block everything out. This is weird, but I feel entirely washed out by emotions, drained, exhausted, nauseous.

The comedown to reality is a lot harsher than I expected, and I need a moment alone to place everything that happened in the last three months in one box, then take stock of where my life will be at when I return.

This Christmas was spent at the top of a Swiss mountain in a dreamlike setting. The Christmas Day beforehand I dropped 13 ecstasy pills with a bunch of self-pitying friends who were also distant from their families. We called ourselves 'The Orphans'. I hid in a cupboard at my mate's house, tried in vain to sleep while flies hovered around me, then spent half-a-week constantly reassuring myself I wasn't dying or going crazy – or both.

Chances are Lucy and I won't continue. I'm not really the type of guy for her. Chances are that human nature and pessimism will ambush us both before we can be reunited in Australia. I doubt all these people who we became great friends with on tour will ever get in contact again.

It's time to face the fact this trip has been an alternate reality, one that ends right at this precise moment.

*** *** ***

I'M distracted at dinner, to the point where Jerome pries for more information.

"Mate, one day left before you go home and you're quiet as a mouse Loxie," he says over a volcanic prawn vindaloo. "Did you meet a girl or something?"

The look on my face beholds the truth and my friends pester for more information.

"I'll tell you what, if there's anything between us when I get back to Australia, I'll tell you then. I'm finding it hard to fathom and not be skeptical right now," I counter.

"C'mon buddy," pleads Ferris. "Don't be so hard on yourself. Live a little."

Close to midnight we return home. For my final day in England all I've got planned is a trip to the Tower of London, then an early sleep so I can head off to Heathrow Airport around 3am.

However, when I open my emails, there's a message from Lucy:

"I know this is highly uncool of me to touch base so soon, but I wondered if you'd like to come explore the city with me before you go home? Just you and me. I've blown off my plans for tomorrow and hoping you might be able to do the same. You can stay the night with me before you fly if you like?"

I bang on the door of Jerome's bedroom and explain the situation.

"Go for it brother," he yells triumphantly in return. "I'm so proud of you, all grown up now."

*** *** ***

JAY collects me at Brisbane Airport at the end of a return flight which feels at least half the length of my outbound journey.

We drive through the Valley, past the nightclubs I've been haunting for the past few years, then stop to grab a beer in the mall.

"So, how was it?" Jay asks simply.

"Amazing. Complex. Strange. Probably the best thing I've ever done if I'm to be honest," I say in a measured, laconic tone.

"How so? What was so weird about it?" he follows up.

"Like everything. A lot of luck fell my way. There were too many coincidences. I met some really great people. I saw and did things I never believed I would. It's kind of made me rethink where my life is going. I need to set my ambitions higher and learn so much more than what I already thought I knew. I've come back with a new faith and appreciation," I blurt out.

Jay smiles a gigantic smile. "That doesn't sound so weird. That's almost exactly what I suspected would happen. You needed to do this. I'm really happy for you. I secretly thought travelling would be the tonic to set you straight," he confesses.

"But you know the weirdest part of all?" I continue. "I think I've met someone. I think I'm in a relationship with a girl, a woman, who at this moment is half a world away and yet, I feel like it's going to be okay. I feel like I might have met someone who loves me for being the freak I am."

Author Bio

Loxton Berg is the pseudonym of an Australian sports administrator and journalist.

www.ingramcontent.com/pod-product-compliance
Lightning Source LLC
Chambersburg PA
CBHW051933290426
44110CB00015B/1966